Ecumenical Adventure:
a Dunblane Initiative

To a great successor
Ian

Ian M Fraser

an ACTS Publication

First published in 2003

ISBN: 0 86153 402-6

Printed by Govan Litho Printing & Design Co-operative
Unit 10, 6 Harmony Row, Glasgow G51 3BA

In glad memory
of two imaginative, committed ecumenists

Rev Dr WG Baker, and
Gillian Carver

Special thanks to:
Shona Paterson for processing, layout and cover design,
and to the Carmichael Montgomery Trust
for financial assistance

The illumination on vellum by Helen Lamb on the outer cover depicts three phases of Christian Enterprise based on Dunblane: the arrival of Blane and his Celtic monastic community around 600AD, the 13th century cathedral, and the comtemporary initiative of churches together.

Contents

Preface

I first hit Scottish Churches House, or rather it hit me, in the late 60s, towards the end of Ian Fraser's time as Warden. 'Bliss was it in that dawns to be alive!' I don't remember the content of my first experience there, but I do remember the sense of energy and freshness and determination to get to the bottom of things, of there being no holds barred, of encounter.

Reading this account of the first ten years of the House gives a clear sense of what undergirded this atmosphere – a strategy of joined-up thinking and practice which had a colossal impact on many areas of Scottish life and on thousands of Christian lay people.

Several things struck me with great force as I read, fighting temptations to nostalgia or idealism, both of which would be grave sins against the ethos of the House.

The first was how close the project was in spirit and in time to 1948, the great explosion of ecumenical energy which brought the WCC into being. International volunteers helped to landscape the grounds. WCC leaders outside the door blessed the venture with prayer as the stone 'oikoumene' symbol was unveiled. Local and national consultations were regularly enriched by input from WCC programmes, and vice versa.

The second was how professional it was. No dilettantie 'talking shops' could be proved, and a constructive role for the House be identified. There was often a year or two's preparation before a consultation began, finding the right combination of people, commissioning preparatory material, identifying the initial agenda. Several themes ran for six or seven years, making a cumulative contribution to a field of social or cultural or religious concern. Rigorous scrutiny was always involved by the House Policy Committee as to when a task had been properly finished, or was ready to hand over to some outside body with more competence or resources to fulfil a named remit.

The third was what a sensitive finger the House had on the pulse of the society around it. Key issues about the arts, consorship, industry, education, housing policy, drugs, leisure, the media, many of them still with us, were explored, always in the company of those most directly involved, from every relevant walk of life.

Significantly, the aims of the House programmes were prioritised as follows:-

- To serve the world with integrity, especially using lay resources.
- To let the churches meet honestly and humbly about what separates them.
- To make fresh discoveries in the life of prayer and devotion.

This was no accident. The primary concern of the churches was not the life of the churches, but the life of the world. The shape of church life, of worship,. of ministry was to be resolved by the question of how the world's life was to be given the value and enrichment and transformation God sought for it. Religious self-preservation came nowhere on the scale of values: 'life is not for hoarding, but for risking' was the underlying evangelical axiom.

There were central, recurrent strategies.

One was to bring together those who normally didn't meet one another, either because they come from different places in the social strata – public schoolboys and apprentices for example; or young people from Easterhouse gangs of the '60s together with a Law Lord, a criminologist and representative of the Scottish Education Department: or because they worked within self-contained professions which didn't normally link with one another, or with the voluntary sector.

The 'cast-lists' for SCH consultaitons are memorable. Often they involve a mix of Christians, agnostics and atheists. Invariably they involve imaginative combinations: so, for rural affairs issues, - weep your heart out, Countryside March – people came from the National Farmers Union, The Scottish Association of Young Farmers' cubs, The Scottish WRI, The Council of Social Service, The Agricultural Colleges department, landowners, educationalists. Concrete realities are acknowledged, like having to time this one before the ploughing starts! Sociologists and social anthropologists, and those who can make comparisons with mainland Europe are filtered into the process. Historians and geographers come on board. A task force creates a needed bibliography.

Or again, for a meeting on 'Lawlessness in our time', there are Lord Kilbrandon, three sheriffs, two criminologists, one chief constable, six police officers, a Director of Education and five teachers, a social scientist, from the Discharged Prisons Aid Society.

Poets, dramatists, artists, entrepeneurs, scientists, politicians, musicians tumble through the pages of this record. The cross-fertilisation was a central aspect of the creativity of the place. But there was nothing self-indulgent about the encounters. People were asked because they had specific experience or skills.

One of the most striking things is that bosses and industrial leaders were asked to release and subsidise those who could never normally have attended midweek daytime events. The boldness and energy with which grants were sought or trusts approached to subsidise the participation of economically powerless youngsters was impressive.

It was, of course, a different world. The tighter constraints, for example, on academic time, the institutionalised appraisals of manageable target-meeting, the Thatcherite models of economic justification as the bottom line for every social enterprise were almost unimaginable in 1968! A phrase like 'The instruments of social compassion' can be used confidently. Discussion about the school curriculum is in terms of 'helping young folk to cope with adulthood and gain a rich maturity'. (Two years ago, the Convener of The Scottish Executive's Education Committee, when pressed, said that the purpose of education was 'to equip children for the global market' – and this a Labour MP!)

Nothing was done *for* people or *about* them without their presence and participation in the process. If it was about hymns for young people, they were encouraged to write them, and assess them. If it was apprentices sitting up all night gambling in the House during a consultation on industry, they were asked to negotiate a code of conduct about limits and rules.

Central to the vision was the confidence that we need one another. Adolescents need adults and vice versa. Skilled professionals need grass-roots responses and vice versa. Learning is always collaborative, involving the life-experience of ordinary people and the expertise of specialists. So, in the area of sexuality, "just as adults need young people to..... bring realism into their consideration of these matters, so young people need adults to round out their inexperience" Or "The professional theologian is a cripple without the laity......... and the lay person is a cripple without the professional theologian...."

At least 50% of the House time was given over to such programmes of empowering exploration, on a galaxy of themes. Many were sustained over most of the decade, involving serious work and strenuous commitment from paticipants. (Today only 10% - 20% of the House programme is initiated by the House, with the vast majority being hospitality to groups who come to spend time there on their own agendas, secular, professional, religious or whatever. Whether that is gain or loss needs weighing. It is certainly a huge difference).

No-one can doubt that the ethos derived in large measure from the persons of Ian and Margaret Fraser, though of course their appointment reflects a level of adventurousness and freedom in the Scottish Churches Council which is fairly breathtaking. A Warden who can say: "Write it on toilet paper. When it has fulfilled its purpose, it can be flushed away!" is not your average church executive.

Margaret had to be in the background, because she was still busy with bringing up family (It's an interesting sense of the shift in forty years that that would *not* now seem self-evident to many: and the book's unreconstructed non-inclusive language: 'mankind', 'stimulating man's coming of age' 'An understanding of Man – Theological and scientific' signals how innocent of feminism even the radical end of the Scottish church spectrum was for most of the '60s.)

What is clear to anyone who knew the House at that time, though hardly explicit is the book, is that Ian couldn't have been Ian without Margaret. And the House couldn't have developed as it did without Ian,

Margaret was a feisty lady! Her commitment to risk, to living on a shoestring, to the 'going for broke' which informed all their shared life was as much part of the House's spirit as Ian's upfront and bullish omnipresence. Margaret's welcome was quieter, but no less vital.

In the different context of Iona, Brian Woodcock, then pastor of St Mark's Greenwich, arrived in 1986 with a party of parishioners for a week hosted by Ian and Margaret:-

> "There was no programme there that week, and we had been too busy and too exhausted to arrange one for ourselves. Up to our necks in neighbourhood provision, planning and hassle, we needed a break from responsibility. We came seeking space, leadership, fresh ideas. What we got was Ian and Margaet Fraser, inviting us to tell our story to the other guests, so that they could help us identify enough issues to keep everyone in the Abbey occupied for the week.

Two things impressed me deeply. One was how Ian and Margaret worked together, complementing each other with their skills, insights, pastoral support. The other was the way they got us, in our near burnt-out state, and without our quite realising it, to do the work ourselves. They started it off, of course, and were there for us all the time. But it was we who had to draw up the agenda, find the resources, discover answers, set goals. Perhaps we were too tired to notice. But not by the end of the week. We went home energised and motivated, dreaming of an enabling church."

Dunblane in the '60s made the enabling church concrete. We need to explore, re-discover, re-commit to the hospitality, challenge, world-attentive nature of the gospel for a new century.

This book should help us all take on that task with exhilaration.

Elizabeth Templeton

"Come and See....."

Jesus' invitation to Andrew in John 1:40 freed him to make what he chose of Jesus' life through direct acquaintance. That is the kind of invitation now extended to the reader concerning events in the first decade of Scottish Churches' House.

On two counts this may have value. Those who longed to see the churches using a common house for service and testimony in Scotland were still alive in the 1960s, and could check whether development in Scotland concurred with their longings and also opened new and welcome vistas. Also, it was not just a matter in 2002 of depending on distant memories. Every event was not only recorded but reported and a tape recorder was used to preserve the flavour of particular contributions. This book draws on that material directly.

So, come and see how Scottish Churches House shaped out its life in the 1960s, especially its engagement with Scottish culture and industrial and social issues; and its dealing with denominational differences and with the retreat tradition.

Starting Out

The seed from which Scottish Churches' House grew was sown at the World Council of Churches Assembly at Amsterdam in 1948. The Scottish representatives to the Assembly came back convinced that they must begin to grow together in their own country. Thus the Scottish Churches' Ecumenical Committee came into being and along with it the more informal Scottish Churches' Ecumenical Association for individuals and groups committed to Christian unity. From the experience of these bodies grew the belief that what was needed in Scotland was a House which the Churches held in common and where they could begin to learn to grow together, and together serve Scotland.

The Russell archive in St Andrews University Library contains correspondence detailing the search for a suitable House. About ten possibilities were considered and rejected often because they were not central enough. There were times when church representatives felt like giving up. Then Dr Nevil Davidson, as chairman, would quietly announce that the next item of business was finding the right kind of house in the right kind of location. He stuck tenaciously to the conviction that the way forward was through the establishment of a house of the churches together. Dr Robert Mackie acted as a kind of mainspring, moving things on when they might have flagged.

It was not till the mid-1950s that attention began to concentrate on a row of 18th century houses, then derelict, which made up one side of the Cathedral square in Dunblane. They seemed to represent a forlorn hope. The Town Council had made up its mind that they were to be demolished and replaced by a war memorial. The Friends of Dunblane Cathedral contested this decision and argued for the retention and restoration of the buildings. When the matter was taken to court, the Council won the right to demolish. But with great courtesy, they allowed the Civic Trust to make a fresh assessment of the situation. Their report proved to be decisive. The row of houses were not only capable of restoration but worthy of restoration. They provided a humble foil to the cathedral, giving the cathedral its full value as a distinguished edifice. If the decision to demolish were implemented, a very similar row of buildings should replace them – the war memorial would be lost in the space which would result, should the alternative plan be followed through. The verdict was accepted. The Town Council and Friends of Dunblane Cathedral handed to the Scottish Churches Ecumenical Committee the parts of the row of houses which they owned. Mr Monaghan, local builder, was delighted to be given the job of restoration. Not only did he bring professional skills to the task but invested heart and soul in the enterprise. He was a Roman Catholic. He was aware that, at the start, his church found difficulty in owning a House in common with other churches, although all kinds of informal participation was possible. He gave himself unstintingly to the project as one who fully shared its objective.

Dr Mackie was mandated to approach Margaret and Ian Fraser to see whether they might be prepared to head up the enterprise. They had served in the parish of Rosyth for twelve years and were considering a request to set up a new department in a Canadian University. Dr Mackie felt he had to give the full picture – there was no money for such an appointment! Margaret's response was immediate "That's for us!" At the time she had come out of the Western General Hospital for an hour, where she was being treated with an unusually severe dose of radiotherapy to attack a life-threatening cancer. She did not know whether she would survive the months to come. On such venturing does the cause of the Kingdom flourish.

Ian was appointed Warden in March 1960. To get income to bridge to the time when money came available, he took on an assistantship in Dunblane Cathedral for 8 months. The Lodge of Deanston House Hotel, Doune, was rented for the family. Generous gifts from the Russell Trust and the Historic Buildings Council allowed the restoration of buildings to be tackled, and a public appeal provided what was needed to complete the furnishing for residential use of what was now called Scottish Churches House. Miss Allison Harvey 'upped sticks' and moved to a house in Dunblane simply to be available for any help for which she might be called on. She gave an immense amount of voluntary work in the early stages of establishing the House. She also brought with her an invaluable gift in Miss Maisie Masson (later Mrs Shields) who become Domestic Supervisor. By the middle of 1960 everything was in place.

A 1970 document gives this description of the objectives which the churches wanted to pursue through the new instrument which they had brought into being: Three aspects of the enterprise were identified from the beginning and shaped the life of the House. They were "the need of the Churches to serve the world with integrity, using their lay resources with a new and fresh subtlety and flair; the need for the Churches to meet honestly and humbly about the things which separate them and the unity on which they may go forward together; and the need for fresh discoveries in the life of prayer and devotion." Besides those events which were initiated from the House, it existed to serve the direct needs of the Churches and other bodies whose policy was in line with that of the House.

All the co-operating Churches in Scotland along with the inter-denominational bodies such as the Young Men's and Young Women's Christian Associations set up Scottish Churches' House together and hold it in common ownership. The original seven churches – the Church of Scotland, the Scottish Episcopal Church, the Methodist Church, Baptist Union, Congregational Union, United Free Church and Churches of Christ were joined in 1962 by the Salvation Army and a little later by the Religious Society of Friends.

There was significance in the fact that the 'little houses of Dunblane' lay between two bases for mission for the church through the centuries. In 600 or 602 AD Blane and his Celtic monks established a community at the top of Holmehill. In the 12th century the cathedral was built.

World Council of Churches Blessing

The first great occasion in the life of Scottish Churches House occurred when the Central Committee of the WCC interrupted its meeting in St Andrews in July 1960 to visit Dunblane

There was a service in the Cathedral, the unveiling of the Oikoumene sign on the gable end of the House by Metropolitan Juhanon of the Mar Thoma Church, India and the dedication of the enterprise by Bishop Sherrill of the United States of America in the name of the World Council of Churches.

Among members of the WCC Central Committee who visited were Bishop Martin Niemoller, an ex-U-boat commander who stood up to Hitler, Bishop Hans Lillje of Hanover, Dr Franklin Fry, the chair of The Central Council, the Archbishop of Canterbury, Geoffrey Fisher and Dr Hromadka of Czechoslovakia

Robert Mackie, Archbishop Athenagoras and the Archbishop of Canterbury converse about the enterprise of the churches and its promise.

For the first and possibly the only time in its history, the Central Committee was able to inspect a World Council of Churches Work Camp which had taken in hand the wild ground behind the House and landscaped it for use.

The House itself had to be restored professionally.

Amateur volunteers from many countries and a whole range of denominations were able to make a pleasant garden area, under the watchful eye of Mr Ross, master builder from Airdrie, who progressed the work as it had been planned by Eric Stevenson, architect.

Work Campers were asked to keep on their working clothes to introduce visitors to the Work Camp, following a service in the Cathedral

The Work Camp

The 'little houses' were in a state of dereliction when they were handed over to the Scottish Churches Ecumenical Committee.

The row of houses as they were

The wild ground at the back posed many problems and was tackled by a World Council of Churches Work Camp of young volunteers coming from as far as Japan.

What became a staff room registers the state of disrepair which marked rooms before they were taken in hand.

The builders punched corridors top and bottom through the back of the premises and, where there was a window, built a room with corridor access.

Some of the building at the north end was in too bad a state to retain and had to be demolished. At one point the roofing was still good and was jacked up. The warden wickedly launched the rumour with foreign tourists that this was the way we built in Scotland – roof first to protect workers from the weather. The original length was re-established in 1966 with a dining room on the top level and accommodation underneath.

Ian Fraser, Warden, consults with Mr Bell of the neighbouring Schoolhouse about the work to be undertaken.

Eric Stevenson, architect, meets Work Campers and a BBC representative (far right) to explain plans for tackling the task. The Work Camp accomplished five times the amount of reconstruction of this site which he believed to be possible in the month available. At the end of the month Eric was quite taken aback by the extent and quality of their accomplishment.

There were representatives of 11 nations and 15 denominations. Co-leaders of the Work Camp were:-

Richard Wagner from the former GDR (East Germany) and...

.....Ian Fraser from Scotland

There were three major levels at which work had to be done-

The back wall of the House was damp. Earth had slipped downhill and covered the wall up to the windows. A track was cut through earth and rubble, at a distance which would give good access, the earth being thrown further up the wall.

In the cleared space a retaining wall was built. The earth was then cleared from the house wall and piled behind this new construction.

To hold the banking firmly it was found to be necessary to make an additional wall further up the slope.

Once the House wall had 'time to breathe' it was found that the dampness now disappeared. The rubble construction had been so effective that a damp course was not needed.

The plan of work produced by Eric Stevenson had to be amended on the very first working day. From the back door of the House, seven or eight steps led upwards, met a mound of earth and ended there. But digging uncovered a whole succession of steps which continued upwards towards the ivy covered wall, set in higher banking. Neither the co-leaders nor the work campers had any idea that there was a building behind the ivy,

But as the thick ivy was cleared, first a window then a door was revealed, and an arched room silted up with rubble.

When this was cleared away, traces of the original floor appeared, and a new floor was laid at the same level. (Later, for cleaning and safety purposes, this was given a cement coating). Outside a skin of stone was built and the detritus barrowed into it. When this was topped with stone it made an access platform. The Ministry of Works said that this work of amateurs was totally appropriate. It fitted in with the stonework around. "If this had been done by professionals they would have given it too tidy a finish!"

Mr Ross supervised the building of the platform.

At the top level, the roof of the arched room was dug out, exposed for the first time in centuries,

and cemented
in to make it
secure

Water still penetrated from the surrounding banking. After two amateur
attempts, the building had to be dug out completely to make it waterproof.
Under Mr Ross's supervision this was attempted by further work camps. But,
in the end the building had to be tanked in professionally.

Surplus earth from the top
level was tipped over the
wall,

and used to landscape the adjacent ground which was then given a winding path to lead from the lower to the top level,

and steps were furnished to link the two levels together.

The Work Campers were by now calling the vaulted room 'the chapel'. Of their own volition they made a cross and raised it on the platform outside. They decided that the conclusion of the whole venture should be a Communion Service in which everyone would take part.

The whole background area had been transformed by the time the Work Campers downed tools.

Other Work Camps which followed completed the work.

Allison Harvey and Maisie Masson, here photographed when helping with a work camp excursion provided sterling support at this and later phases of the work.

During the Week of Prayer for Christian Unity in January 1961, Scottish Churches House was dedicated as a House of the churches together by Rev Dr Nevile Davidson, chairman of the Scottish Churches Ecumenical Committee. Dr David Russell, whose magnificent gift, with that of the Historic Buildings Council had made it possible to embark on the venture, had died before he could see it take shape.

But his son, seen here with The Earl of Wemyss was able to take part in the ceremony.

The Earl of Wemyss and March declared the House open for residential use, expressing thus the hope which the enterprise could have for the future: "In declaring the Scottish Churches' House open, I hope and pray that Dunblane may henceforward become the cradle of a new Christian unity to the blessing of man and to the Glory of God".

The Chapel

To begin with, the accepted local wisdom was not questioned. The vaulted room was believed to be the under-croft of a house. Over many years it had become silted up with rubble inside and overgrown with ivy outside until it became lost from sight and from the memory of most people. Miss Elizabeth Barty, local historian, reported to the Society of Friends of Dunblane Cathedral on an examination of 'The Dunblane Cellars' in 1953 (vol VI part IV). She had looked at the vaulted room in the hillside, but had not even parted the thick ivy to venture a step or two into the dark, dripping cavern beyond. She recorded then "It is thought to be the remains of the House of the Archdeacon or some other of the Cathedral Clergy."

As time went by it became clear that this guess did not fit the facts, either those external, or those internal to the building.

Maps make it clear that all the cathedral clergy houses were grouped round the cathedral facing the river, the Archdeacon's house on the north side, the others on the south side. None were at Holmehill. Twice, under the expert eye of Mr Ross, amateurs had dug out the chapel; and eventually a professional team had tanked it in. It was then clear that there had never been a house at the top level. The wall existed to protect the vaulted construction in its own right against the banking. Above the door are two roughly carved niches which might have supported figurines. They are clearly distinguished from holes left when substantial roots of ivy were hacked out to clear the face of the wall.

As the inside of the room began to be cleared, a well was found on the left hand side, with a small stream feeding it. It was about eight inches across and had a natural capstone an inch or two larger than the diameter. Work was halted and the Ministry of Works asked to send someone to advise whether it should be preserved.

The advice given was to floor it over to complete the flooring at the original level. The well would have been inadequate for household purposes, but a small bowl could have been lowered down to get water to add to wine. The window, with ivy removed, was seen to be ecclesiastical in character rather than what would suffice for household use. On the back wall is a cross-piece, deliberately set there and clearly distinguished from the rest of the walling around it. The cupboards at the back are too shallow to be of use except as aumbries which could hold communion vessels, bibles and prayer books.

A water diviner had been called in to check on flows of water before the tanking was tackled. Once he had done his job, he went across to the table altar and said 'Do you know that you have a body buried under here?" The burial was in an east-west direction as favoured ecclesiastically. His word had weight. If Councils wanted to put the road past where there had been a disused cemetery, they would call him out to confirm where graves ended. Monica Clough, who also had 'the gift' identified the burial separately. It was decided not to disturb the grave. What became clear was that the churches together had not discovered a treasure in a hillside and brought it into use as a chapel. The discovery had greater significance. What they had found was an ancient place of worship, a gift from the past to the present.

What period might it date from? There is no certainty. Certainly the form of building, with its 'Indian feathers' character where the weight of the wall is shared between a copestone and stones in a vaulted semi-circle above, replicates that of the 13th century bishop's palace whose ruins are alongside the cathedral hall and that of the dungeons of Doune castle nearby, also 13th century.

What might it have been originally?

Given a rather earlier date might it have been an annat? The word itself simply indicates an ecclesiastical enterprise, the income of whose first year was set aside for the pope. It was typically marked by the conjunction of a chapel, a burial and a well or stream. In an article in the 1936 magazine of the Society of Friends of Dunblane Cathedral (Vol II part III) Dr J Hutchison Cockburn observes: "Very rarely is the annat associated with any name of a saint, but both in Ireland and in Scotland 'Annat' means the church of a patron saint or a church holding the relics of the founder". Might this have been a chapel which allowed people to pray 'in the presence of the bones' as was the case in Iona before Columba's relics were removed from the small chapel attached to the Abbey? It is as certain as could be that Blane's relics were returned to Bute. Who might be the anonymous subject of the burial? It must have been someone closely associated with the ecclesiastical development in the area.

An annat could be a forward post, presaging a later development - maybe established in anticipation of the building of the cathedral? All this is conjecture. We have no firm evidence.

The marvel of the discovery itself was matched by the brilliance of the architectural plan which had been produced by Eric Stevenson to furnish the Chapel.

As one enters, one is met by a standing cross. It immediately provides a reminder of the original Celtic mission. On the dun or fortified hill small dwellings would have met the simple needs of the community itself – individual cells and meeting/worship place(s). On the level grounds where the Cathedral now stands a cross would be erected and people in the surrounding area be brought within hearing of the Gospel. An illuminated vellum by Helen Lamb in Scottish Churches' House tells the story from Blane's birth till today. It reminds contemporaries that the teams of Celtic monks were multi-skilled. They not only preached where they settled. They went into the surrounding countryside with teams in which there might be only one evangelist. Others would be skilled in teaching, building, agricultural improvements, healing. Nothing less than total wellbeing was taken to be God's will for people.

The table-altar was designed to be used from the front, back or side to meet the needs of any ecclesiastical tradition. Communion vessels were placed in the cupboard or aumbry behind it. Eric Stevenson had designed silver vessels, but pottery was considered to be more appropriate – silver could only too easily be stolen and that would lead to locking up a Chapel which should be open for personal prayer as well as for common worship. Dr Archie Craig presented a reading stand which swung on a metal arm and could be tucked alongside the wall or brought forward for use.

The seating was designed to allow people to gather round the cross and encircle the table altar at the same time. The skill of the plan is shown in this: if two or three are gathered together they do not feel that there are large empty spaces around them, yet 40 can be accommodated without discomfort.

A final touch of brilliance is provided by lights scattered over the vaulted roof. "I had the early chapter of the Book of Revelation in mind" said Eric "the angels of the Churches as stars and Churches themselves as lamps." So the prayer and worship of the Church on earth is brought within the shining ambience of the communion of saints, those beyond death being knit up in life with those on this side of death.

There was significance in the manner in which the Chapel furnishings were provided. A woman was looking for some way to mark the life of her beloved husband, who had recently died. She saw the needs of the Chapel as an opportunity to do this. He was not notable in the eyes of the world. He was just a beloved man. So the dedication of the Chapel for ecumenical use by Dr Kenneth Slack of the British Council of Churches made a link with the House itself whose previous occupants had also been not notables in the world's eyes but families of artisans and labourers.

The Dedication party
L-R: Doctors Craig & Slack, Helen Lamb,
Mrs G Macfarlane Russel, Mr FR Stevenson

There was an unspoken declaration in this that the enterprise of the Churches together was rooted in the life of the common folk and had to be for them, not just for specialists and dignitaries.

The Early Days, from a later perspective

Looking back in 1990, when ACTS became the successor to Scottish Churches Council, the first Warden provided the following recollection:

'Fresh from the pub, swaying on the pavement opposite us, Addie delivered his verdict with all the authority of the inebriated. "It'll no work" he declared as we Work Campers sweated to unload heavy building stones from the parked lorry. "Yer Scottish Churches Hooses thing 'll niver come tae neathing".

But the wisdom of the wise is foolishness with God.

Work Campers transformed the back area and Monaghan and Co rehabilitated the row of Houses for their new purpose under the imaginative planning of Eric Stevenson. Alison Harvey brought her vision and with it the gift of Maisie Masson (commending her with some diffidence because of their close companionship – it was as if the Queen, giving away the Koh-I-Noor, apologised that it had not been dusted that day). Margaret charmed people with the grace of her presence so that they felt welcome from the moment they came in the door. Jack and Betty Stevenson, Archie and May Craig built into the enterprise their love, prayer and service – and Leighton House and the Flower Garden of Scottish Churches House. Marie Brotherston in the kitchen made sure that Blue Angels returned to their respective countries furnished with a much more vivid grasp of English than any language school could have provided, able to tell of the 'collieshangies' they had worked their way through and what had 'scunnered' and 'fair chuffed' them about Scotland. Fittingly, Bill and Barbara Baker are rounding off a life-investment of support with the gift of the new ecumenical library. We were actually in business for day conferences in 1960 though the official opening was not till 1961. The arrival of Gillian Carver in 1965 added strength and imagination.

Decisive parts were played by Nevile Davidson and Robert Mackie in the total enterprise. Nevile assumed the main public ecumenical role while Robert made sure that a head of stream was kept up in the boiler house, where Mabel Small did quite a bit of stoking. When the new Scottish Churches' Council came into being in 1964 Lord Wemyss chaired it through its first years. The churches now had a marvellous double instrument. Scottish Churches House could develop a great variety of initiatives in the life of the churches and of Scotland on an informal basis. The Council could deal with relationships at the official level.

In the 1960s it was the House that was the dynamo. Willie Robertson of Development and Industry called it a "decade of quite incredible creativity." When I returned after 14 years in the World Council of Churches and Selly Oak Colleges, the Council had fittingly assumed a much higher profile and a much more important role. With the advent of ACTS, the informal and official developments can interplay so that they empower and fertilise one another with telling effect.

In all this we were not sure whether we could pull anything off! But then neither was Abraham (imagine a long-distance lorry driver being given his instructions).

Cultural Concerns

"When I first went to Scottish Churches House, I went with many preconceptions and suspicions. I found only great tolerance, friendship, and a lasting impression of committed and serious engagement with the social and moral questions of our time."

James Morrison
Artist, Montrose

Artistic Perceptions

It is mid-1964.

A group of artists and art-teachers, members of the Scottish Art Teachers' Association, are meeting with representatives from Church and public life on the theme "The Autonomy and Responsibility of the Arts."

They are a mixed bag, Christians, agnostics, atheists. They are new to one another. The artists are not very sure what they have let themselves in for and are alert to any attempt on the part of the churches to exploit the situation. The very idea of meeting in a House of the churches is odd to them, indeed that the churches should be seriously interested in the arts is a new thought to most of them.

Step inside now.

The first session is being introduced by a consideration of two cases which have raised censorship problems. In his play "The Workhouse Donkey" John Arden had to modify a scene to please the Lord Chamberlain. The objection was to nudity on stage. Shortly before the consultation gathered, John Arden had been interviewed by "Peace News" and invited to comment on the changes he felt he was forced to make. In this article he declared that his intentions were

    i)   to allow the audience to enjoy quite openly the pleasure of watching pretty girls get undressed.

    ii)   to make a dramatic point at this stage of the play's development

    iii)   to make the audience aware of the essential dreariness of a strip club.

"One might ask questions such as the following about a playwright placed in his position. Is his intention valid and appropriate? Can it be effectively got across – when it reaches the audience, is it in fact simply treated as a peepshow? Is the dramatic point he would like to make worth making? Who is to judge – writer, critic, audience, Lord Chamberlain?", says the report.

The second issue raised was an old chestnut for those concerned with drama and censorship – bawdy in Shakespeare.

"Could it be left out without loss? Yes, if we were meant to be self-protective and self-concerned. Yes, if there were virtue in closing ourselves against the whole range of the springs of human nature and action. Yes, if we are to type-cast people and choose or reject their company accordingly. But the Christian faith insists that life is not for hoarding but for risking. It discourages us from keeping ourselves respectable, from keeping ourselves to ourselves, from treating people as stereotypes. The bawdy element in Shakespeare helps to remind us that life is to be understood and appreciated in its full-blooded demand and promise, and is not seen at all unless it is seen as a whole. It reminds us of the variety of human existence and the different layers of affirmation and denial in people. Thus the essential response to life may not be the one which immediately appears (publicans and harlots go into the Kingdom before the righteous). It reminds us of our need to be concerned for others *as they are,* without first making them acceptable by dressing them up in presentable clothes.

So Christ was open to people and situations, not prejudging or pigeonholing – himself coming into judgement as being "a gluttonous man and wine-bibber a friend of publicans and sinners". Shakespeare's bawdy belongs to his integrity. It is a sign of his openness to the whole range, the whole depth and height of those things which make up human existence, (A side point which may be made here is that what is often taken to be low or "blue" talk, jokes etc., is often simply masculine, and cleaner than much polite conversation which is free of coarse images and words.)

The Church needs the world. It needs the world to take it to task, to challenge its understanding of faith and morality, to examine whether, when it says it is basing itself on the truth, it is simply relying on convention. Searching thinking and experiment in any field of enquiry can help to save the Church from tendencies to narrow the horizons of understanding of human nature, to rely on restricted habits of conduct, to put life on tram rails.

Human life in all its dimension and richness needs to be presented through art, drama, films and books. This must be done in such a way that it will disturb and shock us by breaking open the small worlds we contrive for ourselves within which to protect our security. It must stretch our understanding and give us new horizons. It must enlarge our compassion and keep us open to people of all sorts. How may this be done so that real courtesy is extended to people who are of different ages and at different stages of maturity, who find themselves at the receiving end?

The discussion began with a questioning of Arden's honesty. Whatever his rationalisations, was he not simply putting on an exhibition, the kind of thing which would attract people initially but not keep them, if they were worth their salt? Was this not simply box-office stuff? Bergman's film 'The Silence' (which had been referred to in the introduction to the session) could produce an irrevocable trauma in the mind: it looked as if Bergman was losing his creative drive. 'Uncle Vanya' is in fact more sexy than Osborne. We must not identify the sexy simply with the visual and obvious (which appeals particularly to the adolescent). At different points of the consultation John Arden's integrity was strongly defended. The point was made that writing for money is as likely to help as to hinder an author to maintain integrity.

That there is moral content in art, an indication of life's purpose and significance, must not be assumed. Spike Milligan's philosophy is: 'Whistle a few merry tunes till the bomb falls'.

Art offers means of sublimating primitive emotions which are often repressed, and plays its part in disciplining these. Various levels of presentation of sexuality could be discerned in the arts. There was that in which the immediate external impression given was of sexiness – X certificate stuff, illustrated by 'Tom Jones' which had a rip-roaring full-blooded healthy handling of the sex theme. Camus' 'L' Etranger' and de Beavoir's 'The Mandarins' went deeper showing people attempting to construct viable relationships of some kind where healthy relationships had been beyond achievement. On the other hand there were plays, films, and books which, to all immediate appearances, were above reproach, but when you looked at their attitude to life and people were blasphemous: 'Ben Hur' was such in the speaker's opinion. *We had to be sensitive to those productions which did not set out to provide moral answers but simply excavated a moral area* and called for an understanding response from us.

It was asked whether the modern artist was not in fact a religious visionary working in a materialistic world which does not want his vision.

It was asked whether those who made a fuss about the nude at the Drama Festival did not do so because they felt their repressions threatened. "The Happening" affected what it sought – it reanimated discussion". Thus the report.

Well, how does it strike you?

At a place called Scottish Churches' House, owned jointly by nine denominations and a variety of interdenominational organisations, would you expect to find as blatantly direct a discussion of the presentation of the nude in drama? Would you bargain for such a mixed bag of participants?

Some might well ask what the churches hope to gain from such an encounter. Are they trying to show that Christians are as broad-minded as anyone else? Are they guilty about a Puritan past and anxious to show that they have a much more permissive attitude towards the Arts than was the case in the past?

Or have they just lost all sense of the distinction between the concerns of the Christian faith and the concerns of the world?

* * * * * * * *

It all started with the Scottish Art Teachers' Association conference in November 1963. From the floor, the "Calvinists and fuddy-duddies" of the Church were well and truly slated (although interestingly, it was insisted that the world Calvinist be withdrawn as an inaccurate one!)

At this point, as one who knew how one presbytery had been maligned, the Warden made contact with the secretary of the SATA suggesting that, instead of there being the slanging match from a distance, Scottish Churches' House might provide a meeting ground. A delighted and affirmative reply came immediately, and after some meetings of small groups to make contact and isolate main issues, the consultation on "The Autonomy and Responsibility of the Arts" took place in June 1964. John Arden's brush with the Lord Chamberlain and the problem of bawdy in Shakespeare were tackled in the very first session on the theory that if there is a nettle to be dealt with you are better to grasp it right away rather than dance round it apprehensively. The effect was shattering to the art teacher who was responsible for leading off the session on the following morning on "Violence in Art". He had to spend part of the night re-writing his script. "I came along with the deliberate intention of winkling out some entrenched church people form their fox-holes", he explained – "and I found them at my elbow charging alongside me!"

The opening out of people towards one another at this first gathering produced a kind of comradeship-in-exploration which strengthened over the years.

Atheists, agnostics, Christians shared insights, listened humbly to one another and made some progress on finding a common mind on issues which faced them.

Here are a few of the points: The consultation struggled to see how different responsibilities could be reconciled. There was the responsibility of the artist, painter, script writer, poet, to be true to a vision of life, whatever that vision conveyed of significance or sordidness. There was the responsibility of the producer to consider the medium used and the audience reached (for instance what can be shown in the theatre, which people go to of choice, it may be unfair to bring into the home – by means of television: switching on or off does not represent nearly as deliberate a choice as movement from house to theatre). There is the responsibility of the viewer or hearer to be discriminating or to be instructed (people who never imagine that, with no previous experience, they can sit down and play the piano right away, are prepared to stand before a painting or to hear a poem or see a play and dismiss these as 'rubbish'. It is the personal judgment which then deserves to be called 'rubbish').

Related to the concern that the artist should find his, or her, true social role was a concern that the Church should discover its true role in relation to the arts. This was surprising in this respect: atheists and agnostics who were concerned with the arts, as well as Christians, felt that they were being let down. In particular they felt the Church had a prophetic role to fulfil which was closely related to that of the arts; and that, should it choose to do the work, it could provide a significant framework for life within which the artist (not without challenging the framework) could find a place and part and not feel the need to take on the whole burden of discovering a viable context of social values and relationships within which make a contribution. Jim Morrison expressed this most clearly:

"One of the main functions of the artist is to be critical of his or her time. One would think that the Church existed to fulfil this critical role, and ought to be better equipped to do it than the artist. But what is the Church for? You would think it would exist for attacking stereotypes but in fact it accepts stereotypes. The Church and Art should and could be doing each other some good, the former learning to recognise and admit the multiform expressions of art and the latter agreeing to some ordering of its social image. The artist had a responsibility not to be simply negative but to affirm his positive vision. Men of goodwill of all kinds needed to get together to create a social climate in which the artist's testimony to the truth he sees is relevant. Wesker turned to the Unions and took folk songs seriously; it should be possible for people like him to turn to the Church and find in it an awareness that art was relevant –beyond its usefulness in glorifying its own buildings."

John Busby affirming as a Christian that "the Church has lost through neglect, misuse, mistrust, the richness of its inheritance" shared exactly the same concern from his own different angle. Thus "the artist is turned out in the same mould as the biblical prophet: he has to serve the world given him. Yet we must not take it for granted that creative activities by themselves are means of salvation. The artist found himself in the position of the despairing psalmist who cried out "Will the Lord absent himself forever?" The lack of a Way, the lack of meaning produces a sadness in art today, even though it is vastly exciting."

The timeliness of undertaking voyages of discovery in which Christians and others shared the rations and the risks, in which the venturing was like Abraham's who went out "not knowing whither he went" confident that there was a "a city which hath foundations" to be discovered, was evident to all. Said George Bruce at one point "It belongs to creativity that one does not know where one is going." Said Robin Philipson, "one cannot create, knowing each step beforehand; much reasoning comes after the creative act." At the same time it was pointed out that this agnosticism concerning where exploration might take us must not be used as a cover-up for the inarticulate, the unworthy and the sloppy. Bringing this group of people together had itself been a particular kind of creative act. Here is an excerpt from the discussion:

"It was suggested that the greatest enemy to art and possibly to religion was certainty. Analytical cubism really consisted of the painting of uncertainty – and above any other form of art it encouraged a breakthrough into new fields of thought and expression. But what was called uncertainty might be better described as humility. In the nature of things, design obliged one to be completely humble, open and teachable. When one was on the ball most, one felt most that one was no good at the game. It was often at the very point of defeat that things came out in the end, and some statement was made. This willingness to wait for light, this receptiveness, were basic in both Christian life and art. In many ways a parallel could be distinguished between movements in art and in literature, and movements in the Church. Both were on the question, where is mankind trying to go? All over the place this kind of question is being raised e.g. in the Buchanan Report it is shown you can only deal with traffic problems after asking basically what human life is for. Questions of politics and economics are alike on this basic level of questioning. The concerned person has always to take the rap from a society which does not want to be too deeply disturbed."

Robin Philipson made the plea that religious painting be interpreted as painting which probed the deep roots of human life and not that which illustrated religious subjects. His wife instanced Rembrandt's 'Night Watch' as a step forward in probing into the truth, found within the Protestant tradition. There is some awareness in Scotland that artists have been neglected, she pointed out, but great difficulty lies in distinguishing between those searching for truth in some way equivalent to Rembrandt's which was new to his society – and deceivers. Nothing less than a wide process of education could help people to appreciate the search for truth in new directions and to distinguish this from the phoney.

The need to have fresh insights into the way in which humanity is placed in this world today and to take the risks involved in stretching minds to appropriate such insights is illustrated by a contribution made by John Calder and the discussion which immediately followed. He started with a reference to Samuel Beckett:

"Beckett stated the compulsion laid upon him in these words:

'The expression that there is nothing to express, nothing with which to express, no power to express, no desire to express together with the obligation to express'. In Beckett you sense a cosmic anguish. He is not sure what he is trying to do and yet he does something in spite of that uncertainty. In the process of writing he works out some clarity of thought and direction, which he did not have when he started. He was significant for us because art today is no longer a hunt for beauty; rather it consists of the posing of an unposable question and the search for what would turn out to be an unacceptable answer. Art makes us aware of the human condition – including its selfishness, callousness and cold-blooded barbarity. It becomes the conscience of its time – but not by seeking to be that conscience, only by describing the reality of life, and expressing the horror of finding oneself a member of the same race as destroyed men's bodies and spirits in concentration camps and dropped the atomic bomb. The function of art might not be to bring happiness into ordinary people's lives but rather to destroy their inner peace. Nihilism in Art should not be despised – it got over to us an awareness of the full horror of the human condition.'

Here was the moral problem: Is it good to make people more aware than they are? Don't you open a Pandora's box of ills and inflict greater suffering on people by enlarging their awareness?" His own position was that one can never unthink what one has thought, one can never turn back history. Everyone has a right to face the full dimension of life's potential for beauty and for horror. If he were dying of cancer he would want to know this, to go through the experience with open eyes – as a responsible human being he felt it was his due that he should be told and not have the facing of this great climactic event denied him by people trying to cover it up.

In discussion it seemed clear that people thought that the risk of heightening human awareness of the dimensions of His life was one which had to be taken. One had to face the worst. Nothingness is very close to being. When Jesus Christ made himself "a nothing" (Philippians 2:7) we saw real humanity. They way to the Cross was both a stripping and a realisation of humanity, finishing with the paradox that it was through death that life came.

In a later consultation on "Creativity and Communication" a revealing experiment was made. Four people were selected for a panel – one trained in both theology and education, one both a teacher and administrator in the field of physics, one a painter and a teacher, and one the executive president of an industrial council who found developing technology absorbing much of his thought and energy. A larger company of people drew them into discussion to get them to express basic convictions as those who work in these different fields and they were invited, without using many technical terms, to speak from within the particular thinking of their own discipline using a language which would be understandable to those familiar with their own discipline. There was accordingly some rigour in the conversation (since those who took part had begun to relate to one another as human beings and could have communicated with one another easily on matters of common human interest). What emerged was unexpected. There was a clear affinity between theology, education, physics and painting. This affinity had something to do with the use of imagination and a concern for human dignity. Thanks to the discipline of the four panellists it became clear that the absorption of technology with the 'how' rather than the 'why' of life produced a gulf of intelligibility when communication was attempted. This attempt to discover authentic bridges which crossed gulfs produced by different thought forms and compulsions, is a world away from that lack of communication which is based merely on ignorance and neglectfulness

Thora Philipson's conviction that a broad education to help people to appreciate the many fields of study which need to be related, was shared by many as the only solution. Quite detailed work was done on the aims of education, the release of people into life abundant which it should seek to effect and the examination systems, their horrors and alternatives. Some attention was given specifically to art education in our time; and this brought Scottish Churches'

House into an area in which it both saw a service it might render and the difficulty of providing that service.

Over the next few years consultations followed on "The Arts in Scotland", "The Arts in Society", and "Creativity and Communication"; and there was also an attempt to form an informal group on the art curriculum which would pick up educational matters already discussed in this field with the Inspectorate. In these gatherings film, poetry and painting were given specific attention. No other group of reports of gatherings which took place in Scottish Churches' House can match this collection in significance.

Those who took part in consultations on the arts found their way into a variety of other consultative work promoted by Scottish Churches' House. From the fresh thinking and new contacts made, TV programmes on the understanding of authority in our time, on the relationship of art, technology and theology, and on the human condition were produced. A group which dubbed themselves "Agnostics Anonymous" (though one has fallen by the wayside since and joined the Church) offered to paint out the common room of the House, "just to show how much the place means to us". Best of all was the realisation on the part of many that a house owned by nine churches as a common point of meeting and initiative had shown a fresh concern for the arts and a willingness to re-assess the church relationship to them. It was hoped that this could mean a fresh climate in all the churches which stood behind the centre. There had then been a sign of hope in the Church of Scotland's use of the Gateway Theatre; and there were fresh signs in the appointment of a lay expert to advise the Church in questions on developing technology; and on plans to build a centre for the arts in Edinburgh's Royal Mile.

By 1969 there was every sign that the fellowship of exploration begun in earlier years would continue; and that engineers and technologists would attempt, in concert with painters, poets, film-makers, dramatists and theologians, to find means to communicate intelligibly with one another and share their concern for human well-being in this age, particularly in their own nation, Scotland.

Music

Following on the Memorial Service in Westminster Abbey on 8th February 1983 for Erik Routley, music maestro supreme, friends of his on both sides of the Atlantic agreed that a book should be prepared covering some of the enterprises in which he had been engaged in his busy and joyous life

Ian Fraser was asked to contribute a review of the 1960s Dunblane consultations which, in the words of the editors, provided 'the spark which set off the so-called hymn explosion'. This was his offering:

"I know that Erik looked back and found Dunblane unique, something he did not manage to recapture elsewhere." Thus Alan Luff, Precentor of Westminster Abbey, looking back on his personal experience of the "unique creative atmosphere" which marked the Scottish Churches House hymn-writing initiative. "It was from the Dunblane enterprise that the world 'hymn explosion' took off" I am told on all hands. The beginnings? It was given to me to load a starter's gun and to Erik to fire it. All I said was "Let's stop moaning and get down to the job." All Erik said was "Let's; now!" We were off.

It was 1961, Scottish Churches House was just beginning to find its feet as a house for the co-operating Churches in Scotland – a place held in common which gave them opportunity to move, together, into fresh fields. During a free period between sessions of a consultation on evangelism, some participants exchanged harsh comments on some 'modern' hymns recently published in a Church magazine. Their criticism was mainly that these retained all the old stereotypes. For the umpteenth time, the cry went up "Nobody's getting down to writing the hymns for our time". On this occasion, the cry was heard.

Erik became the real catalyst and inspirer, while I acted as back-up. He cheerfully described my role as that of gauleiter – I was to prepare the working sessions, and produce reports, but especially was to breathe down the necks of those who had agreed to do some portion of the work, and see that it was made available in time. Did you ever happen to notice Erik's hands? He had sticky fingers for work but buttery fingers for praise. Credit directed to him was always diverted to someone or somewhere else. But the flow of ideas and encouragement came quite specially from him.

When it was agreed that we get down to the job I was asked first of all to take soundings; then, if these proved positive, to bring a consultation into being in 1962. Reggie Barrett-Ayres, Head of the Department of Music in Aberdeen University, acted as convener, and Erik became Secretary of the Working Group.

The first consultation took place in early October 1962. Jock Wilson, reporting for the *British Weekly*, put it on record that two dozen ministers and organists of the Church of Scotland, the Congregational Church and the Episcopal Church met to "take a radical look at Church music today".

Ian McKenzie, at that time of the BBC, then Scottish Secretary of the Student Christian Movement, opened the consultation. He likened the tension between high-brow and middle-and-low-brow music to that between creation and redemption and made the plea:

> "As our Lord consorted with publicans and sinners without making any demands that they should first of all change, so we should open ourselves to the young people of today and let them bring what they are and what they have..."

At a later session, Erik applied CS Lewis' literary criterion to the work of judging new music (he illustrated with a number of tape recordings), i.e. "the capacity for receiving all the best the reader can give." Later he reminded the consultation that it is always the immediate past which we want to scrap and the contemporary which appears revolutionary. He warned against two stock phrases: "I don't like it" (said because "it" has impressed us as fascinating and dangerous and has threatened our self-preservation) and "only the best is good enough" (which he called "almost idolatrous"). David Hamilton observed that, since singing had become about the only thing left to the people themselves, it was no wonder that they resisted innovation.

Reggie Barrett-Ayres was asked to take the final session. He spoke of:

> "....the polyphony of the 16th century... its sense of unity: the forthright music of the Lutheran tradition, where new reform with economy illustrated strength; and, finally, the folk element in hymnology, that part of our humanity, "the milk of human kindness" which is Love. Unity, strength and love were the three vital virtues which were worth keeping alive." These were then illustrated from compositions by students and staff of his University's Music Department, concluding with a Cantata by Reggie himself......."

It was observed in discussion that a great deal of strain stemmed from the tension between the "establishment" in the Church and the creative artist. At that very first consultation, the possibility of an ecumenical hymn book was mooted. An alternative was also advocated – John Cheyen put forward the idea of a loose leaf publication (so that pieces could be tried, affirmed, changed, discarded until what was wanted and needed was found) rather than a new hymn book which would "solidify the conventional set-up".

A further consultation was agreed on for October 1963, and the agenda proposed as follows:

(a) Evidences will be looked at from churches already "on the job". This session will give opportunity to participants to share insights, needs and fruitful lines worked on locally.

(b) Composers are being approached and asked to be prepared to be associated experimentally with a local church. What link up will prove most effective? What kind of experimentation is likely to prove significant and where? We must share ideas on these.

(c) Re folk-songs and folk-song groups: a contribution is being sought from Sydney Carter regarding the social and musical significance of such groups and music forms. Consideration should also be given to the place of "disposable music".

(d) Is good music a bourgeois cult? Erik Routley will raise this question.

(e) What are the prospects for an Ecumenical Hymnary? Anglicans and Presbyterians meeting in Scottish Churches House recently were agreed that fresh confessions or even the revision of existing confessions *undertaken denominationally* no longer make sense. Is this equally true of denominational hymnaries?!

The 1963 consultation illustrated features which became characteristic of Dunblane gatherings, namely: a) seminal contributions from people on the march; b) specific tasks (such as the project of producing a new *Church Hymnary*); c) plans for getting more people creatively involved.

The report records:

'In a sparkle and fizz of bright images Erik Routley presented the thesis that good music was a bourgeois cult. Hymns, it was said, had to be by great composers, and there had to be an exactness in producing the music according to the best traditions! The reality is that many of the composers of hymn music remain anonymous, and would have had no great mind about whether this or that way to play their work was the right one! What 'better' music demanded was attention: one had to gather one's faculties and do justice to it. But Bach, Brahms and others did a bread-and butter job – they turned out the music which was required for the immediate purpose which faced them......'

Modern Protestantism is pretty firmly in the "good music which requires and deserves serious attention" tradition. Most people who do not have our background and do not have their minds trained as we do, either enjoy music in a different way or feel that their way of enjoying is inferior – and want to move up a grade so that they can at least appear to enjoy it the way we do! There is no reason for believing that the common enjoyment of music is of less value than "appreciation of good music". The ordinary chap and his missus relish a bit of moderate background noise in a restaurant, since it provides them with a bit of privacy and at the same time saves them the awkwardness of silence. They love a good crowd sing. Do we try to go where they are? Or do we try to get them to come where we are? Is there some point or points of common meeting? Or is this all we can say – that we must be much more humble and teachable before an enjoyment of music which is not of the same kind as our own?....

Tom Keir introduced the question of producing an ecumenical hymnary:

He noted these factors which had to be taken seriously within a general ecumenical concern such as he himself held:

(a)   there were financial considerations, particularly with churches which had produced new Hymnaries in recent years;

(b)   a book produced commonly would lose its point if it were not used commonly: the ecumenical advantage would be lost. The 1650 Psalter was intended to serve this purpose but the Anglicans did not pick it up, so that no common purpose was served;

(c)   There were theological difficulties. Would Baptists happily have in their Hymn Book hymns which understood infant baptism as a proper form of Christian baptism? Would Anglo-Catholics want a transubstantiation slant to Eucharist hymns? Could the Feast of the Blessed Virgin Mary be included without alienating certain Churches; or excluded without alienating others? We would arrive at a very lowest-common-denominator level if we rejected hymns which might offend one Church or another; and would produce a very small hymnary indeed;

(d)   We already used the Psalms in common. We had a common structure in Holy Communion basically. We needed a common lectionary – which would appear to be a more profitable next step. And we needed to avoid standardisation which curbed vitality.

(e)   We had to watch our timing, and the time did not seem to be ripe at the moment. Churches are only now discovering their brethren and discovering themselves in ecumenical debate. This must go on for some time.

The report proceeds

> Erik Routley was essentially of a different mind although he appreciated in a new way certain of the points made. There seemed to him to be a Scottish culture which transcends denominational boundaries and a Scottish Churches' Hymnary would be welcomed.

But we were persuaded to stay on safe ground rather than risk skating on the thin but inviting ecumenical ice of that time. I believe we followed the logic of the situation; and I believe we failed to produce fruits before our time – something we were called to do in face of the logic. From this point, a definitive Hymn Book was not on the cards. Supplements to Hymn books and loose-leaf items of praise were concentrated on. The consultation planned forward thus:

> Erik Routley was encouraged (and any help that was needed was offered to him) to proceed with the linking up of composers with congregations to undertake experimental work. If this could be developed, it would produce a very useful ferment which could help other things of musical interest to sprout.

A Working Group was set up comprising Reggie Barrett-Ayres, Erik Routley, Jock Wilson, John Currie, John Cheyne, Stewart Todd, Tom Weir and Ian Mackenzie. They were asked to find/produce twelve hymns with thirty-six tunes by February 1964, the projected first meeting date of the Working Group. Items wanted fell into two categories a) hymns which the group identified in the Revised Church Hymnary whose words deserved better tunes b) new hymns, particularly on themes which were not dealt with adequately in the hymnaries. Among themes suggested under (b) were baptism in relation to Christ's baptism and baptism as incorporation; the Church militant in the

Communion of Saints; eucharistic hymns; marriage hymns; hymns dealing with the mission, ministries, reconciling work of the World Church; the mystery of the Godhead; the Holy Spirit in exciting Pentecostal manifestation and in the corporate action of the community; eschatological hymns, processional hymns for various occasions.

It was planned that this material then be tried out in congregations, between the time of its evaluation in February and the autumn consultation. Tapes of the material could be circulated to help any interested minister or organist to interest, in turn, congregation and choir.

Before the October 1964 consultation, all participants received a sizeable batch of hymns, songs, words, tunes – assembled by the Working Group – to try out, criticise, amend, replace or whatever. The names of the composers of the music were concealed. Participants were asked themselves to contribute: and material they supplied was also sent out beforehand. The early part of the 1964 consultation was given over to the evaluation of work submitted.

Links were made, through Erik, with the proprietors of Hymns Ancient and Modern at this point, since they were eager to work along the same lines. The enterprise was becoming British, not just Scottish. Sydney Carter shared in the 1964 consultation.

He took a session, and shared with us some of his experience. He pointed to the way in which submerged belief and unbelief were becoming articulate among groups he frequented. People wanted to make sense of life – and they could not get away from life! Folk Song groups brought together people of quite different convictions and backgrounds. Meetings in pubs or coffee bars created a fellowship which was in many senses like that of a church: from time to time, moments of unity were experienced and those present became all of one mind, almost as in an act of worship. A network of these circles existed all over the world. Wherever you went, you felt you belonged. Community was real; people offered hospitality to others freely when they could, and willingly shared what money they had.

Folk music was experiencing a boom in the USA. Twice as many attended a Folk Festival as attended the Newport Jazz Festival. In Britain a good deal of what was available came out through Radio Caroline (the pirate radio station).

In Scotland traditional music never came to a full stop. There had been a clear break in England. An impetus at the beginning of the century, especially through such people as Cecil Sharp and Vaughan Williams brought a revival down south. It had quite a flavour of English nationalism about it. But then the whole thing "went educated", and lost a good deal of its impetus. Some of the native stuff could not be put down on paper! It was introduced into schools and taken up enthusiastically by school ma'ams. As might be expected, words and music were emasculated.

Skiffle brought something almost equivalent to a religious revival. One of the useful things it did was to stop the word "folk" being a word of opprobrium. The word gained an acceptable image. An interesting thing about those who have developed it from that point, is that very many of them are visual artists whose interest has been captured by the possibilities music offers, rather than literary people.

What is it in folk music that grips people? For one thing, it is about honest things presented honestly. You get reality in the treatment of love and work, for instance, which you do not get in the Top Ten. Also there are elements of magic and poetry in it of which many people are starved. It appeals particularly to the under-twenty-fives. Those who appreciate it often appreciate classical music and, surprisingly often, church music. But folk music is not really pure music – rather it is drama, to which the music (or even music and words) is secondary. And it may depend for its effect a great deal on the person who is presenting it. It has echoes of the most primitive forms of drama. It does not differentiate the arts but uses them in proportion. By word, sound, movement, vision a total assault is made on the senses. Musicians want to make the musical interest paramount: very properly they are denied this in folk music.

Out of this movement an approach has developed to music and song which is radical and almost (in relation to what musicians feel is their proper sphere) subversive. It attracts a motley company in which for instance, Communists and Roman Catholics almost balance one another out for numbers.

To follow Sydney's shared perceptions, records were played – records of Bob Dylan on the Bishop of Woolwich and George Fox and a new setting of "Teach me my God and King". These provided an interval to reflect and absorb.

In the consequent discussion the question was raised whether it is possible to have religious songs which are anti-Christian, to provide a certain bit and realism in worship. It was also observed – some things which are needed are not singable in Church. Where truth seems to be emerging in some kind of drama form, does it not belong properly to religious theatre rather than worship? In later discussion it was observed: 'Folk is a root from which contemporary things can grow."

At the end of the whole gathering it was debated whether another consultation should be held.

a)   it was agreed that the process of creating, judging, making available material for songs and hymns of our time cried out for further investment of time and energy.

b)   Jazz still had to be looked into.

c)   Colin Day suggested that there be a contribution to the Perth Kirk Week 1965 – and that would require further work. A fresh Working Group comprising Erik Routley, Margaret Dickie, George McPhee, Douglas Galbraith, John Geyer and John Currie was appointed to carry the work forward. Deliberately it was decided to draw on the experience of unbelievers too. Some common thinking was also to be done with the Corrie Trio (later to become the famous folksinging group) and with Ian Menzies and the Clyde Valley Stompers.

A fruit of the Group's work was a first publication, produced early in 1965, *Dunblane Praises No 1*. Music was hand-written, and the whole production deliberately suggested an unfinished, non-status, try-it-and-see approach.

By 1965 a groundwork of common perceptions had been laid. Keynote contributions tailed off. Time was more and more occupied with producing and gathering material, trying and testing it out. The wording of the heading of the next consultation, given in the letter of invitation, makes this clear:

"Forty-eight Hours of Composition and Consultation on Music and Words to catch the ear of our time". It was promised that "most of the time will be occupied with hammering out words and music on the spot in small groups or solo – it will be essentially an experimental, working come-together."

An undated flier from Erik, designed to stimulate thinking especially on the part of those who had recently been drawn in, was probably issued as a preparatory document for this consultation. He raised in it questions about the respect and/or disrespect due to existing liturgical traditions. I extract a few points:

> Worship is made up of both certain acts and implied doctrines – what are these? (Do different traditions have a common mind on the essentials, he would seem to be asking).

> Thinking of folk song as Sydney Carter had presented it, do ironic words, descriptive or actual human situations, have a place in worship – say, related to the confession of sin rather than to proclamation?

> Since antiphony "is for some reason repellent to people of the reformed religious culture" do Gelineau and Catholic liturgies provide possible clues for re-examining our hang-ups?

Two sections and the summary, I feel, should be given in Erik's own words. They show how he probed and questioned, shook people up, got them exploring:

Spontaneity?

One of the evocative words among many Christian groups is "spontaneity". The idea of anything in public worship being prepared or rehearsed beforehand is strange to most people. Try out some questions such as these:

a) To what extent is it proper to treat a congregation as people joining in a play, charade, or a kind of socio-drama?

b) If it is, in this sense, proper – and the central act of all, worship, suggests that in some sense it must be – then must not some kinds of congregational activity be regarded as 'preparation' or 'rehearsal' for the drama. Is this a profane way, or a creative way, for example, of looking at "Preparation for Communion"?

c) If that kind of approach which includes anything from a congregational practice to a spiritual 'rehearsal' or 'preparation' – is legitimate: if the learning of the Book of Common Prayer responses and Catechism, for example, makes the public conversation and communal acts come naturally to Anglican worshippers – is there on the other hand any place for the 'pentecostal' in worship? Jazz music depends on improvisation, which must correspond in some way to the improvised, spontaneous element upon which the left wing of the Reformation placed such reliance. Is this right?

Sin

It is very necessary to try to come to some common mind on the question whether experiments with worship are or are not found to be vitiated by a spiritual pride that takes too much in human creative ability for granted

a) Is liturgy (controlled drama, if it be drama at all) a necessary safeguard against the consequences of sin?

b) Exactly what outward activities in worshippers ought to be controlled in this or any other way?

c) On the other hand: is a rigid adherence to principles itself a refusal to commit ourselves to the needs of the time and to the duty of responding to them?

Summary

The Consultation will do something very useful if it can, through corporate thinking and discussion, help artists to see just how far they ought, in writing words or music for the Church, to regard existing liturgical customs as a framework within which they must operate, and how far they are permitted to present material whose use would involve considerable (if temporary) change in liturgical habits.

There is one very great danger, a sense of which has prompted these notes: namely, that Sunday Morning and Sunday Evening become divorced from each other and lead to an aesthetic and social schism in the local community. How much may the informed and responsible bearers of the church's tradition insist on? How much is dispensable? How much requires translation?

The 1966 Consultation did groundwork which allowed the Working Group, in December of that year to produce *Dunblane Praises No 2*, which (still adopting a provisional form) was published in 1967.

By that time, the whole enterprise was taking off in a larger way. A BBC "Songs of Praise", introducing new words and music to the public was broadcast on February 12th, led by Dunblane Cathedral Choir with Peter Youngson as soloist and Erik as conductor.

Material was by now being requested for children – the first steps were taken towards what was later published (still keeping to a provisional form) as *Dunblane Praises for School: 1 Juniors.*

Choirs, groups and individuals of Aberdeen University (under Reggie Barrett-Ayres) and Manchester Cathedral (under Alan Luff) prepared joint work with the aim of recording a tape to introduce fresh material to a wider public.

Plans were laid for the first publication to be deliberately given more definitive form, New Songs for the Church 1 & 2, as a supplement to hymn books (published by Galliard and Scottish Churches Council). Children's' hymns, scrutinised by a professional child psychologist, were included.

The introduction ends: "…..we hope that the use of this book may inject into public worship a new kind of sincerity and gaiety which are the constituents of the real seriousness of the Christian faith." Erik's words.

The need for fresh consultations was not now commanding, and the work flowed into a variety of different channels. Alan Luff has shared with me his own regret that he was not able to develop more of his work on chants and canticles in association with the group which met a Dunblane – he saw no other group which was as creative and had as sure a touch. Otherwise, people seem to have been content that, with a basic work done, they should follow whichever lines most interested them.

One line of development, however, needs special mention. Many of us in the Dunblane group were worried at the number of childrens' hymns which served as adult control devices –suggesting that God's great desire was to keep children in line and get them to be meek and mild like Jesus; tidy, colourless conformists.

It was thanks largely to the energetic work of one member, Gracie King, and the co-operation of an Iona Community Family Group that the first volume of children's hymns was produced. Two criteria were set for work which could be published – either children supplied the words or children said "yes" to them. The introduction explicitly states "the present volume consists partly of ideas and words provided by children, integrated in form with the help of an adult, and partly works of adults which had been tried out with children. One tune was composed by children."

The new book was firmly in the Dunblane tradition:

'This is a try-it-and-see book for junior pupils. Day schools and Sunday schools are asked to bring it into use, allow time for children to familiarise themselves with words and music, and judge what meets the mind of children and speaks truly of the faith, and what does not.

They are asked to enter further into the spirit of experiment which produced this book. Is this note or that theme missing? Why not get children to share their thoughts about life and shape these into verse? Or let an adult try to frame words and music which catch the imagination of children. As *Dunblane Praises 1 and 2* were try-it-out publications which led to the more definitive *New Songs for the Church* (Galliard Press 7/6) so we hope for a ferment of creation of schools praises. Original words and music can be forwarded to Mrs RM King, c/o Scottish Churches House. Out of what stands the test, when tried out with different groups, a more definitive volume of new praise could emerge over the years.'

Gracie King culled musical and spoken ideas from individual children, some of them ESN (educationally subnormal) pupils, and sometimes from a whole class working on a "round robin" basis. She would then clothe the ideas in useable form.

The resulting song would then be tried out in a variety of classes and schools. Wherever class after class made the same "mistake", Gracie would correct the song, not the singers – thus speeding up the "folk process". The final version would then be used in a variety of town and rural schools for school worship. The song would at that point be rested. Only those songs which were remembered and re-requested in several schools or Sunday Schools would be submitted for consideration for a *Dunblane Praises* publication. Those songs that were not asked for again were jettisoned. In this way child creativity, adult experience and popular acceptability were married to form child folk hymns.

Some years later a sign and outcome of the Dunblane approach to worship happened in a small rural church. Gracie King was asked if she could "do something with the children" for the church's centenary. The result was a service "Praise through the Ages." The items were linked by bible readings and commentaries on local history given by the teenagers. By the time the (conventional) congregation were asked to sing Tallis in canon (unrehearsed) they quite took it in their stride. They had gained confidence to be active music makers themselves.

The Dunblane Method of Working

In working through the documents, it struck me that aspects of "the Dunblane approach" were registered quite clearly.

1. The aim was to get people involved in finding new words and music and not to do this for them. In preparation for the 1963 Conference, Erik set out the mind of himself and his colleagues in the following words: "we are looking for a new simple music, without a traditional ecclesiastical accent, perhaps making use of instruments other than piano or organ (recorder, trumpet, clarinet, strings?) of which we could say "Try this". He adds that it must be free of copyright "so that it could be freely used at once."

   In a letter to me a year or two before he died, Erik speaks in some astonishment regarding the extent to which early productions of members of the group found favour in different parts of the world and made their way into a variety of hymnaries. What we turned out was not thought of as substantive in itself. It had the aim of getting people goaded and encouraged into creative action. Members of the group would have been quite content if the fruit had been people who said "I could do better than that", and went on to do so.

2. The whole experience was undertaken in community. No doubt there were individuals who had set out to break the mould in earlier years (cf. hermits and the Celtic church). But, as far as I know, no such ecumenical "intentional community" existed previously. The accent was on gifts brought together to serve one another and build one another up in a common initiative to which all sorts contributed. In the preface to *Dunblane Praises No 1* it was said "Hymns and tunes which carry the reference 'Dunblane' in these pages, instead of the names of their authors or composers, are often the result of communal thinking and criticism." In the report of the 1963 Consultation, those who were prepared to turn out words and music were asked to hold their hand before giving their work a final finish. They were invited, instead, to "give it a run", testing it out in experience, and exploring, with others, possibilities which might emerge only from actual production and use. Once a

communal mind had been brought to bear, the rounding off could be completed more efficiently.

It was quite customary, when the Working Group met, to take material which had been sent in and say "Here is a bit of music with possibilities which have not been quite realised", or "Here are words which need a good working over to give them full effectiveness"- and hand over the item to a member of the group to work on for an hour or two hours, and then bring back for group judgement. Even if the author were present, the assumption would be that he or she stood too near to the product; that someone else might provide a fresh perspective on it.

It was this way of working which goaded Erik to write words for a hymn for the first time in his life. Alan Luff can tell the full story because he was the miscreant who unwittingly challenged Erik to move into new fields:

"We had a session to identify gaps in the existing hymnaries. A hymn or ballad which would be useful in a Christian Aid context was called for. We were all sent packing to see what we might be able to produce. It turned out that Erik and I had been given adjoining rooms. Now, I had never written any kind of hymn, ever before. I wondered how to start, and began looking up biblical texts. I landed on the feeding of the five thousand and the words in the New English Bible translation 'Where can we find bread to feed these people'. I made that the first line of the song or ballad or hymn. Then I found that the only way I could work was by creating a thread of tune on which I could string the words. So I hummed over and over and over again this little bit of a tune as I looked for the words I wanted. Poor Erik next door, was put entirely off the task of writing his own tune. He gave up, in the end and went on (and I say, 'Praise the Lord'!) to write his magnificent hymn (the first for him as well) 'All who love and serve your City.' I was sorry when I found the frustration I had caused him. But, in the end, I rather feel more proud of my humming and doodling next door to him, because it expanded his own creative work. I think there was something of Dunblane in this whole incident. Coming into the group, you did not think you had anything to give. Yet you were challenged or encouraged or whatever was needed, to meet the situation. Somehow the Holy Spirit was abroad and things happened. The whole thing could come out, as in the case of Erik, in a way quite different from anything which was intended."

3.   Whatever was produced was floated on the waters. The copyright remained in the hands of the author, while freedom was afforded to interested parties to try things out. Only when a publisher secured copyright was an item withdrawn from general circulation.

Techniques were sought to get musical life flowing. In the letter already mentioned in preparation for the 1963 consultation, a particular possibility is presented:

'We think that the most fruitful way of making such an experiment would be to put you in direct touch with a source of demand that lay near to where you live, so that if you wished you could personally supervise the initial production of what you wrote. A demand might come in from, say Drumchapel: and we might write to one of you and say "Here is the demand: here are the resources: would you care to write something, fairly quickly, that they could try out?" What you sent would have to be sent without prejudice. We should have to face the possibility that it might not come off. But would you please let us know whether the principle of the thing seems to make sense to you, and whether the idea of participating appeals to you?'

People were also encouraged to work on new types of musical production. The report of the 1964 consultation includes the following: "The good songs at present are those of seekers not finders: and for this the 'cabaret' song is a fine vehicle." When Mrs Margaret Dickie stressed the need to keep such experimentation clear of the disciplined march of eucharistic worship, there came the following counter-assertation: "If the liturgy has in it basically the re-enactment of the works of creation and redemption then it could be that the 'cabaret' material could be a vital disturbing explosive preparation for the Eucharist or the sermon."

4.   Those who responded to the invitation to produce material were encouraged to believe that what they attempted could have merit even if it were of a limited or transitory character: "The intention is not necessarily that the music should have a long life: it may well be used for a time and then discarded. Do you think it is possible to have a 'disposable' music that is free of the pretentiousness of 'pop' as it is normally understood? We think that there is a legitimate relation between this idea and that of (say) film music". There was quite a debate about this at one point, on the part of those who thought that they were being encouraged to write ephemeral stuff. There was no such intention. What was meant is illustrated by a conference I shared with Methodist Laymen in Swanwick, where a hymn was produced which spoke to the people of the conference but would not have spoken to those who could not share what they had experienced in the conference. "Write it on toilet paper" I used to suggest for such occasions "When it has fulfilled its purpose it can be flushed away,"

5.   Straight speaking was promised and, from the start, was a feature of the group's way of working. If members of the group and others associated were to have taken umbrage when their work was criticised, there would have been no possibility of giving it more effective form. Introducing a session of the 1963 consultation, Reggie Barrett-Ayres proposed that the Working Group be set up both to produce new tunes to existing words and to create altogether new hymns. He went on: 'These would be submitted to the most rigorous criticism in terms of their theology, their music and their capacity to communicate with congregations and to be sung with understanding and spirit by congregations. They could be worked at experimentally over a period between the time in the year when they were submitted and the autumn consultation." In that consultation itself, members recognised the need for self-criticism and balance. Thus, from the report (Erik's words, I'd guess):

We have to be aware of adjective "Christian". So often it has meant a form of lasso with which we hope to capture things within reach which appeal to us, and dress them up our way.....

Humour is a way of acknowledging one's insufficiency. The medieval carols made this point. It might be that the person who can write hymns is the person who can write good light verse – verse which is light but deep, making an immediate impact which gains the attention and then reveals level upon level of meaning.

6.   People themselves were to be the judges – congregations, groups who wanted a good crowd sing, all sorts of folk using their own judgement and depending on whatever was their musical taste. That included children. Confidence was given to ordinary folk to create and to evaluate.

I may illustrate from my own experience the way in which those who had never thought of themselves as possible contributors to the musical praise of the Church were drawn in. What happened may be expressed thus: awareness of the potential of church praise-forms, as vehicles for words and music, began to take up residence in the forefront of people's consciousness instead of staying in the background. Add to that, that the Working Group bestowed, in a very direct way, a reassuring and encouraging sense that many non-specialists could perfectly well have a stab at this work. That the group would criticise it rigorously was also encouraging: it meant that second and third rate productions would not be allowed to pass.

Thanks to the influence of a perceptive English teacher at school, I was given an early habit of savouring words, rolling them around on the tongue of the mind to appreciate their flavours. I gained the habit of experimenting with words, phrases, ideas to see how they could be set in creative relationship.

When the Dunblane Group started its work, three phrases were interacting in one magnetic field in my mind. There was Jesus Christ as "the Sun behind all suns." There was Blake's "Tiger tiger burning bright." There was TS Eliot's "In the juvenescence of the year, Came Christ the tiger". Previously, the fruit of that interplay might have been expressed in an article, a sermon, or simply some doodles.

Now it sought a poem/hymn form. All I could bring to the task in terms of knowledge of style was to say things as clearly, tellingly and economically as possible. On the way to a Presbytery meeting of all things, I found myself with two lines which began to create a basis of new perception:

> Christ, burning
> Past all suns

I saw Christ as the Lord of the world's jungle, flaming through its thickets of darkness, lithe and powerful, fierce in his love for his own. But he is not only a jungle-presence, I had to remind myself. Risen and ascended, he is in control of the whole created order, above all the jungles of the Universe, over the Universe itself:

> so
>
> > stars beneath your feet
> > like leaves on forest floor
> >
> > > came next.

It is in contrast to his burning love and might that our human predicament is to be seen. We have dangerous longings to act and be "as gods", to take absolute charge of our world – who were meant to take charge *with God*. Yet it is the will of God that we be curious, satisfy our thirst for knowledge, exercise power! The next lines came out:

> We, turning
> spaceward, spurn
> knowledge incomplete
> fevered to explore

Realism required me now to set the hope for creation represented in Christ dialectically over against the threat we human beings pose to creation.

> Christ, holding   Christ, festive
> atoms in one   in quick bird
> loom of light and power rush of river flood
> to weave creations life: glances lovers dart

52

man, moulding	youth, restive
rocket, gun	seek new word
turns creation sour	beat of life in blood
plots dissolving strife	ashes in the heart

What relationship is there between the mighty work of Jesus Christ in and over the universe and our human ability to use the gifts and power entrusted to us to destroy or spoil the marvellous work? I had to find some correspondence. It came in Christ's determination to take our side, whatever the consequences. That was the root of hope.

> Christ, humble
> on our side,
> snatching death's foul keys
> cramping, Satan's scope –
> we gamble on our guide
> inch our gains of peace,
> work a work of hope

(From the first roughcast to the finished product took months, off and on)

I even got courage, as someone who had no musical training, to attempt my own tunes. I became annoyed at the way in which musicians developed their musical creations and attempted to tack them on to my words. My only resource then, as a musically uninstructed person, was to live with the rhythm of the words for some months until they declared their own tune to me.

"Christ burning" did not catch on. Another Dunblane gift – I had now a perspective for such an eventuality. Maybe my work was not all that good, or did not communicate. Maybe it would be more authentically presented as a poem than as a hymn (Erik wrote at one point to say that he could not get Americans to appreciate my poetic hymns; and I myself believe that good verse provides the usual vehicle for hymns). Someone else might be stimulated by it to do better. The time for the hymn might be in the future rather than in the present. "Work in as imaginative and disciplined a way as possible; then sit lightly by your work" was one of the lessons learned by those who came to Dunblane.

Personalities

"The time would fail me .... " It is very difficult to select, from the many people involved, who should be mentioned particularly. Yet this whole enterprise depended on the drawing together of people with special skills and the ability to relate creatively to one another. I hope I may be forgiven for mentioning but a few and therefore leaving out many.

Reggie Barrett-Ayres was convener. Reggie had quite an unusual gift for drawing musical quality out of very unlikely characters. His interest was in the area where music and drama met, and that was the direction he took off on, at the end of the 1960s.

Stewart Todd was deeply concerned that all church music should be subservient to the Word of God and serve the Gospel, not drawing attention to itself but being modest and humble in its service.

Peter Cutts joined the Group when his talents for clothing words with music were coming to full fruitfulness.

Alan Luff joined late, and brought gifts from that fact – as from his musical ability, and conviction that chants and canticles must find their place and the initiative of Gelineau be accepted as an encouragement to break into new territory.

Eric Reid's "Trotting, Trotting through Jerusalem" found its way into hymn books in many parts of the world. His death in car accident really bereaved the group. He was an immensely fertile composer who had a strongly academic and modern background, and a common touch. He had done his thesis in Germany on the work of one of the avant-garde Second Viennese School of Composers. Yet, at school where he taught, the development of brass band and other musical work put him in deep community with children and, from that, with ordinary folk of all kinds.

Alan Luff reminded me of the way in which, quite often, productions developed at Dunblane or in relation to it, took serious account of the violence in society. He noted that few of the hymn books or supplements picked up material which had life's rawness and crudity about it. For me, Peter Youngsons's "Body and Blood" was the best neglected piece of writing in the whole Dunblane repertoire. Peter had been a Communist in his young days. He had a very powerful voice and heckled Donald Soper at Tower Hill unmercifully. At one point Donald stopped and commanded him to lose the power of speech. He went dumb. Early the next morning, he appeared at Donald Soper's door.

What followed produced his conversion. He was parish minister in the territory of the gangs, Easterhouse, when he participated in the Dunblane enterprise.

John Geyer refused to allow us to ignore what was developing in teenage culture, or to dismiss new sounds if they did not fit in with previous ideas of harmony.

Caryl Micklem brought a feel for the music which best clothed words (eg "Christ burning") ... and so on.

The Still Centre

Alan Luff: "I was always very much taken up with the worship in the little chapel cell up behind Scottish Churches House. It was the Iona forms of worship we were using, and that had a fresh heightening impact on me. The very simplicity of that place, as we sat around ... It often had been all words and talk during the sessions. Simply to be there and to be very quiet, got deep into me. Then various people, Erik very often led us – with few words, but very perceptively. The musical input in those services was very scant indeed – strange, considering what we were engaged in. But the acts of worship and waiting on God were very much the heart of what was going on at Dunblane. They were the still centre of the operation".

Publications
Dunblane Praises No 1, 1965
Dunblane Praises No 2, 1967
Dunblane Praises for Schools 1. Juniors, 1970 – all three provisional-style
Publications
New Songs for the Church Book 1. Psalms, Childrens's Songs, Ballads, Hymns.
New Songs for the Church Book 2, Canticles - published in 1969 by Galliard and
Scottish Churches Council.

Drama

Music and Drama are closely related. An insistent note which was repeated again and again during the work on music was that we needed to recover a dramatic view of worship. Worship was 'real happening' made vivid by symbol and movement. Reginald Barrett-Ayres, convener of the Music Working Group took the lead in initiating thinking and experiment in the fields of religious drama.

In the summer of 1967, after some careful preparatory work, a conference on contemporary religious drama was held entitled 'To Believe is to Act'. The working committee which prepared the conference made it clear that its intention also was to get people writing and trying things out themselves. Those who took part were invited to contribute any dramatic works they themselves had created. They were also invited to try out and comment on the work of others. An element of 'instant drama' was included – a group would be given a situation and, on the spot, would be asked to think out a way of handling it and developing it dramatically. All this was very promising and initially attracted the kind of interest which suggested it might provide the same kind of growth-point as had the interest in music.

The opening statement to the invitation to the 1968 conference makes the purpose of it clear: "Christianity is concerned with the wholeness of life. Drama is concerned with the art of living. To discover to what extent and in what way we can use this medium of communication as an instrument to pose problems, to express faith, to aid doctrinal teaching are the main aims of this consultation".

A Working Party prepared the conference for 1968. But at a crucial point Reggie Barrett-Ayres took ill and the conference had to be cancelled.

One key question which occurred is similar to one which cropped up in the field of music. There one had to ask whether there were not to be found, in communities outside the church, the authentic notes of prophecy in our time. To take the French theatre alone, Samuel Beckett, Jean Anouilh and Jean-Paul Sartre are exploring the human condition in our time most sensitively. Their approach is inescapably theological. Atheists have to make it clear what God or gods they reject. Are they the writers of religious drama who should be getting attention?

The Mass Media

In the consultation on "The Autonomy and Responsibility of the Arts" one statement which gained wide agreement was "We will have to cope with an entirely differently conditioned society in the future because of the increasing use of visual media". It was the visual media which proved to be pre-occupying in many consultations at Scottish Churches' House.

In September 1962 material from the Pilkington Report provided the basis for the theme 'The Creative Use of Television'. The report from Uppsala, 'The Church and the Media of Mass Communication' provided substance for a consultation in November 1968 on 'Towards a Responsible Society – The Role of Television'. Between these two came 'The Bases of Discrimination – a Consultation on TV Programming and Viewing' - in October 1966 when there was a good deal of public controversy about the policies of TV companies, particularly the BBC. In all these consultations there was the fullest possible co-operation from the BBC and the Independent Companies. In 1962 they came, eyeing one another, to the starting gate, alert to any lining up of the consultation which would give the other a head start. However, the impartiality of the proceedings early on produced confidence. They appreciated the opportunity of thoughtful residential meeting with concerned representatives of Church and public life. In addition they savoured the chance provided, through informal contacts, of discussing problems with one another as professionals. At the 1968 consultation Scottish Churches' House was asked to provide for this type of encounter biennially and a small advisory group of three was appointed to alert the House to any developments between times which warranted additional consultative work.

Right at the end of the working paper for the 1966 consultation two quotations were recorded which struck the note of challenge which many felt the Church should be hearing today. One was contemporary and came from TS Gregory in 'The Tablet'.

"Ecclesiastical authority will need to change, as indeed it is changing, from the authority of safety to the authority of creation. We shall see less and less of the frightened nursemaid who dares not allow her charges out of her sight and more of the dynamic leader demanding enterprise, fearless of experimental mistakes impatient of holy dislikes and pious inertia".

The other was the familiar words of John Milton: "Though all the winds of doctrine were let loose to play upon the earth, so Truth be in the field, we do injuriously, by licensing and prohibiting, to misdoubt her strength".

The contribution to the 1968 consultation of Tom Fleming. who, as a professional actor, has tried to take the measure of the potentialities of the medium, and, as a Christian, has tried to relate these to the calling of the Church, was considered to express the hopes and fears of many:

"Ours is a situation in which the Church should be saying "Hurrah! Everyone is talking our language these days". The Church should surely share the scientists' assumption that things are not what they seem, and find its eyes brightening at the prospect of new angles of exploration into reality. The tragedy is that the Church is stuck on what it is familiar with. Sadly, it must be said that the Church is not different from common humanity in its attitude. All human beings need to appreciate the voyages of discovery which are taking place. For many musicians, music which is immediately familiar must be a stereotype – and they rightly set themselves to extend the frequencies which the human ear can assimilate and appreciate. Picasso has seriously and responsibly departed from a reproduction of exact likeness (which the camera can do better in any case) to probe into the nature of human beings – their tensions and contrasts and harmonies deep down. The theatre has never seen such a generation of responsible servants. Actors did not need to know much about ordinary life before, and could turn out performances whose impact produced no questioning or search – now they must know what is in life and try to understand human motives and attitudes, simply to fulfil their own remit (there will be chancers and phoneys in every profession, some of whom will contrive esoteric situations, producing as much a closed shop as an act of worship must appear to be to many), Shakespeare's greatness comes out when one realises that, age after age and generation after generation, he reveals what people expect to do as actors, or to receive as audiences. Prospero's unlovable traits are revealed right at the beginning of "The Tempest" (which actors and public alike often feel tempted to cut). Caliban can be made a monster and dismissed – or can show up Prospero's self–preoccupation (over all the years they live together he was unconcerned to give Caliban any education to live an adequate life). School children are sensitive to the nuances of deep human relationships e.g. the need for forgiveness, when adult audiences are often hardened against it: they can have sympathy for Caliban.

The church's divorce from the arts is no more than the divorce of the people in general. Yet, through television, millions are getting used to dramatic form. The dramatic type of presentation simply must be becoming more acceptable and better understood.

Religion must move into this whole rich field. The Church must not be a watchdog on television or the arts, only ready to growl at the appearance of scandal and sex. It can help to bring subtle influence to bear which illuminates the worth of human beings and ask questions about life's meaning. To look and listen critically, then fasten only what one detests, then make loud judgements is entirely inappropriate. To look and listen sensitively and take what judgement is made on ourselves, while appreciating the whole range of programming, is a true task. The Church must not yield to the temptation to supply judgements without knowledge. Nor must it act as a pressure group in a way which it itself would resent if it saw this pressure coming from another quarter, eg Communism. It must get to know those who are making TV programmes and appreciate their situation. It should give thanksgivings for what is well done. It should at times encourage scriptwriters, producers, directors etc to take more risks.

The trouble with religious programming is that you know where you will end up before you start – on safe ground. There is little expectation that unpleasant truths may emerge, little sense of a voyage of discovery in which you don't know where you will end up. This comes at a time when all sorts and conditions of men are on the search. We should rejoice in this search. We should team up with others, whatever their basic life-conviction might be, and belong to the venturing company of mankind.

Television offers a wide field for communicating the truth of the gospel and allowing it to make impact - but as exploration into God, and not from the basis of old structures and old ways of thinking."

Prophecy and Conformity

In all the consultations people wrestled with a serious tension produced by seemingly contradictory responsibilities. To be worth its salt television had to be prophetic and to treat its customers as adults; and at the same time had to be sensitive to the possibility that the very programmes which enlarged the experiences of some would make a disturbing impact on others, gratuitously and unfairly threatening their values and standards. The Uppsala report had some strong words on the need to treat people as adults:

> "If mass media, particularly radio and TV are to be more than merely the means of passing the time; if they are to deal with reality, to move and awaken the imagination, to convict the conscience, to inspire and possibly to ennoble, to help people grow, there must remain a place for serious and adult programmes. On occasion such programmes may offend some listeners or viewers. Media which never offend are themselves offensive." ·

It was realised that human beings need to be disturbed out of their small, complacent worlds; that they need their minds stretched and their experience given new dimensions. The artist also needs to be free from what Sir Hugh Greene calls, in "The Conscience of the Programme Director": "A dangerous form of censorship, censorship which works by causing artists and writers not to take risks, not to undertake those adventures of the spirit which must be at the heart of every truly new creative work," This could be agreed and at the same time another side of the coin be seen and appreciated.

All who took part were aware of the difference between going to the theatre or the cinema to see something of choice/and having visual material come straight into the home. As far as children were concerned a responsibility was shared by the programmers and parents, the former keeping material which might be harmful to children out of an agreed "pre-bedtime period" and the parents seeing that the children were not allowed to watch simply anything at any hour. At the same time it was clear that, with television in the home, a programme could develop in a way which no one could anticipate and damage be done before the set could be switched off. It was felt that the resilience of human beings and of children in particular, provided it was buttressed by the watchfulness of programmers and parents, could produce quite a healthy state of affairs. However, not much light was shed on possible ways of protecting inadequate adults in whom unhealthy fears and worries, instincts of violence, tips for crime, incitement to sexual adventures, might be encouraged by certain types of viewing. The biggest protection is to help all people to "come of age".

In each consultation time was taken by the professionals to explain the processes whereby there was a continual checking and sifting of material before it reached the screen. These processes both in the BBC and the commercial companies need to be much more widely known and appreciated. Those who took part in the consultations thought they were not only adequate but imaginative. Bill Cotton junior illustrated vividly, from tussles he had with script writers in the field of entertainment, the difficulty of drawing a line at the point where the desire of the creative artist to write to express his convictions slides into a determination to see how far he can go and get off with it. Oliver Whitley, Assistant to the Director General of the BBC, drew attention to the importance laid on conventions by Robert Bolt, "one of our more confident playwrights". Without conventions, said Bolt, "it's very difficult to get any tension into the individual work of art..... If you have a firm convention, all sorts of forceful and delicate things can be done."

> "The artist is by his nature bound often to offend. It isn't his function to operate within the limits of contemporary taste or convention. Craftsmen can do that, and must do so. The artist probes around the outer edges of acceptance, increasing the range of man's understanding of himself, and his environment. Outriding his less

perceptive and gifted fellows, asleep in their covered wagons, he is often an uncomfortable herald. This is his offence.

Of all people Christians should be least surprised, and least dismayed, the most understanding why the artist may cry havoc at the status quo, and the first to see that the BBC should let him do so. For prophecy shares with art the leap in the dark and the suspension of personal judgement in the creative process. The Old Testament is full of prophets refusing to take direction to defend the good old days and ways. As for the New Testament, it is not pleasant when Christians have to be asked by others whether they have forgotten which prophet gave the greatest offence and why."

To this was added the comment by another participant: "Undesirable and unfamiliar aspects of society need to be presented. Responsible people must be made aware of the dehumanised existence that is the only life open to some!"

Violence on Television

In consultations on television it proved to be as difficult to assess the effects of the presentation of violence as had been the case in consultation on the Arts. There was a fair amount of confidence that the stylised violence of fistfights and cowboy gunfights produced no deep traumas (nothing compared with the effect of Grimm's fairy tales on children's minds, it was contended); yet the revulsion felt by those who witnessed the killing of Nancy in the "Oliver Twist" serial suggested that the effect of stylised violence might be to insulate people against the actual violence which is endemic in society. Commenting on the film 'The War Game' Peggy Philips, television critic of 'The Scotsman' said that, in her judgement, it looked contrived: whereas film of the actual war in Vietnam made a sickening impact. A variety of different factors had to be taken into account. Stylised violence might offer sublimation for aggressive tendencies, but might also encourage people to live in a world of unreality. The nauseating things that happen in the world had to be brought home to people because we had to live in this time with the sickening things human beings did to one another (the value of Edward Bond's play 'Saved' was that it made us remember 'the monster behind the mask in every one of us") On the other hand the portrayal of violence had no automatically healthy effect on viewers, and could insure and accustom them to violence as if it were an acceptable part of life.

The Countess of Mar and Kellie sketched features of teenage society which should always be kept in mind:

> "The social problems of our day are boredom and lack of involvement in society; and, because teenagers are more affluent, their problems are in some senses more acute. If their boredom exists in an age which is skilled in commercial entertainment but not in creative leisure, violence may well be the consequence you would expect.
>
> If in TV programmes and films you get a climate of violence and the solution to problems is expressed in violent terms, there develops an underlying emotional content to social expression which encourages belief that solutions by violence are appropriate.
>
> Violence in programmes is a danger to younger rejected teenagers with adventurous or aggressive tendencies when these tendencies are linked with hero worship for a violent film or TV hero."

Objectivity in Presentation

It was clear that all television companies had a responsibility to present news and information in an unbiased way. For instance, it had to be made clear what belonged to a factual basis, what came under the heading of interpretation of the facts, and what was comment on facts and on interpretation. This was no easy matter to accomplish. The integrity and vigilance of the professional team were continually called into play. So was that of the viewing public. Members of the consultations were impressed to discover the impact on policymakers effected by a well-argued case (compared with a general roar of invective) and of the effect of reasoned letters from people who were obviously showing a sense of responsibility.

The integrity of the TV team, the way in which they were prepared to apply themselves unremittingly to get a really quality product was impressive. Peggy Philips had pointed out (in a column in 'The Scotsman' some months before the 1966 consultation) that the most effective sermon can be a documentary which simply deals with a situation, presented with integrity, as material for a TV programme. She wrote:

> "Don Haworth's documentary 'Casino Society' on gambling clubs in the 'North' (ie Manchester) was as gruesomely moral a tale as could be found outside the Victorian nursery shrivellers about hell fire for disobedient children. It peeled off layers of cynicism,

hypocrisy, ruthlessness and sucker-stupidity with a sardonic insight that stimulated the alarmed viewer to thought, far more efficiently than earnest denunciation could have done.

That a booker of strippers could complain, apparently woundedly, that the girls were irresponsible, lacking in loyalty and respect for him, was a wonderful plumbing of the absolute depths of male naivety."

Integrity in viewing – viewing which was both appreciative and vigilant – was given a good deal of thought. This raised questions about the discipline to which viewers must subject themselves to have informed judgements, the relationship of criticism offered to the range of viewing experience, and the advantages of look/listen groups. Informed viewing came from: concentrated viewing (half one's attention was not good enough); yearbooks of the companies which should be more widely read; a reporting back to the bodies represented at Dunblane, of the main points of this consultation; the readings of Penguins on the popular arts; invitations extended to those in the companies whose particular responsibility it is to meet with groups and speak about their work.

The Influence of Television

One area in which research seemed to make no headway at all was in the assessment of the influence of television. The Noble Committee had been rewarded with very little hardtack evidence. In an earlier consultation Dr John Highet had pointed out that statistics could be given not only for sales of 'News of the World' but also its readership, but no statistics could indicate whether the kind of stories it purveyed provided an outlet for sexual and other fantasies so that people were purged of them, or were provided with an incitement to immoral conduct. In a very similar way the effects of the representation of violence, sexual looseness, trickery and crime, drinking and gambling, racketeering of many kinds on television could not be directly the cause of certain forms of conduct in society. To take one instance: television was blamed for hooliganism among young people, yet they were the age group who watched television least.

In the very first consultation the impact made upon people by television was considered to be much greater than that made by other media. The visual power of creating images makes more compelling appeal to the imagination; the impact is immediate; certain values are affirmed, not directly, but wrapped in the performance of screen personalities.

As Peggy Philips had asserted, no medium in history has been as pervasive as television. It brings its influence to bear in those areas of human life which were previously considered to be most private. To continue to try to estimate this influence so that it can be controlled for the enrichment and not the impoverishment of humanity remains a major commitment for the people in the companies and responsible people outside them.

Religion and the TV Companies

In all three consultations some attention was given to religious broadcasting though it was not a major preoccupation. In the 1966 consultation it was pointed out that provision for religious broadcasting in the United Kingdom was quite exceptional. Yet four points were brought forward to justify this part of the company's policy:

1) it is necessary to provide programmes for the housebound
2) the language for spiritual matters in this country is the Christian language and it must be kept in currency
3) religion is something which is very much talked about: the debate accordingly must be reflected in broadcasting
4) people whose humanity is enlarged by a Christian position they adopt, in fact transmit this quality and this is valuable.

There was some discussion of the merits of sound broadcasting over against television presentation. It was suggested that radio encourages the use of imagination and preserves the sense of mystery and also the sense of participation – for instance when broadcast services took place. Television was also agreed to have points it could give radio. It could bring people into touch with actual local Churches, present good liturgies from time to time, draw attention to significant growing points in the Churches' life (e.g. New Delhi, Taize) offer vivid commentary on matters of immediate significance (e.g. visually presenting to people material from the Dead Sea Scrolls). It was also believed that television had had an enlightening effect denominationally when people looked not once but two or three times at a type of service with which they were otherwise unfamiliar. Television could make vivid and real the total context of that service.

It will be seen that much of the discussion in these consultations was in harmony with the report of the World Council of Churches at the Uppsala Assembly in July 1968 on 'The Church and the Media of Mass Communication'. The following extracts from that report may make the points:

"Modern means of communication powerfully stimulate man's coming of age. This need not frighten us. What is frightening is that so few are willing to see media's power and to fight for their proper use. Modern life gives freedom at a price – willingness to take responsible, self-disciplined action in defence of our new liberty. Science and technology offer almost unlimited possibilities; survival requires mastery of the art of choice and commitment....

The media can enrich human life considerably. They have done it for many of us. As never before they make it possible for people to share experience with the hope that humanity may grow in awareness, understanding and compassion. The media provide some of the bone structure for a responsible world society. The sufferings of others are swiftly known and may be quickly alleviated....

The media have helped in the process whereby a single system of values and meaning has been replaced by a plural system. The churches have neither the first nor the last word but speak as one voice among many. These are the facts which would need to be accepted and assimilated if the churches are to act rightly in their new situation....

Increasingly the churches will have to learn to live in an open situation where their message will carry weight by its own authenticity, by the inherent quality of the truth of what they say and do rather than from any accepted authority. The comparison with those who speak for other viewpoints raises standards of thought and life within the churches. As a community which makes universal claims the Church must meet this challenge....

Our eyes have also been opened to what God does in the world outside the Church. Christians often have to learn through the communications media how isolated they have been from the modern world and from the living God who is active there. Often films, novels, and other media bring the message of the Gospel in terms more forceful than the institutional Church can find. Artists and journalists have depicted human estrangement with prophetic power. Comedy and satire have celebrated the freedom of human beings with skill and vivid imagination. It is a cause for humble thankfulness that so much creativity and skill is available....

The media play their part alongside the organs of government and political expression. They can help people to know and appraise issues which affect them. Insofar as they stand over against the legislation they can call attention to injustice, corruption, or bureaucratic neglect. They can contribute to responsible international relationships by providing a more objective critique than that of narrow sectional or national interest.

But the media can also stultify human growth. This tends to happen wherever their overriding interest is commercial gain, wherever they are regarded mainly as instruments of propaganda rather than of information and education, or wherever they are content with cheap and unadventurous programmes rather than creative and imaginative entertainment. Unless the public and national leadership is alive to the positive educational potential of the media, their protests will be too little and will come too late."

Journalism

A good number of failures, registered in the experiments at Scottish Churches' House, have been fruitful. One learned from them direct lessons concerning ways of approach which were acceptable or unacceptable, avenues which were appropriate or not, good and bad timing, issues which seemed to be lively or threadbare. In other cases nothing useful developed and no alternative lines showed themselves.

Doctors and journalists probably need to be taken to Iona and a storm arranged to maroon them – they are otherwise so telephone-prone.

About two years after the House came into being, contact was made with a group of journalists who met from time to time in Edinburgh on matters of human responsibility and human relationships, as these cropped up in their profession. The main contact was Bruce Cannon who later moved to press and publicity work in the Church of Scotland. With the loss of that link further contacts proved to be unfruitful, although they had reached the point at which the journalists had recognised the value of having occasional residential meeting in Dunblane to go into the grooves of some issues for which there was otherwise insufficient time. Also amalgamation of newspapers produced redundancies and the group scattered in search of employment elsewhere.

Once this group (called simply the "Thursday Group") dispersed, no other nucleus was found in the profession from which developments might stem.

In February 1967 an invitation was extended to editors to be guests of the House for a twenty-four residential period. Three topics, two of which were case-studies which represented reporting difficulties were suggested by those who took part; and these were allotted to three sessions with a fourth left free. The questions were:

- Is it possible to produce intelligent journalism for a mass audience, thus keeping pace with rising standards of education? (the Randall case to be studied in relation to the question).

- How is the horrifying to be reported in a balanced way? (The Moor's Murders trial forming a case-study).

- How are church matters, especially ecumenical matters, to be reported fairly, especially when some of the most important decisions would make fairly dull copy?

Six editors and assistant editors accepted the invitation. However, they made it very clear from the beginning that they were only prepared to discuss with one another in very general terms: "In this game you play your cards very close to your chest. If you show your hand at all, a rival will soon take some advantage of the fact." Discussion was very general accordingly. A good time was had by all but nothing of significance developed from that meeting.

The advice of the editors was not to bring them together on any future occasion but rather invite them, one or two at a time, to take part in some of the frontier consultations at the House in which they might be interested.

Notes on Process and Participation

In each case the consultative work in this section started by correspondence and a meeting, over a meal, of the principals involved. Once the representatives of the Scottish Art Teachers' Association had found the openness of Scottish Churches' House to its liking, it provided a nucleus of concerned people who were eager to carry on a conversation about the Arts in our time. Very soon the constituency broadened and brought in painters, architects, poets and so on who had no connection with the Scottish Art Teachers' Association. It remained true that the lively group who had first shown a willingness to confer provided a dynamism for later developments.

In the consultations on Television there was at first some doubt on the part of the companies about the value of meeting at Scottish Churches' House. A first approach was unsuccessful – rightly so, since, early on, the material suggested for consultation had been too general in character. However the Pilkington Report dealt with broadcasting responsibilities specifically. When material from this report was extracted and set out in a working paper so that it was clear that the time of professionals in the medium would be well used, there was a growth of confidence. There still remained difficulty in getting the commercial and non-commercial horses to the starting gate; but once they were in the race they appreciated the contact with a variety of people who were really concerned about sound and visual broadcasting, and they discovered the value of having the chance of informal contact with one another through residing on the same premises. There was some difficulty initially in getting the kind of balanced group of people holding different responsibilities, administrative, programme planning and producing, scripting, etc. The temptation was to delegate the matter to the religious departments. However these departments were themselves sympathetic to the wider concern of the House. By persisting in the original intention it was found to be possible to get very good broadly-based participation from both the BBC and commercial channels.

From the first meeting of the small group, who, all unaware of the impact it would make, initiated work in the field of music, contacts developed both by correspondence and by personal meeting. A goodly company of two dozen and upwards assembled for each consultation. This group was very much an interest group. There was no base on which to build and from which to spread, such as was provided by the SATA in consultations on the Arts, and by those involved in television.

The Working Party who were to alert Scottish Churches' House about any emergency work which might be undertaken in the field of television and prepare the material for a bi-annual consultation consisted of Revs Dr Ronald Falconer and George McCutcheon, and Mr A Lindsay.

The Music Working Party varied in membership to some extent over the years. Those who served for most of that period were Reginald Barrett-Ayres, Erik Routley, Peter Cutts, John S Currie (who formed a link with the Church Hymnary Commission) , W Wordsworth, Alan Luff, Douglas Galbraith, Eric Reid, George McPhee and Mrs MM Dickie. Cyril Taylor provided an occasional link with the Hymns Ancient and Modern Committee.

Social Concerns

Serving Needs in Industry

The attempt to discern how a House of the Churches might be of service to industry was in full evidence by the first half of 1962. The ground was sounded out regarding provision that might be made for young people in industry and a consultation for trade unionists was already in hand. Over the years, there developed consultative and conference work for industrial trainees, training officers, trade unionists, managers, and men in industry in general; and there was some exploration in the field of business ethics.

Apprentices and Trainees

When the Policy and Programme Committee was convinced that investigation should be made in the field of industry the normal type of procedure was followed: invitations were extended to a variety of training officers in industry to be guests of the House for an evening meal and discussion. The question put to them was the rigorous one designed to sort out what the House should and should not tackle – is anything needed in this field; and if anything is, can a residential centre of the churches supply it? Quite characteristically the main part of the time was occupied by training officers telling the representatives and one another how adequately the field was already covered and how irrelevant the House would be. Near the end one member said "Let's come clean. How many of our apprentices and trainees get any chance at all for off-the-job training that would broaden their outlook – I would say less than one per cent". From that point the whole discussion changed. Training officers admitted the impoverishment of industry in the kind of meeting which residential provision in Scottish Churches' House could provide and, from that moment, gave their minds to the service which might be offered. By the end of the meeting, in quite a short time, they had sketched out the main lines which might be covered in apprentices' conferences, and agreed to meet between each as an advisory group. They suggested that, at least in the first instance, two conferences per year should be held.

This was the green light that was asked for. But the committee did not act without consulting apprentices themselves. The Sociology Department of Glasgow University was approached and a sociologist who had special responsibility for industry drew up a long questionnaire to investigate the attitude of apprentices to industry and to life. A group of apprentices, about fourteen in number, were then invited to come to a work camp taking place in Scottish Churches' House, spending their mornings in manual work, and some part of the rest of the day in answering the questionnaire in groups. They thus had experience of living in the House and of work and thinking related to the House. Their conviction about the role that the House could play and the excellent insight into their thinking which was provided by their answers to the questionnaire, offered vital clues for action.

The first conference for apprentices was run in January 1963, and, thereafter, in January and June of each succeeding year, apart from one year when special difficulties shifted the June gathering to September. As one looks over the titles for these conferences one discovers that, beneath different titles, there are one or two main pre-occupations: 'Change in Industry', 'The Need for Training and Re-training throughout Industrial Life', 'The Interrelation of Industry with the Community as a Whole', and 'Industry in Britain against a Backcloth of World Needs and Developments' provide recurring refrains. Although each consultation was fully and separately reported, the attempt to help young people to understand the structure of industry, the different responsibilities fulfilled at different points in industry, and human factors and human consequences, would have produced a monotonous re-treading of the same ground – were it not that the resource people and the apprentices continually changed. It was by deliberate intention of the Committee that, instead of having something like an adult education period when interest in the arts for instance might be introduced, industry itself should be the subject. If horizons are broadened and the imagination released in relation to one's own job there is a double bonus – one sees one's own work within a large context of human life: and one goes back to it with a greater awareness of the importance of one's own small part in it.

Almost universally the conference began with a consideration of the relationship of school education and industrial training, headmasters, youth employment officers and training officers from industry being involved in dialogue, on education and training. The responsibilities of management, (top, work and personnel), trade unions and shop stewards, training boards and training officers, the middle line and shop-floor supervisor were presented and discussed along with the specific contributions made by those whose work was e.g. work study, or safety, or research. Subjects which crop up as important ones in the development over the years include a comparison of apprenticeship on the Continent and home, the threat and promise of automation, training and re-training, productivity and people, psychological attitudes to industry, world poverty and world industrial development. Over the last few years case studies have been used on nearly every occasion, and films. In January 1969 an initiative day was introduced. Industrial trainees were sent out two by two to dig up some information about the local community and make a report on that particular facet which would be co-ordinated with some other reports to build up an adequate picture of the life of the community. This also encouraged contact between the apprentice group and the community in which they were set – although there was irritation when some people (e.g. at Dunblane Station) were approached by too many apprentices with different angles of interest (e.g. the railway as a service, commuters, the rail closures, and general transport facilities).

All the bottom bedrooms facing the Square have windows letting out immediately on the Square, and it would have been easy for any apprentice who wanted to, to step outside, not only at any time of the day but also at any time at night. On one or two occasions the police visited, complaining of breakages of glass which could not be pinned on apprentices but which happened when apprentices were in residence. There had been no drink problem at all, almost certainly due to the fact that there was a public house just across the road and there was no incentive to bravado, such as a prohibition might bring. But there was a serious gambling problem. Unless one breathed down their necks, which would be to treat trainees as children, one had to allow for the possibility that there would be some gambling behind closed bedroom doors. However on one occasion the training officer pointed to a much more serious development. He said that one of his apprentices had come back washed out through being at gambling schools through the night and getting quite inadequate sleep, and that he had attempted to fiddle his expenses to retrieve his losses. It was very difficult to know what to do. Clearly there had to be discipline, and equally clearly the young people had to be treated at the

Apprentices enjoying some leisure time

genuine level of their responsibility and not put in a strait jacket. The action taken proved to be completely successful, standing up to the test of several years' experience. Whenever apprentices arrived they were given an introduction to the House and the general purpose within which the setting up of apprentices conferences falls.

They were then put into groups to decide the discipline to be exercised. They were reminded that someone would be responsible for locking up; they were reminded that they were placed in a community which would be affected by their public conduct; they were reminded that they represented their firms and were responsible to their firms.

Then they were told to decide at what hour they would be in at night so that the House could be locked up when, by agreement of the apprentices themselves, no-one would go out thereafter. They were reminded about the serious complaint about gambling schools and asked simply to discuss this and act responsibly in relation to it. They were asked themselves to decide whether they wanted a dance arranged for the final evening or simply preferred a night off. If they decided it was to be a dance they were to appoint their own committee and make their own arrangements. In this one case there were two House requirements which were laid upon them (and which they saw made sense and accepted). One was that girls were to be seen home and boys were to return in reasonable time (a later date for this return was negotiated for the night of the dance). The other regulation was that if any girl was found in the room of a boy he would be sent back first thing the following morning with a black mark registered with his training offer. When responsibility for determining the discipline was given to the boys themselves, in every case they reacted positively.

Normally, in each session, boys were given questions probing subject and were sent into groups to work at these for twenty to thirty minutes. Then, and only then, an expert in the field would spend ten to fifteen minutes developing some main points about the subject. There followed plenary discussion in which the dialogue between expert and trainees was enriched by the pieces of knowledge and the pieces of questioning which the boys themselves had put together. The specialists and the apprentices themselves had from time to time jibbed at this arrangement – the specialist pointing out, for instance, that young people know nothing about management, and the young people agreeing. A discovery of significance was made in the small groups. There were pieces of knowledge which added up to something when they were put together, and questions which were really relevant – which were differently angled when they came from people on the receiving end. Time after time this was acknowledged by those who had the experience. The result, from the young people's angle, was the kind of amazement and pleasure expressed in an apprentice's report to his training offer: 'Here you are treated as if you matter, and as if what you think matters too" (June 1964 conference). The exceptions to this procedure occurred when a film was shown which led to discussion, and when a basis of information had be provided which was simply not normally accessible to trainees such as the terms of apprenticeship on the Continent of Europe or the terms of the Industrial Training Act. A specific request went out with the invitation that young people of all kinds be thought of, not just young church people, and that, if selection should be the reward for good work in the case of one lad sent for the course, the other should be someone with whom some difficulty had been experienced. This guarantees contact with a fair cross-section of the trainee population. On more than one occasion unsatisfactory apprentices have been sent on a course as the very last chance that the firm would give them. Quite significant things can emerge from this experiment. In one case, when the training officer checked afterwards on the behaviour of the lad he had sent, he was surprised to find that he had never used his bed at all but simply slept in a chair in the common room. On investigating, the training officer found that his boy had a poor home background and that he had literally no bed to sleep in – and this put his behaviour at work in quite a different light, and suggested the help that the boy needed.

After each conference a full report was sent to the training officer, a further one for the attention of the Board of Management, and two to the apprentice himself, one of which he could hand on to a friend. These reports were very substantial covering in some detail the development of the discussion. In 1968 a consultation of training officers was asked whether, since the office of the House was snowed under with work, much shorter reports, simply extracting the main points, might not be sufficient. This was rejected out of hand. Training officers pointed out that apprentices were able to go over the reports and put their finger on their own contributions and on the thinking of the group to which they belonged – and this greatly added to the benefit obtained from their lively sense of participation. They also pointed out that since, in most cases, four reports came back to apprentices in one firm, two to those who took part and two spare, the discussions which arose from these reports quite often produced a small ferment among a wider group of apprentices so that the benefit of the course rippled out within the firm. The House, was, accordingly, firmly requested to continue to provide full reports.

Since apprentices came nearly always two by two from firms, they were given double bedrooms and put in different groups: thus, in group discussion they had access to different angles and insights, and, informally, in their bedrooms, they could relate these to, and tie them up with the situation in their own firm.

It is undoubtedly true that off-the-job, relaxed opportunities for consultation give young people time to think their way to responsible decisions. The internal checking of the conference group is quite remarkable. If anyone makes a wild, outrageous, unsubstantiated statement, there is no need to bring the expert in to get the picture straight – other boys are at once on their feet redressing the balance. Thus, on the one occasion in which Scottish Churches' House was taken to task for 'letting kids in industry talk irresponsibly about things they know nothing about' (as the Engineering Employers Association put it) it was possible from the text of the report itself to show how thoughtfully and maturely apprentices had worked their way towards a common mind at this and that point. Among various objections, the main one was that apprentices had said they needed increased wages all round. All that had to be done was make reference to the context in which this came. The experience of boys at this stage (January 1963) was that while some of them had a fairly consistent training programme others were liable, for weeks at a time, to be put at the elbow of a journeyman who was on piece-work. For that period, the apprentice was comparatively rich. But the whole conference came to a mind that they would much prefer to have a clear and effective training programme which they fulfilled, with some increase in the overall rate offered, than have these chances for bigger money at the expense of training. Various other points illustrate the maturity of the thinking – which surprised the boys themselves. For instance, after reacting initially to their schooling by suggesting that it should be dovetailed into the training they were later to receive in industry they ended up convinced about the need for a broad base of education at school without too early a specialisation and also the need for a broad educative basis to training in particular skills. Time and time again they rejected the idea of boosting their wages by piece-work and opted for a set rate and time to do a quality job (bonuses might be appropriate in fourth and fifth years if a stage is reached when quality and quantity can go together). When bonus schemes were in existence they preferred the group bonus – so that older men should not be penalised. One whole conference suggested that a proportion of the apprentice's wages should be kept in hand by the firm so that, if he gets married, or if he is simply stepping out into full adult responsibilities, he will have something behind him; otherwise the money would burn a hole in his pocket. They were quite prepared to see the length of apprenticeship realistically adjusted so that in some cases it could be reduced to three years; and it was astonishing and heartening to find that, quite clearly, apprentices would go for the job that interested them even if it meant being on apprentice rates for two years longer than their fellows in other jobs. The understanding shown of older men who resented the education and other chances that younger people had, who they feared would show them up or take over their jobs, was a further remarkable and encouraging feature of the discussions.

Attendance at prayers in the chapel was, of course, not compulsory. Different groups react differently, some obviously believing that masculinity requires abstinence from worship, others showing the kind of unaffected response that can come from the church and non-church person alike. One non-church young man reported to his training officer: "We went to the chapel for service on Sunday morning. It was funny – it was the most natural thing in the world." When it was natural, as it quite often was, to refer to the bible regarding the meaning of work and of life, it was obvious that religious instruction at school had been a non-starter as far as most were concerned, if it existed at all, and that when biblical testimony was related to the life that faced them, things immediately lit up.

There were no bible study sessions. Instead, bibles were to hand and would be brought out if an illuminating text was identified and shown to be directly relevant. After 4 or 5 minutes the bibles were put back on the shelf and discussion proceeded. This had far more effect than extended bible study would have had. On one occasion, at lunchtime, the apprentices went to the dining room end and the warden in the opposite direction to the family premises. He had forgotten something and returned to the Common Room. There he found an apprentice, circling round, hands clasped in the air in delight, not expecting to be observed by anyone. Without embarrassment the lad explained "When I was a wee boy, the bible meant a lot to me. Then I became an apprentice and realised I had to deal with the real world and kick behind me the fairytale world of the bible. Here I have found I do not need to choose between them. I found the bible is about the real world."

In addition to the work camp consultation which initiated the apprenticeship conferences, two further took place, one a balanced group of apprentices and public school boys in January 1966 when the theme was "Industry and Society", and the other in September of the same year, with police cadets added to the representation from among apprentices and public schools. The results were heartening. A real teaming up took place and a basis of understanding was laid. After the first conference the total company put it on record that apprentices had found the public school boys to be open and approachable when they had expected to find them snobbish or at least class-conscious; while the public school boys recorded with delight the discovery they had made of the quality and maturity of the thinking of the apprentices. Since it was quite necessary that jobs should not be fabricated, and since, at this stage, a considerable amount of fresh work required to be done in the grounds of the House, the experience of these encounters is not repeatable at will. It has to be related to times when a genuine task has to be tackled.

The public schoolboys at work

Attempts were made from time to time to provide conference facilities for unskilled boy, and for girls. First attempts were completely unsuccessful. The rock on which they foundered had to do with a fairly clear-cut industrial attitude. Apprentices were due educative opportunities from the very character of their work; but unskilled boys and girls were production units. Clearly, it was quite unfair to look to some small firms to release young people for courses, whether skilled or unskilled. For others, questions of turnover of labour and the effect of withdrawing productive units were decisive.

On one occasion when an apprentice's conference was being held, two James Bond films were being shown in a Stirling cinema. We took the group to see them. Next day there was an evaluation, probing the underlying assumptions about life implicit in 'Dr No' and 'From Russia with Love'.

At one point the Warden asked what they made of the Bond girls. Tongues moved round lips: "Lush, man, lush". "If you had the chance, would you marry one of them?" With one voice they replied "Not on your life, sir" and the biggest and toughest of the group, who was looked on as the natural leader, added "When I marry I want someone like my granny!"

A breakthrough took place in February 1969. A "Girls at Work" conference was run in conjunction with the Young Mens' and Young Womens' Christian Association in which English experience was used and deliberately built on.

Firms which, in England, had appreciated the value of sending girls to courses, and which had branches in Scotland, were invited to send some of their young workers. The result was a seminal experience. The inadequate parts of the programme had a teaching quality for the future just as the adequate parts had. It was possible to use the type of development which had been established in England and still make an assessment of the extent to which this was valid in Scotland or had to be adjusted. The programme did not concentrate on industry as had the apprentice conferences. A broad basis was laid by a consideration of the world of work, community needs and the service young people might render to the whole community, and current affairs – with, in addition, an explanation from an STV representative of how news is sifted and presented on television. There were matters of general though personal relationships (including sex); and others which particularly related to the work of each day, accident prevention and human relationships at work. The resources of the girls were drawn out by sessions in which they were encouraged to express themselves in words, providing short spoken essays; and particularly in an initiative day for which they had to prepare, which they had to undertake and on which they had to report. The girls were divided into three groups, each one having a share in the overall assignment, one group investigating the history of Stirling, another investigating two new housing areas and how young wives and mothers managed there, the third trying to assess the provision made for young people in the burgh. It was the experience of this initiative day which produced the experimental use of a similar occasion in apprentice conferences.

Training Officers in Industry

Reports of apprentice conferences form a piece of social history. The effects of the Industrial Training Act of 1964 are quite clearly recorded. Until 1965 or so, a sounding out of the apprentices who took part in conferences showed that their training was very uneven. They spent quite a lot of time stooging around without clear work to do. They were put on labouring work of a monotonous and un-instructive kind. They were attached to journeymen who were knocking out the work to increase their wages. From then on it becomes clear that there is much more coherence in the whole field of training, that learning is being programmed and has a rational development, that the quality of the preparation to turn out skilled and flexible craftsmen takes a steep upward quality turn. In this context there is a noticeable increase in interest in the job.

Day Release may have had its part to play in the thoughtfulness of the discussions.

The effect of the Act on the work of training officers was every bit as marked. At first there was evidence of uncertainty about the role that was to be fulfilled in industry by the training officer. There was no sense of security of status within the industrial framework. As time went on, job-definition became much clearer and status and place in the industrial hierarchy much more adequately defined.

The first meeting of training officers was in 1962. Their original offer was to meet between apprentice conferences, make an assessment of the conference work, and advise on future programming. At its meeting in October 1963 the Policy and Programme Committee had received a request that training officers be given opportunity to meet about their own work and be given a chance to think through its developing nature. This was welcomed, and for the first few years thereafter training officers met twice per year – in later years three occasions proved to be necessary. These were 24-hour residential periods when the training officers themselves decided on themes and on specialists they wanted to contribute while the whole programme was administered from Scottish Churches' House. When a Training Officers' Association was formed the first action of the House was to offer to withdraw if its provision was no longer relevant. This brought an immediate request from the Training Officers' Association to continue with the residential meetings since they provided an opportunity of a kind which they themselves could not set up.

A good deal of the early thinking concentrated on the development of the training service in industry. Thus there was discussion on the type of training officer who was needed and how, in an expanding situation, numbers of the required quality might be found. The training of young people, and supervisors, and the re-training of older people claimed a good deal of attention. The training officer's own job analysis and his means of keeping abreast were taken seriously. The implications of the Industrial Training Act and particularly ways in which firms might dodge its requirements were given serious thought. Important relationships were kept under review – particularly that of school especially careers masters to industry, training college to industry, training board to those involved in the training process, and management to the training function and training officer. In May 1968 one of the main conclusions of this continuing group was recorded: Two basic attitudes need to be created in industry:

- All must be given dignity and the chance to be responsible
- All must be oriented to change.

The House proved to be an effective meeting point for principals of technical training colleges, headmasters and teachers on the one side, youth employment officers and adult education representatives on another, representatives of Industrial Training Boards on a third, and training officers themselves on a fourth.

Some of the subjects will indicate content: 'Induction Courses', 'The Expectation of Management re Training', 'The Retraining of Older People', 'The Training of Non-Apprentices', 'Selection and Motivation', 'Communications in Industry', 'The Use of a Module'. More implicitly in some and more explicitly in others deeper issues were given attention – what is human life for, what is industry's proper role and where does it fail in this or overstep it, how are trainer and trainee to be related?

Industrial Workers

General consultative work for people in industry, providing them with residential opportunity to look at many issues which were brewing up and claiming attention, was nearly always undertaken in partnership with some other body during the life of Scottish Churches' House. 'Tell Scotland' groups and Kirk Week groups met in the early years. But the main body in the field remained the Home Board of the Church of Scotland, represented by the Industrial Organiser. The committee on industry of the Home Board was already for most practical purposes an ecumenical committee and industrial chaplains of the Episcopal Church co-operated with their counterparts in the Church of Scotland. At the basis of its work were imaginative laymen who were, in different professions, "at the coal face". It was accordingly well equipped to know which themes were pressing forward and commanding interest, and were helping groups in industry to mature in their understanding of Christian responsibilities there. The natural role of the House was to serve this movement rather that start something different on its own initiative. This is what was done.

The field of business ethics had been under investigation since 1963. In that year the Rev Andrew Wylie (then minister of the Church of Scotland in Lausanne and later General Secretary of the Scottish Churches' Council) made contact with Scottish Churches' House. The International Business College in Lausanne was the off-shoot of the Harvard Business School. Contact had shown the need for work in the field of business ethics and he wanted to benefit from the experience of the House. But the House had no experience! Andrew Wylie was invited to do what seemed appropriate in his local circumstances and keep the House in touch. Messrs WS Robertson and James Gammell, from development and financial interests, were consulted – and they spoke as one man. If any one field cried out for attention it was the field of business ethics: yet, they affirmed, if the perfectly planned occasion were set up, with perfect timing, they could guarantee that the people who most needed to take part would be too busy to attend! In 1964 the matter was kept before the Policy and Programme Committee and contact was suggested with Mr Ebbage of the Commercial College in Glasgow, Professor Hunt of the Chair of Business Studies in Edinburgh University, and Chambers of Commerce. All this led to dialogue with the committee of the West of Scotland British Institute of Management, who, though they were agnostic rather than Christian in committee membership, agreed to hold a consultation in December of that year (1964), after being assured that the whole proceedings would be based on their own experience and expertise and not on some over-simplified version of those that the church might have. This was a most promising meeting, wrecked quite unexpectedly by the failure of the committee to note that their Annual General Meeting would take place before the consultation and many of them might not be re-elected! In fact the committee was substantially changed, new members who had not been through the contacts and discussions wondered what game the churches were playing and the consultation was deprived of its foundation of confidence and of focus. The collapse of the consultation led to fresh contacts and negotiations; but it was not until December 1967 that anything effective came of all the preparatory work. Then Mr John Marsh, Director of the British Institute of Management spent 48 hours sharing large concerns about the way the British economy was moving, and the way industry in particular was moving. He met first with Industrial Chaplains and then with the kind of junior manager who might well be in a senior position in about five years time.

John Marsh, to his credit, held nothing back. He could not quite accept the Christian position, yet was convinced that there was a radical understanding of the world which it had to offer, and which could be decisive. In brief, he contended: that we had lost a world role and had not found its successor; that we were nearly bankrupt but had been protected from a full realisation of the fact; that there was a conflict between technology (which depends on speed) and democracy (which is slow moving); that press and TV were acting as if the only true news was bad news; that the young were protesting against the hypocrisy and humbug of the old and producing a generation gap; and at the same time that Britain was facing a re-organisation of life which other countries would have to face in 10 to 15 years time, so that it was a laboratory of the life of future society. Among power groups the traditional ones of government, employers and trade unions were heard loud and clear – a fourth, the professions, still needed to make its full impact. The present generation of those in control were facing the past and backing into the future; so there was a case for handing over power and responsibility at an earlier age to the future generation. Education is inadequate wherever it is not producing questing minds or long-range minds. The church should be "The Cathedral of Men's Minds"- and was not. From these observations, the drastic questions were presented to industrial chaplains and later to managers, and were given drastic consideration.

This was one of those meetings which depend very much on the character and honesty of the person round which a group is gathered. John Marsh brought thinking on to a level of significance which meant that all those who took part, whatever their personal reactions to his presence and challenge, had to think more fundamentally in future about matters which they believed they had already thought through responsibly!

The question remains, why has it been quite impossible to get consultative work on business ethics established? James Gammell and WS Robertson were convinced that no service which Scottish Churches' House could offer would be more relevant or more appreciated, if it could only get this started.. A disturbing factor would seem be involved. It probably stemmed from too many church resolutions about the life of people in the world which showed a lack of knowledge of complexities involved and the difficulty in discerning the kind of action which is right and relevant. There seemed to be a fear that a church source was likely to try to look for an over-simplification of the problem and attempt to deal with it in a way which is in fact suited only to the ethics of simpler face-to-face relationships such as are found in home and neighbourhood.

Meetings for people in industry took place about three times per year sometimes for general groupings looking at larger issues, but sometimes assembling, say, junior managers to consider specific issues relevant to their specific expertise. These meetings were in addition to those of training officers, apprentices, and trade unionists.

Trade Unionists

Within a year of the start of the House, in February 1962, an exploratory meeting took place with a selected group of trade unionists and Rev W MacIntyre who was then industrial organiser of the Church of Scotland. This was the type of probing meeting which was aimed at finding out whether there was in fact a job that Scottish Churches' House could fruitfully tackle in this field. By September of that same year the first gathering of trade unionists had taken place. At the heart of the thinking was an awareness of the need to restructure trade unionism in Britain radically.

In each instance the advisory group of trade unionists sorted out the subjects they wanted to think through and gathered material on them which was set out in working papers.

The consultation in September, 1962 was on "Trade Unions and the Common Market." At that time, when an application to join the European Economic Community was being made by Britain, it was testified by all those who took part that no other conference opportunity had been set up which would allow them to consider the implications for trade unionism in Britain if Britain joined the Common Market. They affirmed that the House could play a useful part on the trade union scene through an informal type of service. Members of five of the major trade unions were able to discuss, in inter-union dialogue, the consequences they could foresee if the government were successful in its application. It turned out that there had been very little discussion on the theme within trade unions, never mind between them. Mr George Middleton, General Secretary of the Trades Union Congress agreed to be present as the leader of the thinking, but was in the end prevented. His place was taken by Mr John Robertson, MP for Paisley – a man from a working class background who could still speak and think authentically in working class terms. There could not have been a better man for the job. The working paper was based on the provisions of the Treaty of Rome and a very good job was done in sorting out the factors pro and con. But the most remarkable thing about the gathering was the way in which, given a chance to think together, trade unionists together developed different perspectives on the situation from those with which they started. It was clear from the early discussions that the main attitude was one of hostility to joining the EEC. By the time the consultation finished a positive attitude had won the day.

In 1964 there was a consultation on 'Wages'. This concerned itself with a national incomes policy, the tradition of collective bargaining, and the pressing need for trade union re-organisation. 14 trade unions were represented. The idea of, need for, and means to bring into being an incomes policy were first thoroughly debated. Under the heading 'Collective Bargaining' it was questioned whether a uniform wage, negotiated at a lowest-common-factor level, was effective – engineering employers negotiate wage rates which cover marine engineers and motor car workers alike. A case was put for extending collective bargaining so that workshop agreements were made which recognised differentials open to different industries. Other things than wages had to be thought of in this field – proper notice of dismissal, a proper length of contract, a guaranteed annual wage, proper sick pay, and improved pension schemes. In the last session the basic weaknesses of the trade union structure and organisation were examined in groups; a move towards industrial unionism and a possible role of the trade union – more in terms of its past character as a kind of Friendly Society now focussing on the need for industry to be a really worthy human activity – were registered. Contributions of distinctive importance were made by W Monaghan who had been a shop steward himself and was at the time lecturing in the Department of Industrial Administration in the Royal College of Science and Technology.

The 1965 consultation was on 'Power and Responsibility' and was set up in association with the Workers Educational Association through one of its officers, Iain Jordan. He led off the first session pointing out that a fundamental insight of Karl Marx was that the bad thing about a capitalist society was the way in which it alienated people from their work. He went on to ask where people-power lies – with the capitalists? Or managers? Or the state? Or with trade unionists through the Trade Union Congress? A second session on power at the bottom looked at nationalisation and the ineffectual sharing of power with workers produced by it; joint consultation – was it effective and effectively used? the shop steward movement giving power to people who were really in touch with the rank and file. Basic to the discussion was the question whether there was a genuine demand on the part of the workers for a share in the running of industry. The rest of the consultation was taken up with group and plenary work on three main questions: How to integrate shop stewards into the structure of industry and relate them to the traditional trade union structure; how to develop industrial democracy and still get the streamlining which industrial unionism might offer: and how to redesign the whole fabric of trade unionism in Britain probably by giving more power to the Trades Union Congress?

In 1966 the committee accepted a suggestion of Rev George Wilkie, who later became Industrial Organiser of the Church of Scotland, that operations in the field of trade unionism be suspended meantime. He had been invited to attend the Scottish Trade Union Congress and saw the need for developing relationships with people in main positions in the trade union movement so that they understood the kind of interest that the Church was taking in industrial matters. Once there was a base of contacts and a growth of understanding within the trade union movement itself, it was thought that it might be possible to resume this work, approaching the whole trade union situation more effectively. It was thought to be a field in which it would be worthwhile to develop further work.

Rural affairs

The importance of not doing consultative work in any field until it has been possible to determine exactly what can be fruitfully done and what aspects of the subject can be delimited is illustrated by the work on rural life.

In 1963 representatives of the Education for Ministry committees of the different churches had asked Scottish Churches' House if it would look into the ordained ministry in rural areas – which it felt, in many cases, to be in a sad state, with ministers uncertain about their role and relevance. Only one of the churches, the Church of Scotland, had a rural panel; and the matter was debated with them and their advice sought when they met in the House as a panel in November 1963. It was agreed that the following might prove to be a way of getting at the facts and assessing the attitudes of men in the rural ordained ministry. The different churches were written and asked to supply six to ten names of clergy in rural ministries who would be making some worthwhile assessment of their work and its future, and could be relied upon to speak their thoughts honestly. About seventy names were provided. The chairman of the rural panel provided a statement which was a brief, sharp critique of rural ministry – the kind of thing which was liable to get people writing immediately to say "You don't understand the situation at all" or "You are on the right lines – give us more!" This was sent out with stamped, addressed envelopes. Only seven replies came in from the seventy (who, it should be remembered, were specially selected people within their own denomination who knew the field best). It looked like the end of the road, and the Policy and Programme Committee was prepared to believe that there was no sign of the possibility of the response which was necessary, if it were to proceed further.

At this point a member of the committee quietly said: "Is anything happening to the rural ministry which is not happening to rural communities as a whole?" It was at once seen that the field of enquiry was too narrow and a switch was at once made to broaden the enquiry. Contact was made with the National Farmer's Union, the Scottish Association of Young Farmers' Clubs, the Scottish Women's Rural Institute, the Farm-workers' Union, the Council of Social Service, agricultural colleges, the Forestry Commission, departments at St Andrew's House, particularly the Development Department and the Agriculture and Fisheries Department, and representatives of land-owning and educational interest. The timing of the contact was especially fortunate in the case of the Scottish Association of Young Farmers' clubs who were undertaking a survey of changes as they affected young people in rural areas. Material which came from the sources indicated and the eagerness of response which was met with provided an incentive to the committee to proceed. However, it was thought wiser to start with a pilot consultation. To this fourteen people were invited and thirteen accepted – people like the Head Forester of Scotland, the secretary of the Young Farmers' Clubs, an official of the National Farmers' Union, the manager who was at the heart of the development of the Aviemore Sports Complex, the president of the Scottish Women's Rural Institutes and so on. Some of the changes discussed had to do with support industries in agriculture (representing two persons for every one person on the land) the mobility of the farmer and farmer worker so that they were no longer tied to a small geographical community, the development of more and more effective technical methods in agriculture and consequent fast diminution of the labour force, forestry villages, the effect on the rural young people of centralised education, basic attitudes to soil and countryside. This pilot consultation took place in December 1964. Its work was set out in a working paper for a consultation on 'The Changing Face of Rural Communities' held at the end of January 1965 (the speed was necessary since farming folk were available more readily before the main ploughing task had to be tackled).

Before this consultation took place the Warden, when in Rome, had been invited to meet with Dr Yang, chief rural sociologist of the Food and Agricultural Organisation. To his astonishment, Dr Yang had made a plea that Scottish Churches' House be a centre of concern in Scotland for the development of rural studies. Dr Yang had been working on a survey of rural change in Europe, had been unable to get knowledgeable contributions from either Scotland or England, and was concluding that everyone was so preoccupied with urban studies in Britain that rural sociologists were as rare as nightingales. Dr Yang sent a message on tape to the members of the consultation, making this plea. He urged that distinguished sociologists, social scientists, and social anthropologists should be drawn together to make a contribution to the FAC working party on "The Rural Family in a Changing Environment".

The consultation decided to proceed with its original agenda and return to consider Dr Yang's plea in the light of that discussion. The things which go to make a rural community and their presence or absence in the Scottish situation was a major matter for discussion. A consideration of education showed that the majority of the consultation believed it was worth having a higher quality of educational provision, centralised so that young people needed to take transport each day, than to have the kind of dispersal of facilities which is inevitably accompanied by a lowering of quality. Questions of land use brought in not only forestry, agriculture, tourism etc, but town planning – too often builders wanted to build on level ground which was also good agricultural ground whereas land which was more hilly in places could offer the imaginative planner greater scope. The key role of women in community life was given time and thought – their part was too often auxiliary when it should be principal, related to the whole character of area development. The value of ancillary and craft industries to diversify an economy like that in the Highlands was given some attention. Before the end the committee went right back to a basic question – is there any point in trying to preserve rural communities at all:? and discovered, by thinking this through afresh, how crucial in a nation's whole life was the part played by the rural community. The development of factory farming was only lightly touched on, because there was a very strong conviction that intensive methods had to be used if the population were to be fed, and cruelty was not necessarily involved at all. At the very end Dr Yang's message was considered. An approach through the Secretary of State to get the Development Commission to turn its attention to the need to survey changing conditions in the rural areas and to make this contribution to the FAC working party, was agreed.

This consultation was followed by small deputations to and discussions with St Andrew's House Departments which resulted in the formation of a committee of representatives from Edinburgh University – Departments of Geography, Social Anthropology, and History – and St Andrew's House – Department of Agriculture and Fisheries, and Scottish Education Department, the Scottish Council of Social Service, and the Scottish Association of Young Farmers Clubs. The Warden was asked to be chairman. The Standing Conference of Voluntary Youth Organisations later sent a representative. This committee met to co-ordinate information about studies on rural communities or the lack of these, and to isolate profitable areas of study. The areas selected were a rural parish in the north of Scotland, a network of small burghs in an agricultural region, a rural area near a city which exercised a magnetic pull upon it, an area suffering from depopulation on the Borders and an island. In the course of these investigations the complete lack of a bibliography of studies which had taken place in this field over the last 20 years showed itself. Members of the committee were appointed to compile this bibliography. This was done after about a year's work and in itself was a substantial contribution in the field of rural studies - for instance, it could be seen from this bibliography where a survey had taken place in an area, development trends should show themselves clearly. Material fell into four categories – articles in books, official publications, university theses, and material in typescript or otherwise unpublished. Appropriate departments in universities and training colleges were contacted thereafter and the following questions asked:

- Have you any research in progress with a bearing on these interests?
- Do you have any postgraduate students willing to do rural sociology?

- Are you in a position to initiate research projects in the geographical area covered by your university?
- Would you be willing to help in the preparation of questionnaires?

Considerable interest and conviction about the need for rural studies was indicated in the replies. Principal Cotterel was approached with the suggestion that Stirling University, as a new University, could do a new and relevant thing on the Scottish scene by setting up a department of rural studies.

The following matters had become clear through this process of investigation:

- Data was clearly missing in many quarters where it was needed and the studies which were required were those related to developing plans and policies for rural areas, not academic studies!
- There was an obsession with urban studies and a big push was needed to redress the balance.
- Trusts which were interested in work which might also be applicable to developing countries overseas and their need to cope with rural change, would be likely to back financially studies which might have had this wider reference.

When this point was reached the committee felt that it had done all that it reasonably might, and that it should now hand over to a more adequate controlling centre for pursuing studies thereafter with professional expertise and a secretariat as the essential provision required from that point.

Thus a consultation on the need for rural studies took place in May 1966. Out of five possible foster mothers it selected three – the Consultative Council (because of its concern for the effects on youth of rural change) a University Faculty, and the Scottish Council of Social Service. It was agreed that of these the Consultative (Kilbrandon) Council was most promising, not that it could undertake the work directly, but that it could set up means for having it undertaken so that the situation of young people under the pressures of rural change might be understood. Mr Dickie from the Scottish Council of Social Service, Mr Ashley from Moray House Training College, Dr Littlejohn, Department of Social Anthropology, Edinburgh University, Miss Ross, Department of Agriculture and Fisheries, and the Chairman were appointed to pursue this.

By some articles and conference talks the need to have this work carried forward at a more professional level and with adequate secretarial backing was brought before the public from time to time. When a wind of change turns interest from urban to rural matters preparatory material is to hand, already filed, waiting for use.

In January 1969 a consultation on 'Intensive Stock Rearing and Rural Change' took place. It was more like a study group in size but representative of some main interests. It was natural to use bible passages to examine the true relationship of human beings to the animal kingdom. The understanding of the dominion entrusted to us, from this study, was that we had not only to exercise authority over but take responsibility for the whole animal kingdom and its well-being. The consultation then turned to a working paper – "Animal Husbandry in Intensive Farming" given by JM Cunningham to the British Veterinary Association 1968 Congress in Swansea. Existing techniques in intensive stock rearing were examined in the light of this paper and of the biblical passages; and there was a great deal of practical consideration of our responsibilities to our fellow human beings, especially at points at which these might seem to run counter to care for animals.

The consultation then went on to consider the findings of the Brambell Committee in 1965 and the codes of practice which were issued in 1968 as the result of the work of this committee on human standards for rearing and slaughtering stock.

The second half of the consultation was on rural change. The value of community development schemes was underlined by an expert on them; and land use, education, and other factors related to change were again looked into and again the need for adequate study was stressed.

Dealing with Violence

Step inside now.

It is November 1968. Most of the company are young people.

Even when a session is in progress these young folk are milling around. To stay in one place for one session seems to be too much of a strain. Maybe for half an hour they settle. Then, in twos and threes, they move through one of the doors, wander around for a little and move back into the discussion.

Apart from a Law Lord, a criminologist and a representative of the Scottish Education Department, who represent a sensitive listening presence from the nation as a whole, they all come from Easterhouse. These young people belong to three of the gangs who have made that housing area notorious for gang warfare. The other adults are, in one way or another, trying to fulfil some kind of supportive role in this community of over 50,000 people – which is so poorly provided for in regard to the things which make up community life that there is nowhere to have a cup of tea with a friend, nowhere to have your hair done, no social centre in which to establish friendships and get rid of excess energy in sports and dancing.

Listen to their conversation and you will hear the words "Frankie" and "the project" constantly recurring.

Easterhouse had only its bad reputation to live with until Frankie Vaughan, the artiste, appeared – for the alternative was to live on air, i.e. promises of a centre for social meeting and activities which year after year failed to show any sign of materialising. Frankie Vaughan stepped in to try to make a break – to cut the knot of violence and get the young people engaged in planning a programme for a building which would be a centre for the activities which interested them. The idea was to use temporary buildings first until permanent ones were ready.

In the time that he could give, Frankie Vaughan poured himself out in energy and in love for people whose deprivation went to his heart. The handing in of weapons dramatised by television cameras was accompanied by a real truth, real diversion of the strength young people had expended in hostility to one another into constructive channels of planning for their own social needs and those of the whole community.

They have come to Scottish Churches' House to firm up on that planning.

Listen in for a while.

You hear them speak about the drabness of their lives and of the colour and excitement provided if you belong to a gang and find gang fights could flare up at almost any moment. You wonder, with other adults, whether life in Easterhouse would not be worse for young people if there were no gangs – nowhere to belong, no focus of loyalties, no excitement.

You listen to their view of the police, of being picked on when they were up to no mischief, so that it seemed just as well to get into mischief. You would have to pay one way or another and you might as well get something for your money!

The discussion turns to gang leadership. A leader is necessary but there is no great scramble for the position. "He has to be ready for anything and for that you need someone who is a bit thick in the head. He must go on when it doesn't make sense to go on, when the odds are too great, when he stands a good change of getting carved up, when there are too many police on the ground and he is risking quite a long prison sentence. He must be stick-at-nothing, going bull-headed into every situation in which the gang's interests need to be asserted."

You hear of a group of children, five to seven years old, who wander out of Easterhouse into the surrounding fields, find a cow and batter it to death. It is difficult to find teachers to teach in the Easterhouse area, accordingly there is only part-time education; and since there is no work in the place itself, parents are absent, and children are allowed to roam wild.

You hear about dustbins so big and high off the ground that it is difficult to get household waste into them, and of the waste piled up around them; the bins being pulled down, rolled on and played with so that the rest of their contents spill out. You are made aware of the impossibility of making or keeping gardens when any garden fence provides handy stakes for making weapons for groups which meet in a head-on clash. You sympathise with the police who live in the area who are not only jeered and 'got at' but whose children have a very rough passage with local children, because of their father's occupation: and at the same time you wonder what the effect might be if all those who could support the community maybe especially schoolteachers, were to live within it, as some of the police do.

The young people had a fairly clear picture of the kind of centre which was wanted. It would include a cafe (all-night maybe) in which you could simply meet with your pals; a picture house or a place where films could be shown from time to time; a dance-hall, or the use of a hall for dancing; a pub or pubs; a place where you could simply muck around, listening to records and talking with your friends; a floodlit tarmac field in which you could play football, with facilities also for indoor football.

The Home and Health Department of St Andrew's House saw the experiment as an imaginative one and provided enough finance to pay for the board and lodging of the young people and to make up wages when this was necessary.

No publicity was given to this gathering. It was possible to hold it without the press getting wind of it at all. Young people from three of the main gangs in Easterhouse took part along with sociologists, youth organisers, social workers and a psychiatrist. People who had an immediate concern for Easterhouse itself were invited, to represent, as it were, the wider life of Scotland: Lord Kilbrandon, the Law Lord, Mr Avison, Criminologist, and Mr Macfarlane, Scottish Education Department. The one regret of all who took part was that the police did not accept the invitation to be represented.

But is it wise, you might ask to have such characters resident in the House? Risks to property are at least involved – damage to furniture, to windows, gang signs written on bedroom walls with aerosol paints. Is it fair to the local community since they too might suffer?

But also is it not necessary to give young people who have stereotyped one another as enemies the chance to get to know one another as persons? And if a House of the churches is not for such an initiative, what on earth is it for?

As the report shows, it was clear to those who took part in this gathering that similar residential opportunities which allowed traditional boundaries to be crossed might play some part in helping to build a community in Easterhouse. One teenager, who had given it as his opinion that meeting at the House had spoiled some things, answered, when questioned why this was so, "It's difficult to slash a boy (i.e. use a knife or razor on him) when you have lived with him".

Lawlessness and Community Development

The "gathering of the clans" from Easterhouse could be traced to a suggestion from a consultation on 'Lawlessness In Our Time', that we make direct provision for 'social deviants' at Scottish Churches' House, a challenge from a minister on the spot that we pick up the challenge of Easterhouse, and a concern for 'problem families' which itself derived from a concern about the housing situation.

In February 1965 just over twenty people professionally involved with those who felt the pressures of society severely, met for two days to rethink the provision needed for problem families. A great deal of thought was given to the Family Service Unit which combined, in satisfying measure, professionalism and flexibility in its approach. The small case-load carried (ten to twenty families) allowed the professional to encourage the slow growth of responsibility at the speed natural to the family (one of the dangers to be watched was the instinctive desire of the family to incorporate the social worker into the family structure). It was expensive in time, energy, and money to do things with inadequate families instead of for them; but if a constant threat of breakdown could be reversed, this new-found adequacy would make its mark upon future generations and upon neighbours so that there would be a spread of health in society. Experiments elsewhere particularly in the Netherlands and in England were looked at, and then ventures in Scotland including, in Edinburgh, the use of an intensive case worker within the ordinary case work service.

It was clear from this consultation that, as the standards of living of a majority improved, a minority were forced more firmly against the wall. The father might be pushed out of all responsibility since he was not the one who had to make ends meet. There was an inability to learn from experience – the Social Services were designed for 'rational people'! The most characteristic feature was immaturity. There was a strong feeling of inadequacy, and a great reckoning that it would take unusual qualities of mind and spirit to manage on the low incomes which many women had to handle –and those under consideration had less than the average capacity to cope.

Out of this consultation came a conviction about the need for one flexible service, not confining itself to problem families, but dealing with the needs of community. This would imply a different administrative structure, changes in existing departmental services, steps in legislation and a move towards the concept of social education as the determinative one.

A working party was set up to work the suggestions out in more detail. A scheme for restructuring the Social Services was propounded both verbally and graphically, which could be one of the contributions to be laid before the Secretary of State for Scotland as the considered proposals for the re-organisation of the Social Services. The working party, which met two months after the full consultation, pointed out that some pilot schemes could be tried out within the existing framework before changes in legislation needed to be considered.

In November 1966 the consultation on 'Lawlessness In Our time' took place. There assembled for it a Law Lord, three sheriffs, two criminologists, one chief constable and six police officers undertaking juvenile liaison work, a director of education and five teachers, a social scientist, a chief probation officer, three administrators from St Andrew's House, two ministers, and a representative from the Discharged Prisoners Aid Society. Working notes issued beforehand were provided mainly by those who worked in the field of criminology. They divided the consultation into three areas of concern

1) anomie
2) the Kilbrandon proposals
3) the role of the school and home.

'Anomie was described thus: " A society afflicted by anomie is one in which young people do not know what the society expects of them or where they are going. There is a loss of purpose in living. A restless search goes on for identity, security, a niche, a sense of belonging. In this situation young people in particular are under pressure".… "Criminal activity may be started in order to break out of boredom by destructive action. Any outlet for energy, bottled and repressed, may be acceptable." Members of the consultation showed that they were very much aware that trouble was in the very air young people breathed, and it was almost impossible for them to keep out of trouble. An unconscious class bias on the part of police and fiscals, who might let off young people from 'better' homes with a warning when others would be brought to court, might conceal how widespread throughout society was a sense of disturbance. Adults were unsure of themselves and young people were making their own patterns and rules of behaviour. When one came across senseless violence and vandalism one had to ask how much responsibility the young people involved had ever been given, what contribution to life had been looked for from them.

A society which had lost its way and did not include young people in the search to rediscover it was simply asking for a violent reaction from them. "Lawlessness" said a criminologist "is simply the other side of the attractive feature of young people today – their enthusiasm, their responsiveness, their freshness and adventurousness". These qualities must be directed towards responsible participation in the life of society, not dissipated by a feeling of being unwanted.

Lord Kilbrandon expounded his conviction that laws dealing with children should have nothing to do with summary criminal jurisdiction. Lawlessness in young people was primarily an educational problem. Through the use of juvenile panels, which could take time to understand young people and give parents the support they needed to educate them, remedial action could be initiated without waiting for crime to be committed: "At present juvenile courts have to wait until there is a crime; or deal with an accused person; or later, treat with a sentenced person – juvenile panels could be on the job with effective treatment earlier so it was clear to the young

a) that care and concern are being expressed through this method of dealing with them
b) the punishment is so clearly relevant that the person who is suffering it acknowledges its rightness.

Where it is seen that it is treatment that is needed, voluntary acceptance comes in – and consent has a treatment value in itself. Passing sentence lies in the realm of compulsion. Punishment by a judicial body makes it difficult to show that people care. In one important dimension of their work, teachers and police were social workers.

In consideration of the responsibilities of school and home the deeply disturbing effects of broken homes and parental indifferences were noted. A good school could make up for these to some extent. Children needed to be taught fundamental standards of relationship and fundamental elements of group behaviour. There was a trauma in our society produced by the feeling of some young people that they were failures by the age of fifteen and sometimes long before that. An important achievement of school was to respect the attainment of a child at its true level – this was the best gift the school could give. The authority which was effective in both school and home was that which set out to **win** consent.

Other observations included this: that too often the work of the churches was parallel to the problem instead of aimed straight at it.

In February 1968 a consultation on Community Development took place with Miss Ilys Booker from the Kensington Family Study project. There was a balance of people whose fields were social work, education, and youth work. The consultation examined the value of an indirect approach to community development provided by unattached workers who were supported by something like a steering committee (to take an instance, they might be employed by voluntary organisations and financed from statutory sources). Often a community lacked resources within itself to develop points of initiative to provide a more adequate community life. The alternative was too often that some organisation came in and manipulated people to provide means of community interrelationship which looked healthy but did not arise out of the conviction and choice of the community itself. The value of the indirect approach and the unattached worker was that people in a neighbourhood area could be encouraged to take small steps of faith and hope at the speed of their own appreciation of the need for them (too slow a process for the average Local Authority to countenance!). One could register progress when the reaction of people in the area tackled was something like this: "Look at the time she has been around, and note all that has been happening over these years: and see how little she has found to occupy her time with!"

In July 1968 a consultation on "Glasgow's Housing Schemes" looked more specifically at the needs of new housing areas. This was a very practical consultation. It isolated some of the basic questions related to the shape of such areas e.g. – is there a serious intention to bring employment to them or will they always be treated as dormitory satellites? It put its finger on certain fairly obvious but neglected features – such as the delay in providing permanent structures for community activity, accompanied by a refusal to offer temporary structures in the meantime, because the permanent ones were somewhere in the pipeline. The value of youth wings in schools was affirmed, along with a variety of provision which might be dispersed through the community – a place for meeting at a neighbourhood level, youth games huts, play space and 'kick-about' pitches. The establishment of sub-district offices of the Social Services, the Ministries of Labour and Social Security in particular, helped to give a community a feeling that it was being thought about. Where cafes, launderettes, hairdressing and other shops were in quite inadequate supply, private ventures which were not viable without support from elsewhere should be subsidised. The position of the chemist might be used as a precedent – priority in building permission, rent subsidy where required, were laid on. One MP took part in this consultation along with social and educational workers, representatives of Local Authorities, and bodies from the community such as Tenants' Associations.

A consideration of the roots of lawlessness and violence in our time thrust attention to the early formative years in children's lives, and showed the influence of a deprived childhood and a sense of being unwanted in pre-school years on future delinquent behaviour. The agencies for social support, voluntary and statutory, confirmed this from research and experience. Early in December 1967 a two-day consultation drew upon people involved professionally in the Social Services, the different churches and representatives of Playgroup Associations, the Social Work Services Group from St Andrew's House, approximately fifty in all. Father EF O'Doherty, Professor of Psychology at University College, Dublin, who had done considerable field work as well as academic study on young children in the setting of the family, acted as leader and resource person throughout. This consultation showed, at one and the same time, the lack of any proper assessment of the needs of young children in Scotland and a serious shortage of provision for the under-fives by way of nursery schools and playgroups (Local Authority provision, though very good, was not likely to be expanded substantially at this time). An awareness of need was bringing a considerable number of playgroups into being – many of them on church premises. They were of different standards of leadership, of premises and equipment. The Pre-School Playgroup Association was striving manfully to cope. Provision of training courses suitable for paid and voluntary leaders was probably the most urgent need, although there were many other ways in which young children could be given help and support by imaginative adults. The upsurge of interest was timely, since the churches were becoming more aware of the need for the total development of children within a Christian community, rather than with conceptual teaching. The potential for good or evil, including the ability to respond to the Christian gospel in later years, is largely laid down at this stage of life.

Through this consultation a working party was set up to investigate the situation and made recommendations. It met on two occasions. On the second of these Mr JO Johnston of the Social Work Services Group and Dr Haldane, the child psychiatrist were present. They proposed that a continuing working party should be set up on 'The Churches' Concern for Pre-School Children and Their Parents' with a remit 'To assess the needs of pre-school children and their parents and to suggest how the churches in Scotland might respond to these needs.' The working party was in number approximately fifteen and included a psychologist, a psychiatrist, sociologist, social worker, paediatrician, primary teacher, nursery school teacher, health visitor; and representatives from Local Authority, Health and Education Departments, with two or three people from the churches directly involved in such work. An approach was to be made for the backing of the Scottish Churches' Council and the governmental agencies.

On its meeting on 15th June 1968 the Scottish Churches' Council endorsed the working party project with enthusiasm. Since trusts which had been approached had not provided money for secretarial staffing, a financial problem remained. The Scottish Churches' Council sought discussion with the Scottish Advisory Council of Child Care; but in the re-structuring of services the latter Council was suffering a sea-change and the matter had to be left over to a future point in the restructuring. The double aim is presented in the approach of increasing the number of pre-school playgroups and seeing that adequate provision is made in terms of aims, facilities, and training of staff, with standards acceptable to those with experience and authority on the subject. A new Advisory Council on Social Work was to come into being in 1969 and the matter could be taken further with them.

At a meeting in November 1968 two immediate steps were proposed:

a) a leaflet to be sent to all congregations setting out the main aims and methods of good playgroup provision and giving information about literature and organisations which would be helpful and

b) teaching conferences to be set up in different areas of Scotland to encourage the churches in these areas to pick up this responsibility.

In April 1969 five area conferences were held to stimulate interest where this was needed, encourage initiative where it was being taken, and underline the importance of good standards of accommodation, equipment, and leadership.

The concern for the pre-school child should be seen in its total setting. Scottish Churches' House was not a pioneer in the field. Its part was to draw on the evidence provided at relevant consultations and co-operate with statutory and voluntary authorities in getting adequate attention paid to needs, to encourage the awareness that it is the deprived child who is in most need of creative outlet and loving attention in pre-school years, and to emphasise the importance of standards.

Re-structuring the Social Services

It is impossible to disentangle the different threads of social concern which run through the programming of Scottish Churches' House since they are all inter-related. It has already been indicated that compassion for human beings and an assessment of their needs and the provision required led a group of those professionally involved from many angles to consider a radical re-organisation of the Social Services.

This initiative illustrates two important aspects of the work of the House

Quite early on, as a follow-up of Kirk Weeks and as a manifestation of the Tell Scotland Movement, social workers were given opportunity to meet once per month in Glasgow over a meal: and then, at least once per year, they came for a residential period to Scottish Churches' House to firm up on the thinking which had taken place in the short meetings in Glasgow. Thus a useful shuttle service was provided between the local scene and those involved in it and the provision that could be offered by a residential centre. This pulse between the local and non-residential and the central and residential is a significant one to establish. Not all the social workers were Christians: yet the umbrella provided by the churches resulted in a sense of local church co-operation in the Glasgow area, and a House of the churches developed this naturally. The interflow between a centre of the churches and the churches in their local life has allowed a relationship of trust to develop which contrasts with some other parts of the world, maybe particularly Germany, where relationships between Evangelical Academies and local churches are difficult at times.

A second feature is the informal co-operation with government departments. The informality is the gift that the House has to offer. Some small service can be rendered by bringing together people who would not otherwise meet (and who sometimes cannot be brought together officially!) to spend two days residentially working on a Government White Paper. If there is a growth of understanding and a movement of minds, the situation is helped at the official level, even though this help is indirect. Thus a Minister of the Crown may quietly indicate a bit of thinking or study which needs to be done and those who could be usefully invited to do it: or contacts with a government department may show some gap in the field of work being tackled and, on enquiry, in case there should be duplication of effort, it is clear that the House can do some useful work. No official weight is ever attached to such work, but if it is worth its salt it is taken into account by decision-making bodies in the appropriate government departments.

A further characteristic of the life of the House is illustrated in the area of social work. When points are identified where change should take place towards a healthier form of society, it is irresponsible not to do what can be done to give effect to these. Sometimes working parties have to be set up and a quite substantial development (such as Enterprise Youth) promoted outwith Dunblane. But, mercifully, there are many companies of people who, once they have assembled and given their minds to a subject and sorted out their priorities, have means to bring these further in their work. This was so in the case of social workers. What was done at Scottish Churches' House was ploughed back into their own thinking and experimentation as they sought to provide society with adequate services.

In February 1963 a Kirk Week Weekend for Social Workers was held. In May of the same year a Family Case-workers' School and in February 1964 a Social Services Consultation under the auspices of the Tell Scotland Movement took place. Later consultations were held in April 1966 and in November of the same year, promoted by the Mission Department of the Scottish Churches' Council (into which the work of Tell Scotland and Kirk week now flowed). The aim in these was to get into natural association with one another people who had allied professional responsibilities for meeting social need. Professional barriers were broken down and a sense of common enterprise established. This was important for the more delimited work which was beginning to develop and which absorbed attention from 1965 on.

A consultation on housing in 1964 had a seminal effect. It illustrated the possibilities of assessing a difficult situation by using the varied expertise of many people who had tried to cope with it and provided profitable lines of further study and action. Why should the same thing not be done, with problem families as the concern around which people gathered, it was asked? And so the consultation on Problem Families took place in February 1965, and led to a conviction that a realignment of the instruments of social compassion was needed. A working party was set up, as has been indicated, and in March 1965 it drew out a possible scheme for restructuring the review of social provision and would await the conclusions of the Kilbrandon Report. Almost exactly a year before it was published, in October 1965, a further consultation on the restructuring of the social services took place. It had been arranged to suit the diary of Judith Hart, Parliamentary Under-secretary, Scottish Office, who was to have been the chief catalyst. Unfortunately a change of commitments made it impossible for her to come, at the last minute. In a company of thirty almost every organisation which would be affected was represented. Mr Neil Carmichael, MP took Mrs Hart's place.

The scheme for a reorganisation of the social services, suggested in the consultation of February 1965 and given more definition by the working party in March of that year, had been tried out on some Local Authorities and the Council of Social Service. The October consultation believed that it was not comprehensive enough and worked out, in chart form, ideas for structure for Local Authorities' Social Services. It was recognised in this consultation that many people were bound to feel that their own particular sphere of work was threatened, and this fear was taken into account in the discussion. More clearly than ever before the advantage of having "one door" on which any in need could knock and be directly related to some means of dealing with that need, impressed itself upon participants. From the social work point of view this allowed for an economical use of resources; while headmasters and police said that their work would be helped if there were a central point of referral and liaison. Special thought was given to the casework department proposed, the base for research into overall patterns and trends which it offered and problems of staffing and training. The proposals drawn out in the chart offered the following advantages:

a) the rationalisation and better use of available workers, and better training facilities

b) overcoming barriers to communication

c) a centralisation of control of resources so that those were available to all social workers.

Just over a year later, a month after publication of the White Paper 'Social Work in the Community' to which the previous consultations had been a contribution, voluntary organisations in Scotland were invited to consider their relationship to the statutory social services in light of the recommendations of the White Paper. Over twenty national organisations, some church some not, sent 34 participants. It was recognised that the time for study of the White Paper had been very limited. The intention was to have a first run over the ground and then have a further consultation when voluntary agencies had had time to get their immediate reactions put into a fuller perspective. The consequences of the recommendations in the White Paper for Child Care, Youth Work, Family Case Work, Services for the Disabled, and Care of the Mentally Handicapped were assessed by individuals (they made it clear that their judgement was an individual one since there had not been time yet for voluntary agencies they represented to study proposals in detail). Mr Geo Johnston for the Home and Health Department pointed out that what the White Paper provided was only the general framework within which local areas could handle their situation flexibly; and that existing co-ordination would not suffer. The onus was now upon the voluntary organisations to decide whether they were prepared to re-think their roles and develop in new areas of service. Voluntary organisations, for instance, were probably better fitted than were the statutory to build up self-reliance in a community with separate groupings. There was discussion on the ways in which a social work department might service other departments, how stronger co-operation between voluntary organisations might be developed, how statutory and voluntary bodies might work together at policy-making and fieldwork levels, and how voluntary organisations should recruit and train.

The second consultation on this theme was held in March 1967. Co-operation between voluntary organisations, and the recruitment, guidance and training of volunteers occupied two of the main sessions. The other two concerned welfare/medical liaison and community care and participation. A further two sessions were occupied with group work and two were left free to be used in the light of progress made. A host of practical difficulties and possibilities suggested by the White Paper were worked on in group and plenary sessions. There was to be an assessment, when the White Paper was presented as a Bill, on whether the consultation on community development might be fruitful, and whether smaller social work organisations who found it less easy to co-operate might use the House as a meeting point.

A two-day consultation in October, 1967 studied some of the fruits of a year's research work on the Voluntary Organisations undertaken by Mr George Murray within the Department of Social and Economic Research, Glasgow University. In the first part of the consultation the management and finance of Voluntary Organisations was given scrutiny. The middle part was given to a discussion of the support to be provided by churches and membership organisations. The last part had mainly to do with the recruitment and training of voluntary workers. Her Majesty the Queen visited Scottish Churches' House during this consultation.

From this gathering came specific recommendations. These concerned

1) Management: Voluntary Organisations should keep their work under continuous review; an internal study group aided by an outside expert might prove the best way of doing this; managerial salaries should bear some relationship to Local Authority scales.
2) Registration of charitable trusts: this was desirable so that information about them might be spread; and in some cases enquiries into their working would be valuable so that their objectives might be up-dated.
3) A charities official investment fund: this would be particularly useful for smaller voluntary organisations; the pricing of services for local authorities and fund-raising produced detailed suggestions
4) Research: the voluntary organisations would welcome approaches by the universities to carry out research on their work and on volunteers with the caveat that students' research should be limited and carefully supervised and more mature approaches should observe confidentiality and keep in consultation with the organisations themselves.

The needs of the pre-school child, the consultation on Community Development in February 1968, and the consultation on Glasgow's housing schemes of June 1968, all came in direct lineal succession from this work on the re-structuring of the social services, statutory and voluntary – as well as from the consultations which focused on lawlessness and violence.

Housing

It was a consultation on housing held in 1964 which sparked off developments in the field of social work in the second half of the 1960s. The lesson learned was that the possibilities for gripping a situation firmly can emerge if a comprehensive approach is made and if people who hold very different responsibilities all of which impinge on the problem are brought together for residential meeting. Appreciation of different factors and different contributions clearly grows during formal sessions, and, outside these, relationships are established across what were previously barriers and points hammered out in informal discussion.

In the meeting of the Policy and Programme committee of the House, of October 1962 it is recorded, 'The question of housing was raised as an immense and serious social problem which was getting too little attention today....' It was agreed that some probing should be done in case the House could be of service. In February of 1963 the Warden met with five officials over a meal in St Andrew's House, asking the two basic questions: Is there any service which might be rendered in this field through the action of the churches together, and if action is needed is a place such as Scottish Churches' House the place from which to forward it or is that better done locally? Nearly all of the time was taken up with an explanation on the part of the officials of how adequately the ground was being covered until, when it was nearly time to depart, one of the principals said 'There is one thing I keep ducking in my own mind – it is that, whatever government is in power and whatever finance is allocated, hundreds of people will have to live in sub-standard housing for the next ten years at least.' This opened the flood-gates. First one and then the other shared concerns that they had in the field which called for fresh thinking. The conclusion was that they asked that these points made towards the end be set down and sent to them all, that they reflect on them, and that a further meeting should take place in a month or two when they had time to sort things out a bit more. At this further meeting a group which was basically the same started right away to indicate what parts of the problem of housing could with advantage be given fresh scrutiny; and by suggesting the names of people who should be brought in. They started a snowballing process gathering on the way people who should be drawn in and contributions which could be invited from them on paper. Thus, when the first consultation on housing took place in April 1964 material had accumulated on the subjects to be discussed and people had felt participant long before they turned up because they were invited to contribute in the early stages.

The 1964 consultation was certainly a seminal one. It not only suggested lines to be followed up in the fields of the social services. It played some small part in a concerted approach to housing undertaken by both government and voluntary agencies which enabled all concerned, for the first time in history, to take the measure of the housing problem. JB Cullingworth, at that time senior lecturer in Urban Studies in Glasgow University, prepared a thirty-page survey of housing statistics for England and of those which existed for Scotland – simply to draw some kind of map in the introductory session to put the other sessions in perspective. This was the same JB Cullingworth who was to be invited to lead the team of investigation which produced just under three years later, the report 'Scotland's Older Houses', which had a quite decisive part to play in the assessing of the housing problem and plans to cope with it.

Following this introduction, a vivid picture of the effects of bad housing in a community was painted by a member of the Gorbals Group. Thereafter a top official from the Development Department of St Andrew's House spoke on the problems posed to the administrator, who had to remind himself that behind all planning were flesh and blood people who were to be served both by those who were in face-to-face relationship with them and by those who could not be in such relationship. There was a session on new areas, including both new housing schemes and new towns. A substantial amount of time was spent on finance and financing. The report of this consultation is full of insights and recommendations which find expression in government thinking and government documents. This is not to say that the work at Scottish Churches' House provided these: only that, by entering the field at the point of history, a useful contribution was made in the total approach to a serious problem.

From this consultation it became clear that there was quantitative and qualitative housing problem in Scotland which was peculiar in regard to the traditional smaller size of houses and the much greater absence of fixed baths and WCs etc: 'The normal sort of programme applied throughout Britain will not do for Scotland and will not do for Glasgow in particular." There were special problems of sub-tenancy and multiple ownership: and tenants needed to be protected from exploitation.

Building resources needed to be used with economy e.g. private enterprise office development needed to justify itself within a total setting; and industrial building techniques needed to be applied on a much larger scale. More financial and technical resources needed to be directed to solving housing problems including staffing. Social problems needed to be taken into account as well as technical problems about housing and re-housing, particularly since planning can create such problems as well as solve them. Low rentals played their part in worsening the situation. However, the main work of the consultation expressed itself in an examination of specific aspects and the provision of specific proposals regarding matters which came within the general brackets indicated above.

One of the clear gains was in the field of relationships. Not only was it useful for top administrators in St Andrew's House to be brought face to face with the raw problems confronting the Gorbals Group in a slum area in Glasgow; it was useful for that group to be made aware, through direct contact, that administrators are very human, concerned beings, but the way in which they must express their compassion is through the efficiency and flexibility of their administrative work, which is itself a direct way of caring for people. For New Town people from Cumbernauld and Glenrothes to meet with town councillors and officials from Glasgow, Edinburgh and Aberdeen provided a useful link between those holding new town and old town responsibilities. Dr Cullingworth said that he had personally gained two important things from the consultation;

1) a yet more vivid awareness of the lack of statistics which were important if the full measure of the situation in Scotland were to be taken and

2) the confirmation of a dawning realisation that the situation in Scotland was not a spill-over from the English one but had historical, social and psychological factors which meant that it had to be tackled from scratch. Besides this, simply meeting people who were holding different responsibilities in the field had had its value for him.

This was a consultation which did something in itself, which led to work on the social services, which went back into channels of study, mainly governmental, thus playing some part in the shaping of future policy. Since no clear territory for further consultative work showed itself immediately no further meeting was planned, but participants agreed to alert Scottish Churches' House should fresh matter show itself suitable for the House to tackle.

It was three years later, in March 1967, that a further consultation on housing took place. Shortly before this time, the Cullingworth Report 'Scotland's Older Houses' had been issued. It was used as the working paper for the consultation, with a working outline provided in addition, which divided up main issues into the time available. This proved to be a useful encounter, not only in terms of the study done, but in the opportunity offered for a wide range of people concerned with housing, 35 in all, to gain perspective on the proposals from different angles of interest. Besides architects, planners, lawyers, local government representatives, there was a much more adequate representation of Housing Associations and Societies and of Shelter, the campaign for the homeless. Glasgow Corporation took the occasion with particular seriousness, sending a well-balanced delegation of eight. The Minister of State hoped to be present but, in the end, was prevented. The scale of the problem was first estimated. Two full sessions were taken up with issues related to the improvement of old houses. Finance, and in particular rents, next gained attention. A session was spent on the role of the Housing Association or Society. Then Glasgow's housing situation was looked at as a Scottish problem, in itself of quite unusual dimensions and intractability. Finally the Cullingworth summary of recommendations was studied carefully.

Once again the bulk of the report of the consultation consisted of concrete points to be picked up by channels both of government and voluntary agencies. One of the best fruits of this encounter was a better understanding between Local Authorities and Housing Associations and Societies regarding the way in which their work might be complementary, the local authority taking responsibility for large scale building and the voluntary body rehabilitating smaller properties which were going over the edge into chronic disrepair. In Glasgow, for instance, an improved procedure was instituted so that applications for grant money were made in a more rational manner by Housing Associations, and the corporation's procedures were streamlined so that there was a much shorter waiting time till finance was made available. It was as a direct result of working and living together under one roof that this happier state of affairs resulted in Glasgow.

A direct role for the churches emerged from these two consultations, should the churches be prepared to accept it. There was a need to get the whole of Scotland to face its housing situation – and the churches had members in every corner of the land who might be used as information agents. There was a need for Housing Advisory Services – and Stewardship Campaigns in the churches had shown great reservoirs of unused skill in exactly the areas from which helping teams could be built up (e.g. law, psychology, social work, local government). With the arrival of Shelter on the scene, sheer money raising could have a direct effect on the provision of homes for the homeless. It was clear that in the whole field of housing, committed Christians were found at every level, and that the churches were not taking advantage of their gifts by using them for the benefit of the community.

A direct result of the second consultation on Housing came from the awareness of the Housing Associations and Societies in Scotland that they needed occasional means of meeting to talk through common interests. What was wanted was not some form of liaison (it already existed) – but just an occasional meeting to review their fields of interest. In February 1968 the first of these consultations, which promised to be annual events, took place. A representative from the Societies and one from the Associations formed an Advisory Group with the Warden to plan the ground to be covered by each consultation. On the first occasion the role of the voluntary organisation in relation to housing needs was considered; the structure of voluntary housing bodies and the statutory framework to which they relate; problems of co-ordination and procedural problems; the part the churches could play; and observations on government policy. The latter was given particular attention: and representation was made to the Scottish Housing Advisory Committee and Lord Hughes, its chairman, regarding the provision of a better balance of Housing Associations and Societies' projects in the meeting of housing needs, the centralisation of finance, and alternative means to the present ones of undertaking valuations. Mr Cullingworth was to be pressed to do what he could to promote the study of Housing Associations and Societies in Scotland, recognising differences in their development compared with English equivalents. The Scottish Housing Advisory Committee did in fact take the recommendations seriously into its reckoning in its consideration of the Cohen Report, continuing thought being given to these matters.

A second consultation took place in February 1969. The important elements in this consultation were the separate meeting as well as joint meeting of those whose interest was Housing Associations or Housing Societies; the meeting in common consultation of Local Authority representatives and representatives of voluntary organisations; and the examination of some of the features of the Cohen Report which were thought to be most clearly requiring challenge. Matters such as the value of co-ownership and cost-rent schemes were given a good deal of attention, specialist problems regarding management, problems of financing and of educating people on different forms of provision available, the acquisition of sites especially when they were scarce.

Young People in Society

When Scottish Churches' House was brought into being, enough money was provided by trusts for the restoration of the shell of the building, and other money was raised by an appeal for the equipping and launching of the enterprise. But behind the house there was wilderness and wasteland, and there was no money available to deal with it. The site was unsuitable for machines, sloping at a considerable angle with no access (it was years later before the road into the grounds was built). The stage was clearly set (as was realised once people looked back) for using the service of young people in work camps to make the wilderness blossom. In 1960 a World Council of Churches work camp accomplished wonders. A work camp, still partly international, was set up by the House itself in the following year and in 1962 a SCM in Schools work camp took place. These were the longest camps and many short ones followed some being for as little as one day.

The experience of running these camps, and the contact with different organisations which provided advice or volunteers, showed up the isolated way in which different organisations were pursuing fairly similar ends. In December 1961 the first consultation on Scotland 'Scotland as our Heritage' found itself with a vision. Towards the end of the consultation it was as if many bits of insight became fused, a common mind developed and found spontaneous expression. A report in 'The Scotsman' of 2nd January, 1962 puts it thus: "A consideration of our nationhood, the problems of industrial and rural life, our cultural heritage, led at one point to the query 'What are young Scots to think of this?' Where are they to come and share in the shaping of the nation's future?..." "Was there not a way in which young Scots could learn to cherish their homeland, and give it a true place in their affections – by service?..." "What would seem to be needed is a liaison committee of bodies who recognise the possibilities of development of youth service in order to

a)   search out and investigate possible projects
b)   provide the basic organisation and find the necessary finance, and
c)   recruit"

It was also 'The Scotsman' which reported, on April 27th 1962, on a consultation of almost all bodies operating or interested in operating service by young people in work camps involving manual effort or demanding forms of service, short term or long term, to the handicapped, the delinquent, the mentally retarded and so on. It was noted that they hope 'to establish means of co-ordinating their efforts in Scotland in the near future.' The Warden's memo of December 1961 makes the point to the committee 'to me, this is the most important means of ecumenical meeting and service open to youth'.

These events proved to be the seed bed out of which grew a fully-fledged national organisation, Enterprise Youth. Probably better than anything else begun in Scottish Churches' House, it illustrated the way in which a House of the churches could altruistically serve the life of the nation. It must be made clear that the role of the House was to serve a growing common conviction of the independent organisations, not foist its own thinking upon them. Enterprise Youth came into being only because a concern for the whole of Scotland and a developing trust among themselves enabled them to see the advantages of joint effort. It is likely that the committee of the House was rather over-sensitive regarding the independence of the organisations in the field and the need to keep ecclesiastical claws off a development which had its own proper identity and integrity. Thus in the minutes of January 1962 it is recorded: It was decided to hold a consultation of interested parties, in order to set up some machinery for developing co-ordination and promotion, the Warden to fix a date. But this must not become the work of the House or the Warden" When Enterprise Youth first got unsteadily on its feet and the base of development changed from Dunblane to Edinburgh, the House felt it had done its work. It recorded in February 1963 its conviction about the value of helping to bring to birth enterprises which might be significant for the future of Scotland and of cutting the umbilical cord once they had a life of their own. From that point, it was believed, 'apart from the Warden's participation in meetings, all responsibility would then be handed over.' In fact Enterprise Youth was not established at a first attempt. In that first year it almost foundered. The House was invited to help in reconstructing it on a different basis, and the Warden in fact was chairman until 1968, by which time it really was established nationally, in terms of finance, personnel, official acknowledgement and so on. The withdrawal had now taken place: and the original intention of the committee to be of service without retaining any power for itself is illustrated by the fact that Scottish Churches' House had no right to representation on any of its committees. The mainspring of this development was the Countess of Mar and Kellie. Pansy Mar and Kellie with her aristocratic background and plummy voice was one of the last persons you might expect to relate well to young people. But the sheer integrity of her concern got through to them.

A consultation on 'Work Camp Development' held in April 1962 drew upon bodies promoting service among young people, the National Trust for Scotland, United Nations International Service, Friends Work Camps, International Voluntary Service, SCM in Schools and The Church of Scotland Youth

Department: and others interested in the idea, Scottish Association of Young Farmers Clubs, Young Men and Young Women's Christian Association, Girl Guides, Girls' Training Corps, Clubs, SSCVYO, representatives of the Home Department in St Andrew's House concerned with delinquency, and the After Care Council. It was clear from the start that these bodies had a great deal to think through in common, and a fascinating cross-fertilisation of ideas took place. It was clear that they realised that they were making very limited progress in Scotland at that point and that both more projects and more propaganda were needed. At this very early stage matters which proved to be pre-occupying in the development of co-ordinated work already appeared. At the very beginning an awareness of the fact that length of holidays allowed students and teachers to participate in work camps, as most of the members of society could not, resulted in attention being given to the potential represented by industrial youth: and already, thus early, the suggestion was put on the board that an industrial trainee who had a fortnight's holiday might give up one week of it to service, the employer adding a week from the working year. Thus a two week holiday period would become a three week break: only one week of this would be relaxation, the other two being service. Already the resource of retired people who had a lifetimes' experience in areas of work which were relevant for youth service, and who possessed mature skills was realised: and the possibilities of matching them up with inexperienced young people so that there was good oversight and well-directed enthusiasm was being explored. Already the possibility of using organisations which were not in the field of youth service for occasional assistance was being discussed: and the contributions to particular projects which might be given by the Women's Voluntary Service, the Red Cross and the Scottish Youth Hostels Association were being kept in mind. There was already strong emphasis on service not *for* the local community but *with* the local community.

The quietly growing conviction that some means of liaison and promotion would be of profit attained a definite shape at this consultation. A co-ordinating body could search out new projects; team appropriate projects with appropriate organisations; draw in others who could offer experience and leadership (both organisations, and individuals in early retirement): pool resources and promote a search for further resources; provide a map of activity in Scotland; provide one door on which recruits could knock, unless they directly approached organisations – so that there might be a distribution of personnel between projects which had too many and those which had too few workers; attend to the overall financing of the development of these forms of Youth Service; handle requests for information; and publicise the movement. The consultation was clear that it needed:-

1)   an office from which correlation could be developed through administration
2)   an Advisory Body to take oversight of the development.

Representatives were to be sought on the Advisory Body from employers, the trade unions, the social services, education, youth organisations, the Highlands, with others who might help in publicity and finance and who might identify and assess projects, one representative from each serving organisation being responsible for keeping contact between the serving bodies and the Advisory Body. The possibility of setting up this office under the wing of one of the existing serving organisations was considered and dismissed. Some neutral ground was sought and the Scottish Council of Social Service and the Kilbrandon Council were to be consulted and interested departments in St Andrew's House approached on questions of finance.

It was quite clear that the different organisations retained their independence including independence of operation. What they sought was a servant of their common purposes, a catalyst of their common thinking, and a means of promotion and publicity. A great deal of what was sketched out in 1962 stood the test of later years as an accurate indication of what was wanted.

During 1963 a body was set up and the description 'Enterprise Youth' first used. The Scottish Council of Social Service provided office space and part-time help. The Scottish Education Department provided £230 to cover a five month period. By April 1963 when that period finished, the complete inadequacy of a part-time office and the need for a full-time field worker were showing themselves clearly. Meantime approaches were being made to trusts for financial support.

The consultation which assembled in February 1964 was more like a Council of War than anything else. The Edinburgh University Settlement and Community Service Volunteers took a full part for the first time. Fresh possibilities of service were examined, and the needs of the young unemployed were kept particularly in mind. But the future of Enterprise Youth claimed first attention. It had been a year of no progress, of no confidence indicated from government quarters, of negative responses from trusts. Was the whole concept a mistaken one? The representatives of organisations considered the situation radically and came up with a fresh, compelling conviction that a body such as Enterprise Youth was needed in Scotland. It agreed that a field officer was needed: and IVS, most self-forgetfully and generously, held up its own application for a field officer in favour of one who might be appointed to serve all the organisations. A fresh approach was to be made to the Scottish

Education Department for finance for a full-time office and a full-time field officer. The case was based not on mere theory but on the record of work already done by the constituent organisations and their conviction that they needed a promotion of their common concerns and co-ordination of their efforts. £2.200 was asked for 1964 – '65. Besides this there was clearly a need to re-constitute Enterprise Youth itself. This was done. The emphasis was put on the working organisations themselves along with some other bodies closely concerned, and the senior Advisory Group was made into a panel which could be consulted as required. The new committee consisted of representatives of the National Trust, Church of Scotland Youth Department, Edinburgh University Settlement, Friends' Work Camps, Student Christian Movement in Schools, IVS., UNA., International Service, Community Service Volunteers; along with representatives from the Scottish Education Department, the Scottish Council of Social Service, the Scottish Standing Conference of Voluntary Youth Organisations and the Scottish Association of Further Education Officers. Space was left for representation on the part of any further serving organisation which appeared (as Interscot did, quite soon).

The offer of SSCVYO to provide secretarial assistance and office accommodation within its own premises brought a gleam of hope. However there was complete stalemate in finding finance, St Andrew's House saying "We are prepared to put up some money, but only if enough is raised from other sources", and trusts saying "We are prepared to put up some money, but only if the government first commits itself". Each was determined that the other had to make the first move. Since no progress towards financing a field officer was made IVS was encouraged to go ahead and seek an appointment under its own auspices (such an officer could incidentally render service to all the organisations, bringing them in on projects and possibilities for which IVS itself was not equipped). At this point in history the need to involve immigrants and students from overseas and the importance of the Highlands and Islands Development Board for the whole enterprise were being realised.

In early 1965 deputations to St Andrew's House and approaches to trusts continued. A suggestion from St Andrew's House that receiving organisations as well as servicing organisations should be directly represented in Enterprise Youth, was agreed to be wise. In that year the Pilgrim Trust offered £1,000 for two years provided a similar amount came from government sources; and the Kilbrandon Council recommended a grant amount to 50% of the total needed. Enterprise Youth was able to constitute itself a national voluntary organisation, with government and trust money financing it and began to be established. George Foulkes (later an MP and Minister) headed this up.

Enterprise Youth went from strength to strength. A notable drive came from a one-day conference held in Edinburgh in the spring of 1966 which made clear to the nation the great potential of youth service, the varieties of it, the effectiveness of it, given proper oversight and training, and the possibilities in hospitals, children's homes, local authorities etc of making use of the youthful energy which could thrust itself healthily into the community. Professor Robert Grieve of the Highlands and Islands Development Board would have acted as chairman but for an accident to his leg shortly before the conference. Judith Hart provided a warm gesture of support from the government by starting off the conference.

A similar important gesture was made by the Secretary of State for Scotland when he opened new premises in Queen Street, Edinburgh, to serve the needs of Enterprise Youth and three of the organisations whose interest it existed to promote. Enough space remained for other organisations to move in. The advantages were clear of grouping Enterprise Youth and its constituent organisations together, physically, on the same premises, so that natural contacts might underpin the development of continuing consultation and co-operation.

The Queen's inclusion of a visit to Enterprise Youth and the Standing Conference of Voluntary Youth Organisations during her General Assembly presence in Edinburgh in May 1969 showed that Enterprise Youth had now its acknowledged place in the life of Scotland.

Scottish Churches' House continued to meet the needs of Enterprise Youth for some time, in a less direct but still important way. It offered a means of consultation from time to time so that particular aspects of the work could be given the concentrated attention that residential facilities and a sympathetic environment could offer. In April 1969 it was possible to gather an excellent representation of employers, representatives of Industrial Training Boards and training officers to consider the involvement in youth service of young people from industry. There is no doubt that confidence produced in many quarters in industry by work at Scottish Churches' House produced a company that Enterprise Youth itself could not have assembled – thus some forms of specific service were rendered as well as general service.

A constructive outlet for youthful energy was provided by Enterprise Youth and its constituent organisations. This was the positive side. But a great deal of attention was also given to young people at risk in our society and needs for counselling for the young.

Mention has been made of the 'Kilbrandon Council', the Consultative Council on Youth and Community Service. Through its good offices at a crucial point, Enterprise Youth was given a chance to prove itself. In the course of its work this Council decided that it needed a 'think-tank' on the pressures coming on young people in society and the help they needed, and brought one into being for two days in Dunblane Hydro. It was suggested informally at this gathering that Scottish Churches' House might pick up the two aspects, youth at risk, and counselling for the young, and do some work on them which would then be fed back into the Council. These twin areas of concern led to consultative work which continued for some time. The task set was to try to distinguish risks which young people run which are quite unfair, from risks which had to be faced in the normal process of growing up. Counselling needs at every point impinging on the development of young people were to be fully investigated.

An exploratory meeting first took place and a full consultation was held in June 1968. This was followed by two further consultations in November of the same year and March 1969. An Advisory Group was set up to head up the study and experiment, the basis of which was thought through in the consultations. Thirty packed pages reporting the work of the consultations are difficult to summarise, and no attempt will be made to do this: but some main lines may indicate the trends of discussion.

There was plenty of evidence of the unfair risks that young people faced in our society. These included, for instance, those who had to make a double adjustment coming from rural to city areas and from a defined place in the structure of a family and a community to one free of ties (nurses and apprentices often came into this category); lorry-hopping on the part of young people who had had a row with their parents; those who, early in life, had felt themselves to be branded as failures and became social drop-outs. The fences were down in society: there was nothing for it now but to equip young people to cope with adult living. A good part of the school curriculum in later school years needed to be aimed at helping young folk to cope with adulthood and gain a rich maturity. The confusion of parents about their responsibilities and at the same time their clear duty not to give 'instant everything' to young people, not to leave the house to them at weekends, not to allow them to start on pep-pills, were alike evident. Both parents, in their day-to-day encounter with their young people, and schools, in preparing them to deal with the responsibilities of adulthood had to educate young people so that they themselves, of their own choice, rejected fashions of heavier drinking, sexual promiscuity and violence. From early on in these consultations there was concern about stupid drinking – young people who came from homes where drink flowed freely and those who came from teetotal homes were in particularly exposed positions. Educating young people not only in word, but by experiment about the nature of different types of drink and their effect on the person, and planning one or two pilot schemes where there was a carefully structured type of opportunity for young people to drink under unobtrusive supervision seemed to point ways forward. One had to reckon with the need for young people to have colour in lives that were often drab; and recognise that disobedience might come from a healthy non-conformity, and drugs offer a way of thumbing noses at adult society.

Group work in the first consultation concentrated on four different aspects:

1) Counselling, both directive (often through referral) and non-directive (through therapeutic listening): the influence of the peer group was clear, though adults could also prove acceptable if they were prepared to face the length of time it took for confidence to be established.

2) Aftercare: with responsible adults in the background, young people might provide support for those other young people who came out of penal institutions – a risk is involved, but the right kind of risk.

3) Gaps in provision for the young: young people need the chance to create, they need space to develop their own imaginative responses: they might form emergency squads to tackle disasters or to hunt for missing children; the long summer holidays, when nearly every means of occupying time and energy for young people close down, simply encourage the bad social by-products of boredom.

4) Existing provision: there was a lack of finance, and especially of provision for girls.

The November consultation took counselling as one of its main interests. It kept before it the radical question 'Do isolated young people really need help – or are we anxious to practise an adult experiment on them? It was then that the inarticulate way in which young people showed their need for help, and the importance of non-verbal communication for those of low IQs became obvious. Members looked not only at the leadership which was consciously provided, but noticed the informal consultative relationship which develops between young people and barmen, fish and chip vendors, and assistants in public libraries. Those natural points of contact were very important. There was a swing in our society away from providing premises on which young people could be assembled, to recognising the places where they naturally met and offering the service they needed there. Counselling proved to be in its early stages of development in schools although the practice of trying to make sure that each pupil had at least one available adult he or she could turn to was a help; and the way in which parents were participant in this provision and Welfare Officers and Juvenile Liaison Officers made a link between the school and the community was extremely healthy. Again and again it came out that young people need to be given their share of responsibility. Counselling must be thought of as two-way traffic, and as part of a healthy relationship – not necessarily related at all to delinquency.

Further attention was given to drugs, drink and violence. There were leaks through the National Health Service, over-prescribing by some doctors (who were probably overworked), inadequate security in hospitals, the falsifying of prescriptions, patients registering with two or three doctors or pretending they were on holiday. The British Medical Association was to be approached to see what research had been done, what was still needed and what results could be made available regarding such leakages. There was a firmer conviction about the need for pilot schemes to educate young people in drinking under structured conditions; as about the need that the traditional bar gives way to premises for social meeting where there were not only drinks but other beverages, meals, positive policies on drinking instead of the negative ones which had predominated. The relation of violence to underprivilege was noted and the encouragement of violence in the May to September period when young people found creative outlets for energies quite wanting, was considered to be serious.

Various experiments were looked at in which provision was made for young people in need of support, especially after they had served some penal sentence. The small flat (eg with four students and one borstal boy) or slightly larger communal residence, had produced a life-style of its own whose spontaneous development drew its quality from the voluntary character of the enterprise. A further concern was the aftercare of young ex-offenders through people about their own age, who themselves were given support (e.g. by schools). If a relationship could be set up between the community to which the young person will return and the institution some time before release this might prevent his/her going straight back into a delinquent subculture. Pilot projects on aftercare were worked out based on Action Clackmannan and the Coffin – these to be discussed further with the Director of Prison and Borstal Services and taken from that point by Enterprise Youth.

The consultation in March 1969 picked up two specific suggestions of the November group. In an area of Edinburgh, Pilton, and a town with rural surroundings, Tullibody, it was proposed to arrange activities for four to six weeks under the leadership of students from Moray House and Jordanhill Training Colleges. Parents would be brought in on things at weekends, and whatever potential they might have for voluntary leadership would be developed. These schemes would be pilot schemes to show what might be possible throughout Scotland and would be carefully evaluated at the November 1969 consultation.

The other main concern was the drinking habits of the young and this was discussed fully with three representatives of the brewers. Alcoholism and research on it, questions about educating young people in drinking, the need for the control of drinking parties which tended to get out of hand, were among matters discussed. The hope was expressed that the brewers might combine with a group such as the Advisory Group to produce literature on the effects of drinking, There was also discussion about the possibilities of having premises for the under-twenty-ones where beer only was available, of the drawback of laws which encouraged eye-on-the-clock drinking, and of the deprivation in new housing areas where there were no licensed premises for social meeting. The time for discussion was greatly appreciated and it was hoped that the brewers would take part in future discussions.

The Advisory Group which was appointed to carry all this work further consisted of a comprehensive representation of those who were involved with the needs of youth both in the churches and in the community in general. Just over thirty people took part in the consultative work and eleven are members of the Advisory Group.

Would outlets for constructive service on the part of young people be best supplied by the institution of a form of National Service with options other than military and a commitment on the part of young people at an appropriate stage of life to choose one of those and offer service to the community? The committee was sounded out about the possibility of enquiring into this. Some members of the Commons and Lords had made it known that they would welcome such an investigation, but that if any of them started it, it would be branded as the project of the party they adhered to whichever that was. Scottish Churches' House was able to get people with different allegiances to meet around a common concern. Would it be willing to pick up on what was clearly, politically, a 'hot potato'"?

The committee would, but were determined to sound out the ground first. Accordingly a pilot consultation was held in June 1968 to which representatives of industrial education, HM Forces etc were invited. With contributions sent

117

in beforehand it was possible to sort out very clearly the pros and cons of the whole idea, and to look at possibilities of compulsory or voluntary service and specific matters such as ages and stages for undertaking it, selection and placing, length of service, staffing, administration and finance. This pegging out of the ground proved to be very useful. Others besides those who had participated in the pilot consultation were sent copies for comment. It was clear that there was a fascination and stimulation in the very idea of instituting a form of National Service. It was clear from Chief Constables, up and down Scotland, that they were quite unable to forget the quality of recruits who came out of National Service into the police service. One after the other said something like this: "It would do a lot for Britain, and for the police force in particular; but it is too great a temptation – I mustn't think that it is possible in peace time." Alternative suggestions to a year's service came in, probably the most notable coming from the GOC Scotland – that there be a compulsory six to eight weeks of training of a kind deliberately calculated to equip young people basically for many forms of voluntary service they could offer to the community wherever their work led them and whatever its character.

Full consultations were planned first of all for January 1969 and then for April of that year to coincide with parliamentary holidays. Although a goodly company of people accepted the invitation to take part there was no trade unionist, no industrialist, and no member of the Lords or Commons who signed on. It was decided not to hold these consultations since those who could give them bite and carry them through other stages were not adequately represented. It would be a misuse of the time of those who were prepared to come if their work could find no outlet in the thinking of quarters which could promote or deter it. The whole matter was put in abeyance and filed as having reached a certain stage from which it might be brought forward if the conditions should appear in the future which were not then in evidence. This turned out to have a thoroughly healthy effect. Those who wanted a careful examination of the possibilities of a form of National Service to take place, but were not willing to give this a first claim on their own time, affirmed that they felt Scottish Churches' House was the right kind of place to think this through and that they themselves would muster their resources and bring them to bear if further opportunity were offered. The Countess of Mar and Kellie headed up this work and a pilot group that autumn planned a full consultation early in 1970.

If something constructive were to come out of these investigations, it could provide some forms of stability at an important point for young people who felt inadequate, and a broad national base for service on which the voluntary organisations associated in Enterprise Youth could build.

Pressures on Society

Some of the matters mentioned in the preceding section were given more direct attention and fresh matters allied to them were picked up in specific areas of consultative work.

In November 1967 SSCVYO ran a consultation on 'The Menace of Drugs' in association with Scottish Churches' House. A powerful group was assembled round a representative of the Home Office whose special sphere was drugs, drugs squad police, workers in Soho (who had to do something for young Scots who came south for work, got stranded, and got hooked) and youth and social workers. The technical and the personal were given equal attention. The character of different drugs was explained, especially the difference between hard and soft drugs, and illustrated visually. It was clear that there was a wide-spread divergence of opinion about where the line lay between those which were fairly safe and those which were fairly serious. The effects on young people were described and case-instances provided, a young man who moved among drug addicts in London himself providing illuminating insights. The reasons which impelled young people towards drug-taking, the channels they found, the company they sought, the moods they had, the possibilities of rescue, rehabilitation, and prevention – were all much more vividly appreciated by those who took part. Deliberately no publicity was given to this gathering, since any focusing on the subject is liable to suggest its attraction, however unintentionally. Scottish Churches' House was invited to assemble those who had responsibilities for young people of an informal, voluntary or official kind, so that, from time to time, they might be brought up to date about the drugs situation, and given tips about dealing with any manifestation of it. It was agreed that as needs arose these would be planned and no publicity given to them. The Advisory Group on Youth at Risk then held responsibility for further work.

'Sexual attitudes and Habits in our Day' were the subject of study in eight consultations running from 1961 and 1967 inclusive. There was no intention of having a succession of consultations! After each forty-eight-hour period a certain amount of ground had been covered, and the significance of another part of the field had emerged, so that a further job could be delimited. The material from these consultations was drawn together and published by the SCM Press in 1967 under the title 'Sex as Gift'. This book can be referred to for detail. The 'record of work' presented at the front of the book may be quoted to indicate the style and scope of the work. The approach of the committee of the House is mentioned: 'The imaginativeness of the Committee is put on record by the type of consultation which they wished to have brought into being. "We do not want this to be older people talking about how younger people should behave. We want it to be a conversation between older people and adolescents, in which the adults do a lot of careful listening.'"

Youth organisations were asked if they would each nominate one person aged around 17 or 18 who was articulate, could stand up to adult company, and could communicate some feelings about sex which young people have today. Ten young people were nominated – as it happened, all from industry. A letter setting out the nature of the consultation (which lasted, as did succeeding ones, for two full days) was sent to individual firms concerned, and seven young people were released to take part.

From this point, different aspects of the question pointed to different types of consultation.. There was a consultation on the responsibility of schools, undertaken in collaboration with the Association of Directors of Education. The role of the youth organisations was next considered, and the consultation was run in concert with bodies directly concerned. A consultation followed on the churches' teaching and underlying theological issues. The next consultation went into particular points, such as non-sexual motives for sexual behaviour and difficulties faced in education. A second consultation in association with the Association of Directors of Education followed, with a closer look at the kind of material which might be used in school curricula. Since the beginning of the investigation of the sexual attitudes and habits of young people now completed and published as the Schofield Report, we had kept in touch with Dr Kershaw, the MOH in Colchester, who was chairman of its steering committee. He came up personally in 1965 to present the substance of this report and related it to the Dunblane work. Early in 1967 a review consultation was held in which the present material was recorded for publication and was given careful scrutiny.

As the emphasis of succeeding consultations changed, different people were brought into the work, and a large number played some part. There was, however, a continuing core throughout the whole process, basically made up of professional people from the fields of venereology, obstetrics, psychology, sociology, education, probation, police, television, youth organisations, along with the representatives of the 'Youth' and 'Morals' Committees of the co-operating churches, and representatives of the Marriage Guidance Council, the Alliance and the Parent-Teacher's Association. We depended very much on the core of professional people since they represented fully professional opinion, and since they took advantage of surveys and statistics which checked their judgements within their own field, and also undertook some sampling work themselves.

At certain points, particular samples and surveys were used to provide check-ups. A very small sample of the Girls' Training Corps, quite inadequate in itself, usefully put a query against one of our basic assumptions. A questionnaire compiled by Dr John Highet, a sociologist from Glasgow University, was answered by just upwards of seventy young people from the Scottish Association of Youth Clubs. It investigated sources of information about sex. A teacher who had undertaken a survey of unmarried mothers who came into her care in 1962 then undertook a fresh survey in 1966. Comparative statistics were of value: and as, in the last case, a real relationship was set up, although the sample covered only about 70 girls each year, there was unusual adequacy in the information received. Finally, over two and a half days, Dr Kershaw presented the Schofield Report.

We had thought the amount of checking quite inadequate until Dr Kershaw urged upon us the value of our material. It then dawned upon us that, apart from what had been brought to the consultations by professional people, and the samples and surveys to which they had access, apart from the particular samples and surveys we undertook ourselves, we had in fact checked material against the only adequate investigation of sexual attitudes and habits which had taken place in Britain; and, though it was in England that the investigation took place, the report had obviously relevance to the Scottish situation.

Before the material of this book was finally written up, a draft was sent to 35 teenagers with the simple request that they check on whether the substance was relevant and accurate to their mind, and whether it communicated – they were invited to re-write parts if they felt there was a failure on the latter score. The replies were taken fully into account in the final re-writing. When the book came on the market, an experiment was tried. In May 1967 a 'Teenager speaks to Teenager' weekend was held. Young people of 17 or 18 years were selected as being reasonably average and articulate and invited to sort out from the material things which they might want to add. A representative from 'Honey' magazine was present, prepared to write up in an article or articles, anything of value which showed itself. Nothing of value showed itself. What came out of the weekend as a message loud and clear was the sheer immaturity of these teenagers meeting by themselves, and their short-term views which amounted to blatant short-sightedness. The message which came out loud and clear was this, that, just as adults need young people alongside them to bring realism into their consideration of these matters, so young people need adults to round out their inexperience and put matters in a larger perspective.

It has been very profitable at times to team up with secular organisations and undertake study jointly with them. A further consultation in the series on sex was one held in association with the Family Planning Association on 'The Pill and the Unmarried'. As the consultation on a possible form of National Service touched different emotional strings, so did the one on the pill and the unmarried; so that a whole area of facts, fears, worries, hopes was uncovered. Just on 40 people took part, from church and secular types of responsibility, with good representation from fields of sociology, gynaecology, venereology, psychiatry, marriage guidance, family planning, youth and community work; especially those connected with or working in clinics where contraceptives were available for the unmarried. What came out most impressively was the high integrity both of those who believed that contraceptives should be made available to the unmarried if they were asked for, and those who felt that this was encouraging and bolstering loose standards in society. It was clear that a Family Planning Clinic which was open to all was used also as an advice centre by the unmarried – very often they took the opportunity to talk through some difficult situation with the doctor on duty. To refuse to go beyond the mere mechanics of professional provision of contraceptive advice and devices was agreed to be to abrogate responsibility. At the very least one must be present with the enquirer as a human being who cares. Small springs of responsibility can be encouraged and developed and the freedom of the person still kept. The affects of extra –marital intercourse are difficult to assess: the science of the dynamics of marriage is so new. There was however no evidence that the existence of Family Planning Clinics encouraged promiscuity or increased the VD rate. Many related aspects were brought in: for instance, it was wondered whether the furore about the pill had a psychological basis in the fact that the control over conception was being taken from men and (rightly) given to women.

This consultation was to be followed by one on 'The Pill and the Married' which was to be, in particular, a conversation between and with Roman Catholics of different persuasions about the matter. The Warden's appointment to work in Geneva, and the need for this document, meant that this consultation had to be postponed.

From this whole area of concern emerged a reiterated conviction about the need for education in sex in schools, for young people in industry, for students in teacher-training colleges; and on smoking, drink, and drugs – all within the context of preparation for a rich adulthood which should have positive and not only negative elements. The need for counselling provision, and the role that young people belonging to the same age group could fulfil by entering into a counselling-type relationship (two-way) with other young people in need, showed up clearly, as it had in related consultations.

In the summer of 1968 Scottish Churches' House was given an unusual opportunity. Patients of Rosslynlee Hospital, mentally ill and old, came for a period of residence. Everyone benefited. The local community rallied round, came to visit, took people out for runs in the surrounding countryside, invited them to tea, put on entertainment. The staff of the House, who usually have only occasional contacts with guests, found that they were needed as a caring community on the spot and their pastoral gifts were brought into play in a way which both delighted and exhausted them! The patients flowered under this treatment, some who were thought to be almost useless helping others to manage (only a small professional staff were on duty), some who hardly ever spoke a word getting up to sing in a concert. There was noticeable reversion when they went back into the hospital environment (an excellent environment, both in the new standards of comfort and attractiveness being applied and in the personal compassion shown in nursing). But they did not go back to where they started. Potential had been shown where it was not known to exist. Patients, community and staff contributed in a genuine experience of renewal.

Road Safety

The churches paid serious heed to the death toll on the roads in a series of consultations on Road Safety. From the beginning, in June 1961, there was the Pedestrians Association, the Scottish Accident Prevention Council, the Chief Constables' Association, the Institute of Advanced Motorists, members of relevant committees of the different churches. A good deal of technical information regarding road research was made available. Psychological attitudes of motorists were emphasised to take skilling in driving with the same seriousness as other forms. The first consultation in 1961 used as a working paper the BCC document 'Priority for Road Safety'. Among its conclusions was the need for re-testing of drivers on safety – including, where possible, the use of traffic training grounds which familiarise them with road signs. The 1962 consultation considered aspects of traffic engineering, the needs of the old, and desirable legislation to check the alcohol content in drivers who had been drinking, by some such means as the breathalyser test which was introduced some years later. The 1963 consultation used, as a case study, a comprehensive approach on road safety made in Rutherglen; and the moral problem of sheer human carelessness and lack of concern for one's neighbour continued to be looked at in various aspects. Mr George Eyles, Director of Tests, Institute of Advanced Motorists, was the main catalyst in the 1964 consultation and provided a wealth of acute observation on the present situation and drew out the experience of others. This consultation was linked to a broadcast service on road safety form Dunblane Cathedral in which Mr

Eyles took part. The 1965 consultation occupied itself with the human factor in road safety. The Secretary of State for Scotland, in a written contribution, pinpointed the main issue, as he saw it thus: 'How public attitudes to the problem of road accidents can be changed, and a sense of collective responsibility evolved. Most of the measures by which the rising toll of road accidents could be halted or reduced involve restraints on the freedom of one or other class of road user to make use of the highway as they think fit, and the amount of restraint needed to bring about any significant reduction in accidents may be widespread and at first irksome. Such measures have no prospect of being enforced without the consent of the great majority and the active support of a considerable section of the public.' Personality characteristics and their control were examined. Three types of dangerous motorist were identified, the habitually careless, the unskilled, and those with low moral standards who just have no concern for others. Something, it was thought, could be done with the first two groups but the third posed a very serious problem. The effects of drinking (which were much more serious than drunkenness which was not a major factor) and of speed, and in particular the relationship of the two, were fastened on by some as matters of major importance; whereas others felt that, given education all the way through, these were reasonably controllable. A recurrent conviction was that we had to use all our resources and make sure that some very heavy freight which was going on the roads was forced to go by rail instead. The consultation for 1966 on 'Urban Renewal and Road Safety' was to be led by Mr RE Nichol, then Chief Planning Officer of the Scottish Development Department. Although this was a subject of high interest, sufficient registrations did not come in to proceed with it. It seemed quite clear that after five consecutive consultations people had talked themselves out to some extent, and would need now to try things out, forge instruments of propaganda, and keep an eye open for new factors which might emerge. One highly impressive feature of this series was the number of points mentioned throughout the discussions which in fact became law in succeeding years or which were given fresh weight in a growing sense of public responsibility.

Nursing

Consultations for those in the nursing service were held, partly to enable them to take the measure of pressures which came upon them in their work, partly to provide an opportunity for considering ethical issues which faced them. It was from within the nursing service itself that encouragement was given to explore the provision the House might make for them. Over a period of some years small groups which held different types of responsibility in the nursing service were consulted. Again and again it looked as if a fruitful line had been discovered, but it failed in the end to indicate clearly enough the ground which should be covered and the constituency that should be tapped. The determination not to undertake consultative work until its objects were clear, paid off. It was learned, for instance, that any existing association in the nursing world, including Christian associations, would limit the invitation by suggesting that the House was only open to certain types of nurse. Regional Nursing Officers are only too easily by-passed, and this was brought to mind in time. What came out of the long, long trail awinding was such an interest on the part of those holding high administrative responsibility that they formed themselves into an Advisory Group to meet once or twice per year to review and plan events. The group represented not only a variety of responsibilities for nurses in training but a geographical spread throughout Scotland.

The basic method of approach had been to distribute questionnaires to nurses and extract material from these questionnaires which are then set out as case-studies and worked over by groups before being discussed in plenary session. Eventually a pilot consultative gathering was held in November 1967. Twenty-one people took part and a venereologist and a psychiatrist acted as resource persons. It was clear from the start that time to think, away from hospital premises and out of uniform was much needed and appreciated by those who are under pressure in the nursing service. Ward sisters, staff nurses and student nurses attended. This first consultation concentrated on deficiencies in communication and in clear job-allocation and definition, the inadequacies of medical care for nurses themselves, the drawback of not being able to plan leisure well ahead; and the way nurses were bothered by feeling they had an image of being sexually 'easy', the special problems of isolated hospitals, the extent to which one should get involved with one's patients.

Thereafter two consultations per year were planned, that in March 1968 having a consulting physician and a psychiatrist as resource persons. Many useful ideas for the improvement of the working of hospitals came forward. The main emphasis was on the welding of those who had different skills into a consultative team, in which they shared knowledge and checked with one another on treatment. Under the guidance of the Advisory Group the autumn meeting in 1968 was planned for those holding maturer responsibilities, mainly at the assistant matron level. It is believed that if, through questionnaires, the experience of young nurses were put on record, senior people could best take note of these and help changes be made. In 1968 the Director of Psychological Research in the Crichton Royal Hospital, Dumfries joined the Advisory Group and thereafter offered his services in providing questionnaires through which the experience and thinking of nurses could be registered while their identity remained anonymous. The consultation planned for April 1969 did not take place because of a tangle about permission to attend outside conferences and money to pay for these. But as it was hoped that a solution would be found, spring and autumn consultations were planned.

* *

To try to see how theology and sociology should relate to one another, some consultations took place in which people simply tried to discover terms which were acceptable to each other and to illustrate approaches to understanding life which might be complementary. In April 1964 sociologists and theologians were gathered for a first encounter, and in December of that year a consultation on 'Sociology, Theology and Mission' was run as an enterprise coming out of the Kirk Week and Tell Scotland emphases. These were administered from Glasgow. When earlier concerns were drawn into the Department on Mission of the newly-constituted Scottish Churches' Council a small sociology research group met in January 1965 and a meeting of university teachers and sociologists took place in December 1966. What came out of these gatherings contributed to the awareness of all the churches that they had been making unfounded assumptions about communities in which they served and that new surveying work had to be done to make an accurate reassessment of situations. One of the sociologists, himself a Jew, pointed out how thoughtlessly churches moved into new areas, setting up old forms of organisation without asking whether these met the needs of people in these areas. When challenged to give instances of alternative forms of service which might be provided, he said that it would need to be actual surveys that indicated these. Pressed further, he said he was pretty sure that some form of kindergarten run by volunteers which allowed young mothers to have an afternoon clear for shopping and for a cup of tea with a friend, and means whereby people who were thinking of taking on hire purchase commitments could consult with those who could help them to assess their situation, would prove to be relevant and highly appreciated. A similar attempt to relate theology and physics came to nothing because it did not prove possible to get a clear enough work remit for such a group to justify calling together different parties.

In February 1967, through the joint interest of Prof Ronald Gregor Smith and Principal SC Curran (Strathclyde University) a consultation took place on 'An Understanding of Man – Theological and Scientific'. Contributions were made from the fields of genetics, physics, sociology, psychology, and philosophy – each speaker trying to indicate the relevance of his subject, and every listener tearing to shreds the so-called relevance which had been expounded! It was the kind of gathering which called out for continuance; but a long illness from 'flu which Prof Gregor Smith suffered in the following year and his death thereafter meant that the consultation was deprived of its lynch-pin. The next consultation was to have had the relevance of theology as its main concern. It was guaranteed to get as harsh treatment as other disciplines suffered!

The growing co-operation between Roman Catholics and Protestants in Scotland resulted in an attempt to provide for both a vantage point on ethics today. A summer conference on 'The Formation of Ethical Judgements', using as a working paper a report of Edinburgh Presbytery under the heading, had as leaders Monsignor Barry from the Theological College, Drygrange and Prof James Whyte of St Mary's College, St Andrews. This did not pick up the interest which had been expected and had to be cancelled because of shortage of numbers registering. In 1969 a second attempt was made, the subject being 'Authority and Protest' with Prof William Barclay providing bible studies each morning, Dr Bernard Haring lecturing on social ethics, and people concerned with protest in many forms acting as catalysts of discussion. The first of these was undertaken in co-operation with the Extra-Mural Department of St Andrew's University and the second with the same department of Edinburgh University.

Nations and the Nation

International and National Communities

The importance of international affairs to the Policy and Programme Committee of Scottish Churches' House was registered by the fact that it held a consultation on defence and disarmament even before residential accommodation was available in 1961. From the beginning there was self-questioning about whether the House had a distinctive part to play in the consideration of issues of international peace. The British Council of Churches had its International Department, and the separate churches had Church and Nation or Citizenship Committees or equivalents. There could be a mere duplication of work done there and elsewhere. In addition there was a problem of subject-matter – it was difficult in this large field to disentangle some of the issues which mattered and which were susceptible to delimitation so that a group meeting residentially for twenty-four or forty-eight hours had some reasonable chance of tackling them. There was also a difficulty regarding constituency. The aim was to get together, in a concerned relationship, people with very different convictions, particularly pacifist and non-pacifist. Some pacifists were particularly aggressive and non-co-operative. The story, then, is one of experiment, frustration, uncertainly about what to do next and how to bring contending parties together: but also a growing certainty that there was work that must be done, that the House had a distinctive contribution to make, that international peace-making was a top priority.

Early in 1961 Admiral Buzzard came north to be a speaker and resource person for a consultation on 'Defence and Disarmament'. The value was at that point demonstrated of the presentation of a clear-cut position over against which others could reassess their own positions and to which they could bring their own challenges. The contribution of defence to peace-making when there was no acknowledged international force, the dangers of settling issues by means of power politics and the nuclear threat in particular, were well debated. A follow-up consultation was planned for June of the following year but the pacifist/non-pacifist confrontation prevented a real meeting of minds and Dr George McLeod gave it as his opinion that further discussion between pacifists and non-pacifists was non-productive – they must just act separately on the convictions they held. A consultation on International Peace was however planned for a twenty-four hour period in the Week of Prayer for Christian Unity in 1963. This consultation concentrated on two matters:

1)   the gospel and the use of power, and
2)   practical steps towards peace.

There was an attempt under the first heading to see what the Christian revelation had to say about the exercise of power and its inevitable concomitant, the use of force – in particular what does the Cross say in the context of international relations and tensions? Under the heading Practical Steps Towards Peace, the publication of the International Department of the BCC in April 1962 entitled 'A Pattern for Disarmament' was used as a working agenda. Rev Alan Keighly was present as a resource person from the BCC, press and television were present, an equal number of ordained and lay representatives took part, some coming from the appropriate church committees, others being present in terms of a particular contribution. The Society of Friends and the Iona Community were well to the fore. Luther's view that coercion is one of God's instruments for carrying the life of human society forward was debated. It was clear that society needs a degree of compulsion and authority before it will work. Lines which we hoped would be followed up in the future were:

a) the meaning of the Cross and its relevance to international tensions
b) how international relations could work without armaments
c) national sovereignty and a world authority
d) ideological factors in the present tensions
e) another specific contribution such as Admiral Buzzard's.

A small study group in June of that year worked at the role of international institutions, the possibilities of international order without armaments, the test ban treaty, the deprivation of people in poorer countries as a cause of tension, non-violence as a technique.

The next three years were taken up with attempts to find a more fruitful way into the subject. The Warden's Memo of 1963 pointed out the difficulty of getting pacifists and non-pacifists together. The Committee suggested that either a catalyst, like Admiral Buzzard, was needed or a book as a basis of study eg dealing with the effect on an economy of stopping armament production. The Warden was asked to consult with an Edinburgh University group, whose contact was Mr Geoffrey Carnall, and the United Nations Association. All that had appeared clearly to this point was that Christians were fragmented in judgement and the spark, which might set minds on fire, was missing.

Early in 1964 a report was made on these meetings. It was suggested that research was needed on

1) the setting up of an international police force
2) the relation to war of other forms of violence in society
3) the consequences to an economy of its not being dependent on armament production

Professor Michael Howard, Professor of War Studies, King's College, London, was suggested as one person round whom a whole consultation could be grouped. Over a year later, in spite of a visit from Rev Frank Glendenning of the BCC, a clear way of gripping international issues had not yet shown up.

But the Iona Community had been trying to hammer out a policy with regard to peace-making. Permission was given to pick up the main points made in the thinking of the Community (later to become the Peace Commitment) and put them in a working paper. These were:

1) the unprecedented urgency of international peace-making, in one world with weapons so powerful and indiscriminate;
2) the developing gulf between rich and poor countries producing economic, racial and ideological world tensions;
3) the role of the United Nations (the dismantling of other alliances is bound to be lengthy);
4) weapons of mass destruction (they should be abrogated and at the same time: the causes of war, means of removing weapons of war without causing economic collapse and alternatives to war should be explored);
5) the establishment of peace centres to do research (e.g. on causes of war) and to create public discussion.

Dr Michael Nicolson, Fellow in Conflict Studies, Politics Department, the University of Lancaster gave the main lead-in talk on the use of the social sciences to discover how and why people behave as they do. Two things were needed: social understanding to teach us why people go to war, and social engineering to enable us to alter situations so that war is prevented. Because of human irrationality there was a need for money for research and human study-action groups associated with peace researchers. There was need for a broadly-based public movement to focus the concern for more research and constructive action. The first half of the consultation followed up some of the lines Dr Nicolson suggested. In the second half Dr Nicolson expounded peace research as a new discipline for the study of war and peace which a few people had pioneered as a result of the First World War. The consultation gave its mind to the communication and implementation of research findings. Lines of action in Scotland were suggested thus:

1) acting as promoters and agents of peace research, working in association with peace research centres
2) arranging central seminars
3) promoting local study/action groups
4) acting as middle-men bringing together those who had some specialist concern for international peace.

In conclusion it was pointed out that in Scotland some structures of consultation were needed for the churches together; that a greater use of the churches' potential as an international community needed to be made; that more resources should be devoted to international affairs by Scottish Churches' House; and that more support should be given to the Christian Peace Conference in Prague.

In that year, 1966, a 'Scottish Seminar on International Relations' was established under the joint sponsorship of the Conflict Research Society, the Scottish Churches' Council and the United Nations' Association. In 1967 it was agreed that the subject of the seminar would be 'The Causes of Conflict.' A planning committee was set up which met several times in the intervening months and money was sought from trusts to pay for the expenses of those who travelled from a distance to make some central contribution to the seminar. The gathering in September 1967 marked a stage: by now it was clear that Scottish Churches' House was getting on to the right track, finding areas of study and discussion which could be delimited, contacting the people who could provide material of quality, seeing a job which could be done in Scotland at a time when people feared a reversion to parochialism. The Rev Andrew Morton, chaplain to Edinburgh University, chaired. Mr Geoffrey Newnham and Dr Michael Nicolson gave main talks on these two themes:

1) an analysis of conflict; conflict of interests and conflict of emotions; the positive and negative aspects of conflict
2) how far are group reactions analogous to individual reactions; what is good and what is evil in the motivation of individuals and groups in relation to conflict?

Most of the work was done in commissions and the title and leadership of these might sufficiently indicate the ground they covered. That on 'Social and Economic Disparities' was chaired by Mr John White of the Overseas Development Institute, London and led by Mr Roderick Ogley of the University of Sussex; that on 'Nationalism and Racialism' was chaired by the Rev Paul

Oestreicher of the International Department of the BCC and led by Dr Nan Wilson of the Department of Social Anthropology of the University of Edinburgh; that on 'Weapon Possession' was chaired by Mr Stephen Maxwell of the Institute for Strategic Studies, London and led by Mr Philip Windsor of the Department of International Relations, London School of Economics; that on 'theological alignment' was chaired by Mr George Target, author and journalist and led jointly by Dr Fritz Keienburgh of the Evangelical Academy of Rheinland/Westfalen and Rev Lubomir Mirejovsy from Czechoslovakia. A very representative company from the sponsoring bodies was joined by those who had some specialist contribution from the fields of politics, economics, education, psychology, marriage guidance, and television and journalism – to make a company of just over fifty. The Fellowship of Reconciliation played a quiet and important part, mainly through the representative who was treasurer.

For a number of years particularly good contact had been kept with developments in Czechoslovakia. One of the many gifts Gillian Carver brought with her when she came to be a colleague in the wardenship was her membership of the Prague Peace Conference and her many friendships with Czechs and visits to their homeland. When the year 1968 opened with the liberalising movement, the trend of events was already appreciated. Thus, reflection on the 1967 Seminar had led to the conviction that the theme for the following year should be ' A Case Study: Czechoslovakia' looking at this in the context of changes in Eastern Europe and their international implications. The Seminar was planned for September 20th-23rd 1968. A month earlier the Russian tanks moved in. Once it was possible to assess the situation, Mr George Brown, ex Foreign Secretary, wrote to 'The Times' and said that what was needed at this point of history was a Seminar which drew together those who had lived through the crisis in Czechoslovakia and had some special knowledge of it, with all those who, in different fields of study and life, were deeply concerned about developments. It was possible to write to 'The Times' and Mr Brown himself to give the information that such a Seminar was taking place very soon, and that a place was kept for Mr Brown himself should he be able to come! He wrote regretting his inability to be free on the dates in question, but expressed appreciation of the committee's initiative in planning the Seminar. This Seminar must be classed as one of the great events in the life of Scottish Churches' House. Dr Julius Tomin, a Marxist, from the Department of Philosophy in Prague University was flown out, with his wife, to be the centre of the Seminar. Several other participants had been in Czechoslovakia when the invasion took place. In the group of seventy people who assembled for the Seminar there was strong representation from the University of Glasgow and from student bodies in Britain. The Scottish Council for Nuclear Disarmament and the Christian group for East/West Contacts supplied participants.

The priceless contribution provided by Dr and Mrs Tomin was their experience as members of a whole people who peacefully combated the invasion of the Warsaw Pact Powers. It was made clear once again that what had happened in Czechoslovakia was what Marxists were prepared to do to Marxists! Czechs showed a clear determination to retain Socialism, but Socialism with a 'human face'. Every opportunity was taken to assault in debate the invaders; and so successfully was their morale undermined and their understanding won, that the orders of officers to act against Czech agitators were often disobeyed, and troops had to be sent home and be replaced. Comment was made to Mrs Tomin on the effectiveness of their non-violent resistance, and she flamed immediately: "We were not non-violent! We attacked them with words, with ideas, with psychological pressures. It was conflict".

In the first of his main talks, Dr Tomin said that he had intended to talk about Marxism as about a living theory with a future, with hope of its own development, and with a positive worldwide relevance. He had now to ask whether, in the light of events in Czechoslovakia, Marxism remained relevant – since it could not be separated from the actual actions of the Communist movement. He then moved on to a discussion of human responsibility, flayed Christians for not living out the teachings of the New Testament (which he was reading afresh in the original Greek, having been pressed to that by the invasion), spoke on the unrealised possibilities in every human being, and showed that Karl Marx himself was much more concretely concerned with the situation in which we human beings stand than had been allowed.

The Seminar developed in a kind of antiphon thereafter, a speaker on economic realities in Eastern Europe being balanced by one on these realities in Britain; a speaker on political structures in Eastern Europe being balanced by one who examined these in Britain; and a speaker on the intellectual and cultural climate in Eastern Europe being balanced by one who spoke about the climate in Britain. Professor John Erikson of the Department of Politics of Edinburgh University led off on 'International Political and Strategic Implications of Recent Developments in Eastern Europe'. And Mr Geoffrey Carnall led on 'The Strategy of Civilian Defence with Special Reference to Czechoslovakia.' Between these a special session was held on 'The Significance of Student Protest', and a panel discussion allowed participants to pick up with the main contributors matters on which they had wished to raise further questions.

A summary of the main points arising included these: Czechoslovakia is showing a way of life and not a way of death; its resistance to invasion points to a new way in which small nations can contend with great powers on a basis of truth-seeking. Political, cultural and other historical realities set Czechoslovakia in a predominantly Eastern context, and its quest for a new political style is strongly Marxian in its inspiration. The resistance showed a remarkable fusion of spontaneity and discipline. There was a respect and sympathy for the Russian soldiers which was also the ground for attack upon them: "We pity the Russian soldiers enough to be harsh with them" (they were capable of something better). The thought-forms and language of Czech resistance had much in common with other movements, in particular with student protest. The unity of the entire nation behind the Communist Party had been possible only because the party had voluntarily opened itself to criticism. The West, involved in Vietnam and other compromising situations, had its hands tied and had to bear its share of guilt. Physical and psychological factors which made the invasion likely were examined, the role of the mass media, and the strategic dangers (the Warsaw Pact powers were probably weakened not strengthened by being on the Czech borders, with an un-co-operative population behind these frontiers). In the light of all these factors there was some re-assessment of the Russian Revolution.

In January 1969, during the Week of Prayer for Christian Unity, Professor Hromadka visited Scotland to speak on the theme 'The Christian Presence in a Secular World'. This provided an opportunity to discuss with Professor Hromadka the extant situation in his country and the forces which he thought were shaping the future. It also allowed for an assessment of his own brave reaction to the invasion.

The 1969 seminar followed naturally from that of the previous year. The theme was 'European Co-existence – Conflict or Convergence?" It was to include an examination of the meaning of convergence between East and West in Europe, asking 'what is possible and what is desirable?'. Three particular areas of society in East and West were examined:

    1)   industrial and commercial organisation and control;
    2)   participation in political decision-making
    3)   social services.

Aspects of the intellectual and cultural climate evidenced in newer thinking and writing in the East were considered in terms of their bearing on convergence. Attitudes to authority in East and West and their relevance to the theme were examined.

Within the whole context of this concern about international relationships and the need for international peace there came a concern for the poor nations of the world. Mainly this was discussed in the wider context. But on two occasions it was given specific attention.

In December 1966 there was a consultation on 'World Poverty and British Responsibility', the British Council of Council of Churches' book of that title being used as a source book and a summary of its main points in 'Christian Comment' being used as a working outline. Lord Ritchie Calder attended as speaker and catalyst of discussion. The lack of grip of the campaign to get the churches and the nation to take world poverty seriously at this stage, was shown by the fact that only 16 people took advantage of what was a great opportunity. There was comfort in the developing effectiveness of the movement to draw attention to world poverty over the next few years. In the conference the need for a vast investment in human resources, if the world were to be fed, was underlined. The base of social services necessary for prosperity was emphasised. Damage to young lives would produce physically and mentally handicapped and unstable adults in the future. At this point in history compassion and self-interest met: there would be no worthy life for our children unless we fed and cared for the world's children – the backlash of the deprived could be terrible. Where the terms of trade are so drastically against primary products, hard work turns out to be self-defeating. The investment of human resources for developing countries was as important as financial resources. New means of provision of food have to be given high priority.

One of the best jobs done by the Assembly of the World Council of Churches in Uppsala was in the realm of world poverty. To follow this up, a world poverty conference for young Protestants and Roman Catholics together was set up from Scottish Churches' House and carried through at the Roman Catholic Centre at Coodham, the two being joint sponsors. The aim was:

1) to present the problems of the developing countries in their human, economic and political aspects, and to consider our involvement in these problems which arises out of our shared humanity and our understanding of Christian vocation in the world, and
2) to discover ways in which we can become more informed and effective, and attempt to formulate practical steps by which government and public opinion can be influenced.

This gathering drew its direct inspiration not only from Uppsala itself but also from the BBC Youth Conference 'Edinburgh '68'. Contributions from lecturers in the Department of Psychology, Glasgow University, Christian Aid, and a public relations body pointed up the discussion.

There was also joint bible studies. It was clear as a result of this conference that a special appeal could be made to young people within the general concern for world poverty; and Christians of all kinds could bring their minds to bear on the subject, there being no particular denominational barrier of belief or practice.

It seemed likely that, in the future, world poverty would be studied within the context of international relations, and that from time to time there would be points of special focus.

In all this, it was thought to be a great advantage that Christian Aid was integrated in the Scottish Churches' Council.

As a kind of bridge from the international to the national were consultations which had to do with international encounter expressed within the life of the nation. Thus there was consultative work on Hinduism, Marxism and Mormonism. It was clear that a dialogue with Marxists was not only needed but was becoming more and more welcome on both sides. A tentative dialogue developed out of the common concern about international affairs. A visit of the Rev Murray Rogers to Britain made possible a two-day dialogue on Hinduism – in which he used the experience of the Ashram in India in which he was leader to represent the outlook of Hinduism to native Scots. Three day meetings on Mormonism took place in 1963 and 1964. The result of these was both to inform people about the nature of Mormonism, its claims and its approach, and to check on a substantial study document prepared by the Rev Roy Paterson which was later published as a book. While it was hoped that the Marxist dialogue would continue, the work on Hinduism and Mormonism could not be called dialogue but was essentially informative in intention.

Three concerns emerged directly out of the Seminar on International Relations. One had to do with the study, each year, of one of the world's hot-spots. The second and third related to life in Scotland – a concern for the integration of immigrants, and a concern about the Polaris Nuclear Submarine Base at Faslane.

Scotland was favourably placed in regard to the immigrant situation, since the pressures felt in England were not yet reproduced on the same scale. As a result of the Seminar on International Relations, Glasgow Education Department combined with members appointed by the seminar to investigate the situation and needs of coloured teenagers in the Glasgow area. In co-operation with the Iona Community, the Overseas Council of the Church of Scotland and various other interested bodies, the House had its share in pushing for more direct research and specific forms of provision for immigrants. (It was hoped that the Community Relations Committee might co-ordinate the interest and work of various bodies in Scotland in this field, but it did not quite find a clear way of planning an overall approach). Meantime the second need had shown itself – the need to educate people who were much further back in their knowledge so that, at a quite basic level, they began to understand immigrants and feel what it was like to be in their shoes. Such an educative consultation for church people was held in Scottish Churches' House in November 1969.

In February of that year a weekend seminar was held on the Polaris Submarine Base at Faslane. Over 70 foolscap pages of material on the subject were prepared, more than half of this material concentrating on the economic effects of the development of the base and the commercial spin-off which resulted. Apart from this, main contributions were prepared on the British Polaris Force by an RN Captain, Submarine squadron, Faslane, on civil defence implications at the direction of the Joint Parliamentary Under-Secretary of State for Scotland; and theological implications by the Rev T Ralph Morton, supplementary material being provided by the Church and Nation Committee of the Church of Scotland and the parish minister of Rosyth (the dockyard town which services nuclear submarines): while a pronouncement of the World Council of Churches in New Dehli was also recorded and taken into account. Comments on political implications, invited from the different parties, came from the Conservative Party and the Scottish National Party, the Labour Party saying that it had no policy in Scotland distinctive from that of the British Labour Party whose main statements on the matter should be taken as the contribution requested.

Professor John Erickson, Defence Studies, Edinburgh University, led a crucial session on 'Strategic Implications'. There was also a full session on political, legal, social and psychological implications. Films and charts illustrating the working of a Polaris force were provided.

One of the features of this seminar was the full participation of the Navy and the Royal Air Force, and the openness and the honesty which marked their part in the discussion and the frankness with which questions were answered and attitudes explained (provided these were not strictly in the field of security).

The work on economic implications undertaken by a lecturer in Defence Studies, Aberdeen University suffered, as the speaker pointed out, from shortness of time and lack of resources; but it was very effective, not only in giving some kind of picture of the impact of an affluent incoming community in Faslane upon a long-established community, but in indicating the areas of investigation which needed to be tackled by serious and adequate research work. The desire to establish 'A Scottish Foundation for Conflict Studies' was strengthened by this kind of meeting. The areas of enquiry which were shown to be needed had to be left in the hope that they would be picked up by professionally equipped teams from government and university sources. The co-operation which was possible between members of the armed forces and representatives of the Scottish Committee for Nuclear Disarmament was a precedent which could be built on in the future. The existence of the proposed foundation would allow for an alertness to developments and further study as occasion demanded. The group assembled to consider implications of the Faslane Base, accordingly, did not constitute itself a continuing group but ploughed back its work into the Scottish Seminar on International Relations.

Scotland

From the first year of the existence of the House a consultation had been held annually for some years on Scotland. The intention was simply to provide an occasion to assess where the life of the country was thriving and where some important elements in its life were in jeopardy. The very first gathering provided one of the issues which eventually produced Enterprise Youth. But on the whole, what was offered was a place of meeting. Here the boundaries of discipline could be crossed, people who were out of touch with one another could be brought into touch, judgements which were largely based on ignorance could be corrected in personal conversation.

At one point, an attempt was made to follow up the clear convictions of the consultation about the examination system – particularly as this applied to art teaching, and with regard to publicity stated aims of education which could be publicly debated – by correspondence with the Under-Secretary of State who was responsible for education. But when a largely fobbing-off reply came, there was nobody who could pick this up and continue the debate. (An official document showed that the point was taken seriously). The consultation on Scotland discovered its own identity through experience, an identity dissimilar from that of most forms of meeting in Scottish Churches' House - less clearly structured, with less definition of subject matter, with no preparatory papers and, at times, no reporting. The value had been in the direct personal encounter of people who were in every field, literally every field, of Scottish life and who, through personal meeting, could bring these fields into some relationship. Every time the query was raised whether there was justification in continuing the series of consultations there was unanimous conviction about their importance, that conviction being directly related to the value found in sheer personal meeting.

The first consultation in 1961 attempted a blanket coverage, having sessions on Scottish culture and the Arts, Scotland's Nationhood, Industrial Life, Rural Life and Education. Already, in 1961, there were signs that the arts and technology were staking a claim for serious attention. The 1962 consultation looked at Scots Law and its affinity with European Law in general (in contrast to the different foundation of English Law); at the churches' care for the people of Scotland; at the Highlands as an area of special difficulty, need, and promise; at means of promoting local initiative through community development, and promoting national initiative (it was the time of the Toothill Report on Scotland's economy); and signs of ill omen and promise in Scottish culture. Already, at this point, the contribution of the lawyer, the journalist, the local authority representative, the community development expert, the national economic development expert, and the poet and broadcaster were not only being used but were drawn into fruitful relationship.

In 1963 the theme was 'Education for Living'. First there was a review of Scotland's economic prospects provided by a representative of the Scottish Council (Development and Industry). Against this survey of possibilities for the physical organisation of society, the Chief Planning Officer, Scotland (who later became chairman of the Highlands and Islands Development Board) shared his concern that the life of people gain direction and vision, and they discover a commanding purpose to grip the different parts of life in Scotland into significance. A man of letters shared his worry about an unawareness of heritage, a cheapening of what had been native and masculine, in Scottish culture. Only then did the Director of Education for Glasgow and the Principal of Falkirk Technical College lead the consultation directly to considerations about education in general and technical education in particular; and the headmaster of a school which based itself on the art room, well known for his pioneering work, challenged the exam centred educational system which he believed blanketed native abilities and gifts.

The consultation in the following year was on 'The Arts in Scotland'. To it reference has been made elsewhere.

In 1965 a consultation on 'Creativity and Communication' drew together matters which had been raised in consultations on education and on the arts.

It was at this gathering that the experiment was made of trying to see how physics, technology, painting, theology and education could communicate with one another when there was strict attention to the language and imagery normally employed within each discipline. Here too Mr JS Brunton, famous for the Brunton Report which proposed a relation of education much more definitely to the life-interest of young people, and his successor Dr Dickson were present personally to discuss educational trends with members. A professor of theology who was also provost of a large city, set educational needs in the context of society as it was developing at that point of history. Prof Graham challenged the idea that we expect to recognise the real problems of education before having an understanding of social forces. He was convinced that (as with children) we need to have the pattern of life defined to some extent for us, if we are to be free: "People cannot be experimental with life except within severe limits. You need to be partaker of an established common experience to go on into new experience."

The session with the panel, on the Sunday, probed to see if it were possible to communicate across the barriers. Robin Philipson suggested: "The language of materials and space relationships can be a bridge of communication between artists and scientists: "art education should make us critical of our environment". Mr WS Robertson described the role of the theologian as being to work with the layman in giving direction to society. Mr W Ritchie pointed out that science deals with intangibles and offers models of what we cannot even see. Light has to be understood as a wave, as having particle properties – but, in itself, it might be neither. There is an analogy to our attempts to understand God and describe God's nature. The attempt must be made with the understanding we have. But in the end, what we get is a model: and the reality lies beyond.

A challenge thrown out by Mr Brunton to suggest an alternative to the existing system of inspection and examination of art in schools and to the entrance requirements to Art Colleges in particular, was taken up. An informal working party was suggested on which a member of the Art Inspectorate might sit to offer comments and judgements. When, upon investigation, there was no promise that a member of the Inspectorate would be available to render this service, the matter was taken no further, (direct representation was felt to be needed to give significance to the working party's thinking and to check it against actual practice).

The 1966 consultation looked at two other matters which had gained attention – the need for healthy growth in Scotland's economy and the effects, for good or ill, that this might have on Scottish culture. The contributions were shared by a businessman, an artist, an agricultural economist, a lecturer and poet, a theologian and a publisher.

The 1967 consultation provided a point for gathering up reflections on the educational situation provided by members themselves. It was clear from contributions that a great deal of concern existed about the examination system and about stated aims of education which could be publicly discussed. This led to correspondence with St Andrew's House. The education correspondent of the 'Glasgow Herald' started off with an appraisal of the education situation. An artist gave his ideas on education as transmission of culture. The Principal of Stirling University talked on 'University Education – fresh concepts.' A debate, 'Freeing the Imagination – and the Examination System' was introduced by an adviser in science studies and an art teacher; and an open forum allowed opportunity to gather any matter up which had not had the chance to get attention. The final two sessions were on 'Further Education for the Inadequate and Delinquent', led by the countess of Mar and Kellie who had made this aspect part of her field of concern for young people, and a pioneering headmaster; and 'Further Education to enrich the Life of Everybody', led by a lecturer in Further Education who was strategically placed to assess developments in Scotland.

The 1968 consultation concentrated on 'Scotland's Nationhood and her Sub-cultures'. At that point of history, when demands for independence for Scotland were continually strengthening, the dangers of narrowness and parochialism and the prospect of a more positive and dynamic role for Scotland in the world needed to be faced. The core of this consultation was a panel comprising a Labour and a Liberal MP, the Conservative Research Officer, and a Scottish Nationalist Party candidate. Worries and hopes about the different ways in which Scotland might be pushed by her present mood were shared with this panel by people who were given five minutes each to put their finger on one or two issues which they regarded as highly important – including the chairman of the Highlands and Islands Development Boards; the executive president of the Scottish Council (Development and Industry), three people who were outstanding in the field of the arts – a poet, an artist and an actor - the director of Enterprise Youth, and the general secretary of the British Council of Churches. The consideration of sub-cultures covered both those which belonged to small community environments, and those which arose from special circumstances e.g. gangland sub-cultures. A lecturer from the School of Scottish Studies led off in two main sessions, one looking at the way in which young people in particular related within different sub-cultures, and the other at the kind of total communities which showed the influence of particular sub-cultures. In earlier consultations attention had been paid to the raw material, fresh and red-blooded, which sub-cultures could provide if those who operated at a 'higher' cultural level took advantage of such material – for instance, football matches, folk-songs sessions, gang fights – grist for the mill of painter and poet as well as social anthropologist and magistrate.

The 1969 consultation attempted to direct a searchlight on traditional centres of power and examine them in the light of fresh emergent points of power and pressure. The title was 'Power Structures and New Power.' A context was provided by the Wheatley Report with its suggestions for the re-structuring of government throughout Scotland; and existing and new points of power in the realms of politics, culture (picking up on the Duchess of Argyll's observations on cultural power in France – she was one of those who led off) and finance ('The Power of Faceless Men'). After the ground had been worked over, the Wheatly Report was again given attention, the point of focus being elements in a participant society which makes the participation real in education, industry, politics, finance-economics, and culture.

The 1968 consultation expressed the desire that Scottish Churches' House might provide some continuing means for alerting the churches to what was happening in the field of the arts and in the field of technological development. In July 1969 a small representative group assembled to carry this further. The intention was not simply an attempt to sensitise a wider part of the community in Scotland through the Churches to the impact of the arts and of technology, but to keep these concerns in relationship with one another so that what was developing in the one field would be related to what was developing in the other and their inter-relationship could be taken seriously.

The need for the meeting of people from different backgrounds and areas in consultations like those on Scotland underlines the need for other houses like Scottish Churches' House at different points of the nation's life, maybe particularly near Inverness and in the Borders.

Rethinking Faith and Practice

Sharing the Gospel

It is the afternoon of Remembrance Day in November 1967

This time you are in the Chapel of Scottish Churches' House, at the back of the main building. About fifteen lay men and women are conducting a service which they themselves have prepared. At different points of the service this one or that one will give the lead; at some all participate.

The beginning is conventional enough, the hymn 'O God Our Help in Ages Past'. But with that all resemblance to a traditional Armistice Service disappears.

Instead of adoration what follows is a questioning of the affirmation in the hymn that God's saints dwell secure under the protection of his throne. To be one of God's people one has to be prepared to be 'destitute, afflicted, tormented.'

There follows a horrifying incident from Dr Zhivago, the centre of which is this paragraph:-

> 'The orderlies were carrying a man who had been mutilated in a particularly monstrous way. A splinter from the shell which had mangled his face, turning his tongue and lips into a red gruel without killing him, had lodged in the bone structure of his jaw, replacing the torn-out cheek. He uttered short groans in a thin inhuman voice; no one could take these sounds for anything but an appeal to finish him off quickly, to put an end to his inconceivable torment.'

This quotation from a modern writer is followed by readings from the Bible on Gethsemane and the Crucifixion after which there is a considerable period of silence to allow the readings to sink in.

Then "But the Crucifixion goes on" says a voice: "men kill and are killed, are imprisoned, hungry, cold – and others – ourselves – look on". Wilfred Owen's poem 'The Send-off' illustrates and confirms the continuing crucifixion.

A prayer of repentance follows – expressing the amazement of the worshippers at the way in which we human beings grab for ourselves and make war inevitable; amazement at our concentration of honour on the dead whom God has in his care and our neglect of the living. An awareness of bankruptcy which all people share, issues in abandonment to the mercy of God and a plea for such cleansing as will send them out with new strength to bring God's will to pass in the world.

A reading from Dr Hugh Montefiore on Jesus the Crucified's acceptance of all people unacceptable and un-accepting, is balanced by St Luke's parable of the Good Samaritan, a reflection on the cost of involvement in contemporary life, and two minutes silence in which there might be reflection on the waste of life, the unfulfilled living, attending two World Wars.

The ending of the two-minute silence is marked by the singing of a hymn "When I Survey the Wondrous Cross". There is a prayer for those who are suffering under contemporary pressures and violence all over the world, a plea that God's presence might be made known to them, and a petition that ways might be found of living together in a world community, with war outlawed.

The service ends with the following prayer of dedication spoken by the company in dialogue.

A: "To what are you calling us, Father?"

B: "To mature manhood, measured by nothing less than the full stature of Christ."

(pause)

A: "But what does this mean, the full stature of Christ?"

B "He made himself nothing, assuming the nature of a slave, humbling himself, accepting even the death of the Cross."

(pause)

A: "But must we grow up to that, Father?"

B: "He who will lose his life for my sake and the gospel's shall keep it."

(pause)

147

A:　　　"But there is our work to do in the world. Show us the real issues in our lives, the true priorities, the right way of achieving the right goals.

B:　　　He is the origin, the first to return from the dead. Through Him I choose to reconcile the whole universe to myself, all things whether on earth or in heaven, through Him alone.

A:　　　Lord Jesus, like your disciples, we have been loud in our protestations of loyalty to you, and yet we have turned out to be disloyal. You trod the way of love without flinching: we hesitate to tread it at all. We have been afraid of the pain and suffering which love brings."

(pause)

A:　　　"But how can we do these things?"

B:　　　"The secret is this: Christ in you is the hope of the glory to come."

ALL:　　"Lord we believe.

　　　　Help Thou our unbelief"

ALL:　　read together the Nunc Dimittis and leave the Chapel quietly.

We are familiar with protest marches and demonstrations these days. This is a protest service aimed at traditionalist Armistice Day Services. The company of lay people turn customary liturgies on their head, challenging traditional Armistice Services, especially those which evidence an underlying jingoism. The service moves from dismay at the way we live our lives, moves to repentance, ends with a re-affirmation of trust in God. The lay people have a true feel for what belongs to worship – all the elements which matter find their place in a liturgy designed for a particular purpose.

The company of laymen who prepared the Remembrance Day Service, came into being as a result of a shock sustained by the Policy and Programme Committee of Scottish Churches' House. The Montreal Faith and Order Conference had taken place in the summer of 1963. The shock was produced by the realisation that the preparation, through commission work, for this conference had been undertaken by a group chosen so that it might be representative of the World Church: and it consisted of 111 clergy, 5 lay theologians, 3 laymen in secular occupations, and one woman. The Committee of the House were made vividly aware that, though many people were speaking about the need for adequate theological equipment for laity and their adequate participation in Faith and Order discussions, laity were simply not being equipped and were not being made participant in some of the main thinking of the church. It was clear that in Scotland a start should be made to discover means whereby laity might be helped to mature in their faith and contribute to the thinking of the Church (that contribution including radical criticism of the way in which Faith and Order work had been developed up to this point).

During 1964 exploratory meetings took place with small groups of laity and, by the autumn of that year the form of meeting which would allow laity to contribute fully on some of the issues concerning faith and practice which had a commanding interest for them, were sorted out. In December of that year an invitation to meet during the Week of Prayer for Christian Unity in January 1965 was issued to lay men and women who had revealed particular potential in Kirk Week and Laity Forum gatherings and in a Scottish Churches' Ecumenical Association Conference in St Andrews.

The weight of this whole development had to be thrown on laymen and women; so from the start they were invited to contribute material and ideas and take the development of the thinking into their own hands. Over the years which followed they piloted their own way to this and that point of the map of the Church's faith and practice, lingering for several meetings in one spot, returning at times to revisit others. Not only did they map their route by testing out in life and then putting into words their thought about some by element of the Church's belief and its expression, but in between met with one another and corresponded with one another, sorting things out with this one and that one who might have some light to shed on a particular question or whose position was felt to give or need challenge. Thus the group became, in a quieter and more limited than the Music Group, a centre of ferment.

The first meeting took place in January 1965. They had chosen the subject 'Worship' and had put their finger on facets which interested them particularly, but no method of approach had been devised – that was left to the House.

They found themselves thrown in at the deep end. First they were asked whether some statement such as the following met their mind: "The insights gained by Christians in the world as they seek to be obedient at points of pressure and decision, are insights with a theological content. Laymen who gain these must try to bring them to bear on the Church's understanding of its faith, taking care to preserve idiom, language and imagery which is authentic to them and understandable in secular situations. A partnership of the ordained and unordained is required – for the understanding of the Church's faith and the ordering of its life is the work of the whole Church in each generation, not simply of one part of the Church.'

This was agreed to be the basis on which to proceed. Immediately thereafter participants were told that they were to conduct an act of worship in just over an hour's time, dividing responsibilities for it among three different groups into which they were formed. This first act of worship constructed before they got to know one another – although the act of compiling it brought them quickly into sensitive relationship – was fairly traditional. Over succeeding gatherings it was often found to be necessary to sum up the thinking of the group in an act of worship. None of these were 'far out'; but they show evidence of the growing maturity of the group. Their development often had unexpected features, and one felt powerfully the flavour of the real world in which participants were engaged daily as the world out of which worship arose to the throne of God. The weakness of much of the Church's worship was made very clear. It is not the Church's worship. It draws upon the limited experience, imagination and sensitiveness of one man or woman. The authentic worship of the Church is offered only when the hopes, fears, thanksgiving, rejoicings, awe and remorse of the whole worshipping community are drawn into it. A lay group such as this provides a pointer to the renewal of worship as the offering of the people.

The immediate next task of this company was to handle a case-study of a tricky industrial situation where no one clear Christian way out showed itself; and in three groups to consider how they would pray for those involved:

a)   in their personal prayers
b)   in a small committed group
c)   in an act of public worship

Prayers of those different kinds were worked at, written down and submitted. But at the same time, people pointed out that prayer, by itself and from a distance, denied its own character. One had also to make contact with the persons in straits concerning how they should act, be made sensitive to their background and attitudes, get the factors involved in the situation clear, see what support (through prayer, the fellowship of a committed group, money to tide them over - if action were required in the situation which brought work dismissal) should be provided if sympathy were not to be simply a matter of words. The case-study brought the group into rich fields of reflection. At one time they were wondering how the average congregation were to be helped to understand how people were placed in situations of this kind, and act relevantly to them; at another they got into questions of the broad aims of industry, God's purpose in providing people with skills, the stewardship of the whole creation. When an act of worship was compiled to draw into it the thought and experience of the weekend, one of its main notes was awe before God who had made such a marvellous creation and given such testing responsibilities to human beings.

Before this gathering act of worship took place, the attention of the group was turned to a fresh entry into the subject of worship. Two questions were posed:

1)   Imagine that, for the next ten years, you are not going to go to a service of worship of any kind. Would anything important go out of your life: and if so what?

2)   You are working alongside someone who is an agnostic and is intrigued by the act of Christians in gathering for worship, there being a clear element of serious search in his interest. What do you say to someone like this?

Among many perceptive things it was said: "Nothing but life which is authentic makes worship credible". One of the small groups found it impossible to make a straightforward statement about how they would react, and instead wrote out a dialogue between a Christian and an agnostic which expressed more effectively the way in which they might imagine a developing relationship and conversation.

At the end, members stated their intention to stay together and to meet two or three times per year. They accepted 'Sharing the Gospel', as a description of their object since they were setting themselves to understand the gospel afresh in genuinely contemporary thought-forms and language; and they wanted others to share in their journey of exploration. A satisfying variety of lay experience was in fact represented in the group, the bricklayer rubbing shoulders with the scientist. It should be noted that added richness came to the 'Sharing the Gospel' group from the fact that they not only had different lay responsibilities in the world but came from different parts of Scotland.

The theme of the next gathering was 'Jesus is Lord'. A project to be undertaken individually took the place of a working paper: it was set out in the letter of invitation as follows:

"Live with the phrase 'Jesus is Lord' in your own working situation – quite consciously and deliberately asking if there is any meaning in the phrase for most of the people you encounter. Ask yourself whether it is a harmless kind of phrase which people are prepared to accept, provided it does not disturb their life. Is there any way in which you could say that the Lordship of Jesus Christ is being made visible in the industrial nexus?

Then apply this to your home. Consciously examine the set-up, the things which you count important, the relationships closely established; and ask whether there is a note of testimony in your home (which need not be consciously sounded) which suggests that the Lordship of Jesus Christ is the determining influence. What do the words mean for those who have no home? How can you see Jesus Christ invisibly at work in difficult home situations – or can you not see Him at all, and, if this is so, can you be sure that He is there?

Think of your leisure time activities and ask whether there is any way in which these words indicate priorities, and add or withdraw zest/

Jot down all the phrases which come to you from the Bible over these weeks which in some sense provide content for the words 'Jesus is Lord'.

Find out from the people you work beside or meet for leisure activities or in the home whether the word 'Lord' gets across the relevant image. If they do say that there is meaning in the phrase, probe deeper to see whether they are prepared to reckon with larger and deeper demands which will be laid upon them. What particular meaning does the phrase have at this time of space travel and of nuclear weapons?

Please send in any comments you care to give beforehand".

The last part of the consultation which ensued was occupied by small groups making written statements of belief summing up their insights.

The next consultation returned to some of the issues raised in the very first meeting and, using as starters crucial quotations from Evelyn Underhill, John Robinson and Paul van Buren considered what we made of prayer at a time in history when much that was traditionally thought to belong to prayer was under challenge. A working paper issued beforehand drew together reflections of the group and pinpointed the intersection points of urgent interest. The report of the consultation registers deepening experience on the part of the group together and it points to the development of commonly-held insights – for instance, it became clear that prayer need not be answered by direct guidance on every matter, there are situations which can only be held in tension before God. A service was prepared as part of the weekend meeting, and prayers were related to industrial, political and ecclesiastical "hot potatoes" namely the Seaman's strike, Vietnam and Christian Unity.

In October 1966 the early intention to study the meaning of baptism was fulfilled. People were invited, beforehand, to reflect on a) why they would or would not have their children baptised and b) what difference baptism had made to themselves, if they were baptised. In preparation there was a brief pinpointing of some of the contentious points regarding baptism in Christian history from the earliest times and also a gathering of main points in a working outline. The weekend took the form of a project study, a consideration of imagery, and the comparison of existing baptismal rites from different traditions. First an attempt was made to outline the content of a leaflet which could be given to parents who were not (or were lapsed) church members but wanted their children baptised. This proved a difficult exercise but served to raise fundamental questions about the meaning of baptism. After study of relevant Bible passages it was agreed that teaching about baptism should not be dogmatic but a training of the imagination to comprehend the use of images. This led on to a discussion of imagery that can be meaningful today. The emphasis on repentance and the washing away of sin was repugnant to most people when it referred to infant baptism, but some sense could be made of it when one thought of a child born into a community guilty of economic exploitation and injustice. At the end of the weekend one thing was clear; none of the group was convinced about the practice of infant baptism.

A second weekend was spent on baptism in which the group looked at different denominational practices and particularly at infant baptism. This resulted in a tape recorded discussion between four people holding different views, and in an act of worship.

The arrival of Donna Myers, a Roman Catholic who had studied at Bossey and spent some time thereafter at Scottish Churches' House, suggested as a theme for the next encounter 'The Diversity of Gifts and the Unity of the Ministry'. The aim was to face the basic questions: What is the mission of the Church? Who are the missionaries? A working document of biblical studies was sent out which raised questions about the ministry of the whole people of God.

By this time the desire for a group celebration of Holy Communion had been expressed frequently by some members. There were then no Roman Catholic members of the group, though two joined later, and the question was whether or not to ask the Episcopal bishop for permission for an open communion. The group decided against it, not because of any denominational scruples, but because, while some felt that a communion service would be a fulfilment and an expression of the fellowship which had grown up among them, others felt it would be formalising something which existed as a reality. It could add nothing to the normal meals they ate together. Thus it was appropriate to spend a weekend on the Communion.

The approach to the consultation on Holy Communion was prefaced by preparation by participants. They were asked to record as exactly as they could what Holy Communion had meant to them in their own experience; to see if they could find Christian but non-ecclesiastical terms to interpret the simple word 'communion'; and to talk these questions over with their friends so that their thoughts were also taken into account. Communion as a human experience was expressed as: a sense of unity with the natural order; entering into the development of a work of drama; getting over barriers such as those of language and race and establishing real relationship; comradeship between man and man and man and woman. The very experience of meeting, eating, thinking, joking, challenging, living with one another as a 'Sharing the Gospel' group was thought to demand the word 'communion' to give it adequate expression. The consideration of sacramental communion which followed developed on the interplay of the biblical testimony and this human experience, which it seemed to meet at many points. Where the meeting point was the unreality of the relationship of the sacramental act to human experience, this fact was not avoided.

In the autumn of 1968 'Jesus Christ, Son of Man' was the theme. A reading list was provided for use throughout the summer. The liberation produced by the Second Adam who had the power to transmit life and so become a quickening or life-giving spirit provided the dominant note on which this consultation started. Jesus Christ's humanity liberated them as people faced the future, even as he bore the responsibility for all God's creation in space and time. Thereafter, attention was given to the challenge to human beings when they found their lives measured by a true human life and by the free choice of Jesus Christ to be a man for others. The rest of the thinking of the group was gathered into prayers and poetry.

In 1969 the matter which concerned the group was set out thus:

"A human life lived among men is of such significance that it becomes much more than a sign or promise or example: it becomes a way through which the human race may realise its potential and reach its true destiny.

Can we make a fresh interpretation of the atonement, using these terms?"

The 'Sharing the Gospel' group provided a sign for the Church in our time. It had been made abundantly clear that laymen can tackle theological responsibilities and breathe new life into theological thinking from the freshness of their varied experience. Too often laymen and women, have been treated as children in the Church. When they are treated as adults and invited to do adult study and thinking, immense resources are released into the Church. Some members of the group get so little chance in their own churches to work at questions theologically that they find it possible to remain with the local church only if they can go from time to time to a place where they are dealt with at the level of their maturity.

Theology is the work of the whole Church. The professional theologian is a cripple without the laity who bring insights which have theological content from a rich experience of life; and the lay person is a cripple without the professional theologian who puts him or her in touch with the thinking of the whole church down the centuries and across the boundaries of race and nation.

This group met most often as an entirely lay group. At times in the church, when theology has been made the preserve of the ordained, it will be necessary to encourage the ordinary membership to being to recover an inheritance which belongs to the whole church. The authentic notes of daily experience need to be preserved and to challenge the jargon of theology. But before long the ordained and the unordained discover their need for one another and can discover with fresh relish that they belong to one venturing company of study, thought and action with Christ at its heart.

Faith and Doubt in this Age

Early in the life of Scottish Churches' House it was suggested that some festivals of the church – in particular, not only the Week of Prayer for Christian Unity, but Easter and Pentecost – should be regarded as focal points for inter-church initiatives. Attempts to do this were made; but the fact that Pentecost is not a holiday period as Whitsun is in England and that, at Easter, people were either in their own churches or on holiday, meant that no fruitful line was discovered for developing work related to these festivals.

It was quite otherwise in the case of Holy Week. The time remembered then was one in which issues of life and death were fought out and men and women reacted in ways which revealed faith and unbelief in unexpected quarters, with unexpected people, and in unexpected ways. Holy Week seemed to be a good time to bring together young people who were in the last years of their school course to examine issues of faith and doubt in this age. The only problem was technical. Easter wanders about the calendar; and different education authorities have differences in the arrangements the make for Easter holidays. Sometimes, particularly when Easter comes early, it is impossible to shorten the school curriculum to make Holy Week a holiday period. Thus, in 1969, the four-day residential gathering had to take place in June.

The same kind of freedom to explore into matters of Christian faith and practice was provided for young people as was provided for adults in the 'Sharing the Gospel' group. Some material was provided beforehand so that they might have something to bite on from the moment of arrival. There were two catalysts for discussion, one a convinced Christian, the other an agnostic or atheist (for instance, in one case this was an agnostic artist, in another a psychologist and Marxist). The hope was that, as each of these contributed and challenged according to their own view-point, and, as the young people took the impact of points made by film, role-playing, case studies, readings from contemporary novels, bible studies, sharp dialogue recorded on tape – their more superficial understanding of their basic convictions might be penetrated and they might be able themselves to see more clearly where they stood and what life-issues they should be facing. About half way through, one could almost guarantee that a number who were very sure of their Christian or agnostic position had almost reversed roles. This was then, essentially, not an argument between Christians and agnostics, but the exposure of young people who believed themselves to be Christians or to be agnostics to different experiences and insights, together. This age group was treated as one which was so close to full adulthood that the risks of this kind if exposure were perfectly proper. To cling to an infantile faith or to be over-confident about one which the realities of life can shatter is, at this age, to have no faith at all that will last the pace.

A good deal of the time was not definitely programmed beforehand. Material of various kinds already indicated, was on tap and ready for use; but this use was always made subject to the natural development of the group – which no one could predict before they met. Space was deliberately left for people to converse together, walk or kick a ball around together, or go to their own rooms or the chapel to think things through further.

The opening up of thinking was, as will be clear, undertaken in different ways. On one occasion, against a background of folk music, extracts were read of prose and poetry expressing the faith and doubt of writers through the ages. At another time statements by a theist, a deist, agnostic, and an atheist were used to spark off the encounter. William Golding's 'Free Fall', Tennesee Williams' 'The Night of the Iguana', Ian Fleming's 'Thunderball', Albert Camus' 'The Outsider' were used in different gatherings. In one consultation attention was given to 'Playboy' culture – and what it said about the nature of man, woman, and society. A characteristic overall theme was our world – what is valued? who holds power? who are casualties and what responsibility does the community feel for the unsuccessful? what place is given to the arts?

One contribution deserves special mention.

The senior schools boys and girls would be bussed across to Edinburgh for a whole morning with Richard de Marco. He was very gifted in establishing thoughtful relationship with that age-group. He might sit them all before a big painting and ask "What was the painter's point in putting a discarded red cloak in the foreground?" They would try to figure out the intention of the whole picture. Somehow, in no time at all, they would be debating the meaning of life and what mattered in life. Richard might contribute in the debate by referring to the importance of prayer in his own life – what an impact that had compared with the words of any ecclesiastic! He was willing to give time, in successive Holy Weeks, freely and generously for such encounters.

One thing is certain about this kind of meeting. A concerned conversation was started which would go on among groups of friends and associates when the young people returned to their own schools and neighbourhoods. This conversation would be on the meaning of life in the twentieth century. Christians and non-Christians would feel confident that they could explore together.

Possibly one other thing can be said with certainty: all would have discovered the close relationship of agnosticism and faith, including, for Christians, that agnosticism which is proper as one stands before the mystery of God who refuses humanity the security of a belief which is cut and dried.

Spontaneous Combustion

Contact with people in the arts had shown how 'denominationally' the different arts were being pursued. They too needed an ecumenical movement to bring them together. It happened to be at the student level that this showed itself most clearly. By 1965 the committee of the House was considering means whereby opportunities to meet across existing barriers might be provided. A start was made with three groups – Art, Drama and Theological students. The initiative came from the Art students in Glasgow who wanted to investigate questions of authority in our time with people from other disciplines in the same age group. This Glasgow nucleus provided a continuing base of interest which allowed further developments to take place. Drama students early declared their interest and reaffirmed this from time to time, but did not in the end send a delegation any year! Theological students took part from the beginning, but in such small numbers that it was clear that the opportunity for breaking out of theological college ghetto-thinking was not appreciated. Over the years they were joined by student nurses and teacher training students; and some interest has been shown by music students.

The first gathering, early in 1966, had the theme of 'Authority' to give it focus; but the use of time was relatively unplanned and the students found a method which provided so appropriate a framework for their dialogue that it has been used ever since.

The words 'Spontaneous Combustion' had been used to describe this weekend meeting because, apart from that first encounter, nothing was prepared beforehand. Everything depended on whether students who will hold different responsibilities in society can spark on another off. On arrival, they were put in groups according to vocation and are asked simply to speak to one another about what is worrying and what is cheering them. They were then split into different groups in each of which a mixture of studies is represented and invited to talk to one another, this time across the boundary of their disciplines, about the things which matter to them and which worry them. From this point there emerged concerns which are obviously central. Most often one theme presented itself commandingly and, from different angles developed in small groups, the whole gathering searched for more light on the theme. There is one other constant feature. Before the groups disperse they must undertake a project, by means of which they communicate to one another the insights that they have gained (even if these are only insights into the agony of dilemmas which face them). The very first occasion on which student nurses took part they made the issues which have to be faced responsibly in medical practice today so vivid to others, that their concerns became the concerns of the whole group. Thus, not only are students opened out to one another; but those from any point of the student hierarchy (in which nurses reckon themselves to be pretty low down) can capture the interest of the others.

Students were very imaginative about the methods they used to communicate to one another convictions to which their thinking had led them. It was understandable that painting was a favourite mode (one series of about sixteen paintings of a chair at different points of history made clear social comment on the type of society exposed by the style and craftsmanship). A series of cartoons on test-tube babies which stretched the length of the common room, made serious points with a light touch. The need for us to understand the meaning of our living and dying and the relationship of these to one another was presented in an anthology of poetry and prose. Sometimes an act of worship was produced to gather up new dimensions or awareness. At times a dramatic dialogue was chosen. At others, role-playing was used both in small groups and in plenary.

One of the most exciting things which had taken place in Scottish Churches' House was this ferment of thinking and wrestling to communicate across the barriers of different disciplines.

Project on 'A Christian Style of Living'

One of the effects of identifying the lay resources of the churches in Scotland through Laity Forums, Kirk Weeks, the work of the Tell Scotland Movement, and then developments in Scottish Churches' House has been the contact established with lay men and women who were growing into a maturity characterised by a sensitiveness to the world in which their faith was to be expressed. Thus when a request came from the Department on Laity of the World Council of Churches to do, well ahead, preparatory thinking for a session in the Uppsala World Assembly it was possible to assemble a group of mature Christian laity who were able to undertake the work requested. A second pilot consultation was to have taken place in Sweden but it did not materialise.

The question was put in this way in a letter of invitation: "Is there a recognisable form of Christian life to be lived out in the contemporary world? If so what characteristics does it posses? If not, is the Christian way quite hidden except to the eye of faith, or so different in its expression in different situations and ages that no common threads run through?" The invitation was sent out to a very limited number of lay people so as to produce a group balanced in background, experience and expertise. It was made clear to every person invited that they had been deliberately sought out. Accordingly this offer was made: a note would be sent to make a special plea for release from work where this would help, and to make up wages, where necessary. A big risk was, naturally, involved in the latter but the Inter-church Relations Committee of the Church of Scotland offered up to £100 to allow the consultation to happen, and other churches gave a certain amount of backing. It turned out that laymen were so impressed by the realism of this approach that they negotiated a few extra days' holiday or some such thing; and it was possible to meet expenses within the limits set.

In preparation for this consultation, two pieces of advice were given:

1) Not to read relevant books!
2) To live with an added alertness over the period between the invitation and the holding of the consultation, "spotting the circumstances and the context in which your own Christian decisions have to be made........ we need the background of your particular experience, and we need to have you express this in lay language with lay illustrations".

Preparation was, then, to be life-preparation. Written material was provided however, in addition, and consisted of bible studies on 'The Poor in The Bible', a memo of gathered reflections on 'Aspects of the New Life'; an industrial case-study; and some signposts for wayfarers. A programme, dividing out the work, was issued beforehand – with the observation that it should be jettisoned completely if the natural development of the thinking took a completely different line. "We must be prepared to turn the whole creation around and stand it on its head if in the process of tackling some issues we get on to others which really are of major significance". Almost all those who were invited accepted. For four days, thirty participants including Ralph Young of the Department on Laity of the WCC hammered out their response to the questions levelled at them. A considerable document was offered to the WCC as the main document and there was added a group reflection on some of the issues and a chart suggesting developing relationships and communications which would help in the etching out of a new style of living.

Other Laity Ploys

With the restructuring of the ecumenical movement in Scotland which brought the Scottish Churches' Council into being in December 1964 there was a period of readjustment, at the end of which the Laity Committee was more closely related to Scottish Churches' House. In a meeting held in December 1967 a reappraisal of the development of its work was undertaken. The gathering of lay people in Kirk Weeks and Laity Forums had proved a useful enterprise; but the conviction of the Committee was that it was now time to return to the small group (though not necessarily local or even church-based).

In this re-evaluation the Laity Committee discerned three aspects of continuing responsibility:

a)   The task of keeping before the Scottish Churches' Council and its departments lay concerns and lay thought.

b)   Helping and nourishing groups which already exist (some of these groups being prophetic in character and not closely related to the Christian Church: 'ecumenical agnostics' the members were called).

c)   Serious work on the theology of the laity.

The relation of service and mission was a continuing concern: as was the relationship with Roman Catholic laity.

Joint meetings were planned of Scottish Churches' Council and Roman Catholic laity. They found from the first moment of meeting that they were on common ground, facing the same issues in the world, concerned for the renewal of the Church and its service and testimony to the world. A joint seminar was planned for June 1969 at the Roman Catholic conference centre, Coodham, near Kilmarnock. A useful partnership was set up with the Passionist Fathers in Coodham. Besides the seminar indicated, in the autumn of 1968 there was a joint gathering of youth for a weekend on World Poverty and in April 1969 a Psycho-Analytical Spring School. It is significant that decided to have a gathering without outside speakers; and it was therefore a commitment to share with one another the features of difficult situations with which they had to wrestle. Groups meeting in Edinburgh and Glasgow through that winter, shaped the conference and prepared case studies which provided the starting point for discussion.

Visit of World Laity

Lay men and women in Scotland were given the unique privilege in April 1968 of meeting with a company of Christians from Africa, Asia and Latin America who would be returning to their own countries to head up lay training there. The Association of Directors of Lay Centres in Europe and the Laity

Department of the World Council of Churches had jointly planned a course which provided insights from lay training work in Europe. There was no suggestion that training in this part of the world could be applied elsewhere. There was no hidden ecclesiastical imperialism. But acquaintance with work in some centres conveniently grouped geographically and providing a variety of national experience could bring an awareness of a fellowship of enterprise in this field all over the world and provide some ideas about what might and might not be possible in the countries to which the guests returned. As often as not the point of light which showed itself was of this kind: "What you have done would not be relevant in our country because these and those factors are different there; and in any case we doubt the wisdom of policy x and approach y which you have suggested; but in our situation what would fit would be......." Whether by similarities or by contraries an enrichment of the imagination took place. Certainly, although the group was in Scottish Churches' House for a very short time, it was an enrichment of the laity in Scotland to meet with these others and be exposed to an understanding of their situations and the vitality of their approach.

One of the important things provided by morning prayers at Scottish Churches' House, when, each day, a centre in another part of the world was remembered in prayer, was the strengthening of the awareness of this world fellowship of enterprise which was sensed so clearly when people from other continents came to visit.

Examining the Faith

To redress a balance and give full weight to the practical expertise and to the theological insight into God's way with the world available to laity in secular situations, lay men and women needed opportunity to meet separately. But they would recognise as readily as any that the rich mixture comes when the ordained and unordained meet on a common task, bringing to bear their different forms of expertise. In Faith and Order committees and commissions of all kinds the participation of the ordained was outrageously disproportionate. Moreover commissions tended to play their theological cards close to their chests so that there was little widespread discussion in the Church as a whole about the matters of faith and practice which were on their agendas. Early in the life of the House it was agreed that matters of Faith and Order should be given attention by companies which represented a cross-section of the Church so that the discussion, as far as the House could effect this, was got out among the membership. There were the odd occasions when, for particular reasons, the ordained were in the majority; but most of the time, laity were not only in the majority but very substantially so. Those who were already engaged in

162

inter-church conversations and in commissions on similar themes were rarely invited. Consultations began in 1961, but it was in 1965 that the Policy and Programme committee shrewdly formulated the basis on which invitations were to be extended. They were to go to "those so placed as to prolong action in their own environment". Nearly always the churches which hold joint ownership of Scottish Churches' House were represented; and from a very early point the German Speaking Congregation in Scotland, an occasional representative from the Free Church, and Roman Catholics took part.

Two consultations per year were held. It was possible to have a core of people who were continually maturing in their understanding of the faith and its expression in our time, along with a larger group of those who were brought in from time to time and represented a spread of discussion. In most cases working papers were prepared, to concentrate material in certain areas, so that there might be a disciplined use of time. The reports are too packed with meat to be satisfactorily represented by summaries or extracts; but some brief reference might indicate the range of interest and the points which gained most concentrated thinking..

The development sprang from an existing group. The Scottish Church Theology Society, a society of the Church of Scotland, saw the advantages there would be in thinking through with people from other denominations some of the themes which claimed its interest. A springboard was thus provided. A consultation was planned for October 1961 entitled 'Worshipping Together'. Five different denominations were represented at a two-day gathering which set itself to identifying the basic elements of an act of worship. Those who came were surprised at the extent of their agreement. By this time, members of different traditions were probing beyond these traditions, probing back into New Testament practice, and probing deep into an understanding of Christ and the response to him which they were themselves called to give. The earliest meetings of this kind revealed a shyness on the part of people who were not sure where Christian neighbours stood, and a relief to find how genuine the neighbourly relationship was. An immediate gain of ecumenical gatherings of this kind was that every church had assumptions from which it started: when it was doing its thinking on its own these might be taken for granted, but in the company of other Christians that was disallowed, and everyone had to get back to square one. The questioning of unexamined assumptions produced a realism, accordingly, which non-ecumenical meeting could not match. This realism was equally evident in the way in which people of different denominations faced up to differences and agreements. It is recorded in the minutes that what was then called the Policy and Programme Committee had a first evaluation of this form of meeting:

noting 'how out of touch the denominations were regarding their understanding of the faith', yet 'the willingness of people to clarify the convictions against each other with honesty and humility.' The first consultation on baptism, which showed wide divergences between those who held infant baptising and believer's baptising points of view, produced this reflection: "those who took part were further from one another in conviction at the end, and clearer about their different convictions; and at the same time closer to one another in their commitment to one Lord and in the fellowship of one Church".

The consultation on baptism referred to took place in May 1962. There followed in the same year 'Ministerial Order and the Service of Ordination', and the following year 'The Ministry of the Whole Membership' and 'The Ordination of Women.' By the end of 1963 some of the preoccupying concerns were coming to the surface: particularly the loss of a description for the ordained ministry through an awareness of the extent to which responsibilities which appertained to it were seen to belong to the whole church; a realisation that the meaning of ordination had to be thought through quite afresh. Even at this point, although a functional designation of ordination was accepted as basic, it was not thought to be adequate; a unique pastoral responsibility towards the whole church was believed to belong as well; the unity that lay people found in working situations was considered to be of great theological significance, though it was not being given weight in ecclesiastical commissions – and it pointed to the theological contribution that lay men and women already could offer and the need to equip the whole church theologically not just the clergy. No one pattern for a reunited church was believed to be on the cards – Christians must work together in new territory now being provided by God, and allow this common obedience to sketch out some indications of the form of the Church needed to sustain obedient action.

The autumn consultation in 1963 was of particular interest because a consultation four years later on the same subject 'The Ordination of Women' showed a clear change in church opinion.

The consultation in 1963 concerned itself almost entirely with an examination of evidence. Looking at the roles given to women in the New Testament and in the history of the church, members tried to disentangle insights which remained valid from those which belonged to a particular time of history, special circumstances, a respect for conventions of the time, the claims of good order, timing in history; for working out all the implications of the gospel, the different types of responsibility which could be most easily carried by the one sex or the other; and the implications of the centrality of Christ to all relationships now, the new mutuality of men and women in his service within the fabric of new social relationships which belonged to a new creation: new perspectives gained in the ecumenical movement and balancing responsibilities now to change practice in the church drastically so that it expedited progress. The fact that masculine terms were used for the Trinity did not prove to be an impediment. The fact that the apostles were all men was put alongside the fact that they were all Jews and theological amateurs .That fact pointed as much to the inappropriateness of ordaining Scotsmen or professional theologians as of ordaining women!

Working paper material was provided by Marga Buhrig from Switzerland and Mary Lusk from Scotland (who had petitioned the General Assembly of the Church of Scotland for ordination). The thinking of the consultation moved easily into new fields of the imagination regarding the service of women, if they were not restricted to traditional church roles. Then, interestingly and almost amusingly antennae which had been fully extended to explore new territory were sharply withdrawn in the last session – almost certainly because members realised that they would have to return and report back to committees! However, the need not only for continuing study but for pilot experimentation which would allow the ministry of women to be re-minted in this age was fully accepted. The most remarkable thing about the consultation in the autumn of 1967 on the same theme (which used as one of its working papers the Panel on Doctrine's report to the General Assembly of the Church of Scotland of that year) was the evidence of a battle almost won. In churches which had excluded women from ordination there were signs of a movement of thought clearly directed towards their inclusion.

In 1964 the themes were 'Evangelism' and 'The Nottingham Proposals'. Then in March 1965 occurred one of the formative gatherings. The theme was 'Mass, Eucharist, Communion'. During the consultation there was a Church of Scotland Communion Service, an Episcopal Eucharist and a Roman Catholic Mass. The consultation developed with the exposition of different traditional points of view and the way in which these were expressed in different rites. The Church of Scotland position was given exposition: and comments from Lutheran and United Free representatives started discussion on it. The Salvation Army's understanding had that of the Quakers put alongside it. Doctrine and practice in the Episcopal Church was followed by a Methodist comment, leading into plenary discussion. There were observations from a Congregationalist and a Baptist on the interpretation mode within the Churches of Christ. The meaning of the Mass was expounded and this led straight into plenary consideration of implications. Of equal importance in this gathering was the respect shown by members of different denominations for one another's positions, the friendship created by meeting and thinking together, and the determination to let no statement be made without challenge if challenge were needed. It was clear that many people had taken up positions in relation to the practice of other churches which they found had been distorted or unfairly presented to them.

In the same year, 1966, there were further consultations on 'Ordination' and 'The Church and its Mission'. The latter subject was developed, not in the abstract, but in relation to the understanding of the Church and its outreach in our time which was expressed in church conversations or statements. A major contribution was made by laity who were involved in Church of Scotland/ Congregationalist, Anglican/Presbyterian, and Methodist/Anglican conversations. Thus a fresh angle of entry was provided both in regard to theme and to catalysts. A Roman Catholic layman drew on material from the 'De Ecclesia' of Vatican II to provide complementary insights into the Church and its task today.

The work of the World Council of Churches on 'The Missionary Structure of the Congregation', with the document 'Agenda The World' as a working paper and Dr Hollenweger from Geneva as a resource person, was followed up by a consultation on 'Proclaiming the Gospel in Our Time' in 1967. In that year an extra consultation was held to examine the union proposals of the Church of Scotland and the Congregational Church before these went to their respective Assemblies. Dr W Stewart, ex-principal of Serampore College, examined the proposals in the light of a survey of negotiations towards union all over the world which he had undertaken. It was extremely useful to have a comment from a Danish-Lutheran angle from Dr Aagard who was visiting with his wife at the time, as well as observations from the United Free, Episcopal and Roman Catholic Churches. A number of 'Matters to go into further' were sent to the Joint Committee simply as observations. Probably the most important of these were a) the suggestion that the Church Meeting might have a revived significance in a reunited church and b) that the proposals made no provision for the continuing preparation of women to serve in the ordained ministry. (The Church of Scotland's decision to admit women to the ordained ministry came at a later point, and removed this difficulty)

Dr Ian Henderson's book 'Power Without Glory', a critique of the ecumenical movement, came out in 1967. In the autumn of that year there was a day gathering whose aim was to sort out the criticisms which should be taken with most seriousness: and this led to a consultation in March 1968 on 'The Shape of the Church'. A serious attempt was made to get all the main wings of church opinion directly represented: and this was largely successful. There gathered those who believed that the movement towards unity was a diversion from the real task of the Church, those who believed in some federal relationship of the churches, those who held that the way forward was in terms of invisible unity (re-interpreted in the consultation as spiritual unity) and those who thought that organic union had to be the goal. Contributions were made by Professor Henderson himself, Rev Andrew Herron, Dr Alan McArthur, Rev Andrew Macrae, Dr Nevile Davidson and Bishop Wimbush. This was a particularly difficult meeting to assess. Probably the main gain came through the friendly but frank encounter of people with different convictions about the need for church unity. One thing which did become clear was that the federalist position, which was believed to be strongest, turned out to be almost non-existent. Most of those who were presumed to be federalist in their attitude by others, turned out to be otherwise minded when contact was made with them; and others revealed that, while they used the name, they either meant that churches should stay as they are, or that what was called spiritual unity was the way forward. There was probably some agreement that there needed to be more common action on the part of Christians which allowed attitudes to be revised naturally by means of direct personal contact and dialogue.

Also in 1968 opportunity was offered for a study of the confession of the United Presbyterian Church in the USA. Too few people showed interest for this to be carried through. This was read as a signal that Church confessions appearing in several denominations at this point of history were not accepted as compulsive reading.

In 1969 a study document on ordination prepared by the World Council of Churches was worked over and it was agreed that in the autumn of that year a further consultation should take place, specifically between Roman Catholics and Protestants, with questions posed to each in the Study as the subject matter for consultation.

Any series such as 'Examining the Faith' series has a variety of co-ordinates sparked off by, or closely related to, its own development. The one which might most deserve mention examined the growth of Pentecostalism within traditional church structures. Consultations were held to suit ministers and laity, consecutive weekday and weekend periods being chosen. In 1967 under the title 'The Charismatic Revival in the Church Today' the historical background and biblical basis of this manifestation were examined, the present situation was described, and times of testimony, discussion and prayer were included in the programming. A year later the work of the Holy Spirit was the focus and 'The Holy Spirit and Gifts in Revival' the subject. These consultations drew upon those who were already in the charismatic movement or on the fringes of it. In February 1969 some who had reservations about the movement as well as those who were convinced, assembled to assess 'Signs of the Spirit Today'. This consultation came in the 'Examining the Faith' series and gained some of its membership from that group. Representatives of four different church traditions expounded their understanding of how the working of the Holy Spirit was understood in the their denominations. There was then a consideration of the gift of tongues, of prophecy, and of healing today. Finally the hand of the Holy Spirit in the fields of a) the arts and b) politics was considered. This area of work might illustrate the convictions of the committee that Scottish Churches' House could be alert and teachable before every manifestation in the churches today which might be a sign of the presence of God. Such signs deserve humble investigation and, when that has been done, constructive and sensitive criticism. Wherever signs of life were shown in any of the churches, whether these have a left-wing or right-wing character, Scottish Churches' House was called to a work which included both teachableness and honest evaluation.

The Ordained Ministry and Training for it

The above heading indicates a series of consultations which began with the theme 'Recruitment for the Ministry' or 'Candidates for the Ministry' and was most often called, for short, 'Training for the Ministry'. A good deal of the work undertaken by the 'Examining the Faith' consultations covered similar ground; but in this series a particular job was done as a contribution to a larger study.

When the work began there was no indication of what would be its broad context. In June 1963 a one-day consultation was held with representatives of the Education for the Ministry Committees of seven churches, meeting together to consider questions of candidates and recruitment. The basis provided for meeting was: 'The contrast between problems of recruitment in previous generations and today; significant changes in contemporary thought and attitudes affecting recruitment; the changed character of ministry in this age – and what in unchanging; the scope and demand of ordained ministry today; the image of the ordained ministry; sources of supply of candidates; presentation of this as a potential vocation at school and in church; effective training and its relationship to recruitment."

At its next meeting the committee reviewed progress, realised that the direction being taken was an investigation of the ordained ministry and the training needed to equip it in our time, and noted the danger of doing work out of step with Theological Colleges on the one hand and the British Council of Churches on the other. There was uncertainty about ordained ministry in our time.

There was a need for fundamental study. But care had to be taken to prevent overlapping. It looked at this point as if the work would be put into cold storage at least for a period.

However, in February 1964 a request came from the British Council of Churches to supply material gathered through consultative work as a contribution to its own study on the training of the ordained ministry. The Iona Community, St Ninians, Crieff, and St Colms Missionary College were invited to send representatives and other individuals were invited to provide a balance of denominations and experience (e.g. representation was asked from the Gorbals Group). It was agreed that the group should meet at 6-monthly intervals between the times arranged for BCC meetings. What emerged effectively was a Working Party which met on eight occasions. A boost to the whole enterprise was given when in September 1966 a World Council of Churches Consultation on the theme was held in Scottish Churches' House.

The World Council of Churches had set up a special study on ordained ministry and training to equip it. The documentation of the Scottish Working party was eagerly seized upon by the WCC but given little attention by the BCC. This could be because, in the judgement of the Scottish group, the BCC Commission came too quickly to questions about selection and training whereas they felt the need to ask quite basic questions about the purpose of the Church, the Church's ministry, the justification (if such there was) for having an ordained ministry at all, and the role or roles that such a ministry should fulfil – before asking questions about appropriate training. So radically were these matters considered that, after a few consultations, so much was seen to belong to the Church's ministry, which had been assumed to belong to that of the ordained, that no defence could be found for the continuing provision of an ordained ministry! Because the Working Party had the courage to come to this point and to take it with the utmost seriousness, it was able to get beyond that point and discern in a quite fresh way what kind of ordained ministry might now nourish and build up the Church in its mission. It might also have seemed that the process needed streamlining – that the working party was too widely based, too representative of all the denominations and of different emphases within the denominations. The benefit, however, was that one could chart out from progress in the consultations steps which the churches could take together and an understanding of ministry into which they could all grow. Even by the second meeting in June 1964 the following elements of ordained ministry were being sorted out: galvanising, delegating, getting feed-back, really learning with others, being educated e.g. regarding the sins recognised in daily life, sharing in the training and retraining of the church membership. This need for training and retraining was one of three points inserted by Rev

Stephen Mackie in WCC discussions on Faith and Order. Three points were made the basis of the 1964 consultations. The other two were

a) the need to think out afresh the doctrine of the ministry in light of the experience of the ecumenical movement and recent theological study and

b) the manifest need to experiment with new patterns of ministry.

The clutch of questions which were grouped under these major headings were worked over in a working paper and then it engaged the whole consultative group.

In 1965 participants were asked to give ordination full attention and sort out their own position by seeing where they agreed and disagreed with the following composite statement:

"Ordination does not add to the Christian's status and obligations – it refers to a function within the Church to be discharged according to the terms of the Church's discipline – exists for the good ordering of the whole Church's ministry, and the eliciting of gifts employed in that ministry – does not confer a special kind of grace – bestows exousia not dynamis – is for life."

By this time a world of questions released on the nature and function of the ordained ministry had grouped themselves round the significance of ordination itself. This was returned to several times as a crucial point.

By 1966 the following occurs at the end of the March report. It clearly marks a stage:

"The willingness of this group, concerned substantially as they were for the education of the ministry to allow the ordained ministry as has been traditionally understood to go into the melting pot to allow for the thorough examination of what God seems to be requiring in the Church, has paid dividends which could not have been looked for beforehand."

The call to enter the ordained ministry is clearly now not a call to enter something which is cut-and-dried, but to take part in a process of rediscovering the Church's ministry and then distinguishing a ministry of a particular kind to be rendered to and within it. There could be no more fascinating calling than that to the ordained ministry at this time of change and rediscovery, when everyone who enters it has an opportunity to take part in the process of reshaping. The ordained ministry may have a particular contribution in a society in which there will be much more education for many more people. It can be a sign of a kind of leadership which is humble and enabling, which draws out the gifts of others and encourages their contribution as one of worth. This may be particularly important in an age when people feel that, unless they get the promotion and pickings understood to bring status in the rat race, they are without real significance. The compartmentalisation which exists in society as a whole might also get a sign from an ordained ministry which was not concerned to fragment it more, where broad responsibilities were undertaken which draw people into relationship in their communities and put them significantly in touch with one another. To do such work requires a high professionalism, without the narrow range that 'professionalism' sometimes suggests.

What may be becoming clearer, after an understandable period of uncertainty caused by re-evaluation, is that the lay men and women, as they take life in the world seriously, need the ordained person the more.

Advantage was taken of the World Council of Churches consultation, and material from it provided for a full residential meeting of the Working Party. Then in 1967 it was agreed to harvest the material up to that point and set it out in a single document. The possibility (never realised) that this document might be made into a study booklet helped to determine the way in which the job was tackled. An introduction set the scene and indicated some of the recurring concerns which questioned old assumptions about the place and status of the ordained ministry. The churches' ministry as a ministry of the whole people was then considered, and thereafter 'the commissioned ministry' (as it was decided to call it at that point of the conversation). Its function and diversification were reviewed, team and group ministries, tent-making and specialist ministries being considered and a note on professionalism being added. A section on 'ordination', with a footnote on calling, completed three-quarters of the document. The last quarter was on 'theological training'. Here an attempt was made to isolate insights from the whole work of the Working Party which pointed towards elements and emphases which should be noted in the construction of Theological College curricula – without spelling these out in detail since their technical realisation would need to have been worked out with a different group comprising those who oriented the curricula.

The 'basis of a study document' material was considered on the whole to gather up very fairly the work of past years. The working party made adjustments and corrections to it, and left it as a record of their work. They felt that this brought them to a term, and they should be summoned to re-assemble only if some fresh responsibility in the field showed itself.

They were in fact summoned about eighteen months later to do one particular job, which had been given attention otherwise in the life of Scottish Churches' House but not by this particular group – on the Ordination of Women. Their discussion showed the trend registered in other similar consultations – an openness to the Ordination of Women as a normal feature of the church of the future. Some of the factors which provide special problems for and bring special pressures on ordained women were set out as one part of the fulfilment of the remit.

Members of the working party also took part in the consultation on ordination in 1969 which used a WCC study document on ordination as a Working Paper.

Mission Overseas

If one description were chosen to identify the main preoccupation of consultations referred to within this section on Christian Faith and Practice, it would be the church's mission. That this part of the section is headed Mission Overseas does not mean that we are moving on to a new subject. 'The mission is one' is a recurrent phrase in the consultative work. However, the outreach of the church in any one country to people in an another country carries with it responsibility to take serious account of the life and culture of that country and of the preparation needed not only for those who will themselves go to it, but for those who will support them by prayer and finance from the home base.

The series of consultations indicated by the title 'Mission Overseas' took their origin from two sources. Once the churches began working together in a team in Scottish Churches' House, they became aware of areas in which they continued to work in isolation where this separation no longer made sense. Thus, in Scotland, while the Church of Scotland was directly represented on the conference of British Missionary Societies, those belonging to other denominations had no regular means of contact in Scotland for study and discussion of common problems and opportunities. There seemed to be a need to provide a meeting ground. Before the first steps were taken in this direction however, in 1962, the year after the House was opened, Mr George Fraser, the son of the famous missionary Dr Donald Fraser, attempted to institute courses for lay men and women going overseas. He was convinced that the future of the mission of the church lay with lay people (as much of the effectiveness of the mission of the church in the past had). He made two attempts to bring into being provision for Christian laymen who were going abroad to secular posts which might help them to be sensitive to the habits and culture of a strange people and to see in what ways they might bear witness to their faith, with full courtesy to the land in which they served. The first attempt did not succeed; and by the time a second attempt was made Mr Fraser was severely ill and died not long afterwards. He did not win that day; but his conviction has been shared by a growing number of people and the implementation of his dream is a responsibility which the church organisations concerned with mission abroad keep continually before them.

In 1963 a residential consultation took place whose aim was quite simple. Representatives of the different churches and missionary societies were invited to indicate briefly the form of their own organisation and the forms and scope of its overseas work. In addition there was a session on mission/church relationships. A second consultation a year later in June 1964 looked at some practical problems – the communicating to the church at home and abroad of a new image of the missionary; candidates and recruiting; short time offers for service abroad; joint summer schools and so on. At this consultation it was agreed to have regular annual gatherings. This was the year in which the Scottish Churches' Council was formed; and some thought was given to the question whether there should be a direct tie-in of the work of this group to the work of the Council. In the end it was agreed, and this was confirmed later, that the informal type of gathering related to the programme of the House was adequate, at least at present.

In 1965 the changing missionary situation was vividly illustrated by Dr James Taylor from Yakusu in The Congo, Rev Neil Bernard speaking on Zambia and Rev Robert Manson reporting on the state of the Church of South India. This was the year in which it was agreed to consult with Overseas Service (Farnham Castle in Sussex) about preparation of laity going abroad. This approach resulted in a request that the staff of Farnham Castle pilot at least one period of preparation for laity going overseas, in Scotland. This may have given a pointer to possibilities which could be developed from the resources of the churches in Scotland. However, the programme undertaken in Farnham Castle was so heavy that it did not permit the release of staff for this project. At an earlier point in history one or two consultations had been planned in Scotland, but the response was poor.

In 1966 the awareness that the mission is one resulted in the merging of the concern for mission overseas with the concern for mission at home in a 'People Next Door' conference. This was called to assess the effects of the People

Next Door campaign and to see what should issue from it in the life of the churches. 1967 however saw a return to the consultative work on mission overseas. 'Patterns of Mission Today' embraced an examination of the nature of proclamation in our time, of the relationship of lay people abroad to the indigenous church, of world poverty and its claim on British responsibility, of changing patterns of urban and rural life at home and abroad and how these affected missionary approaches. Some of the main notes of this consultation concerned the need for world perspectives in a time of nationalism; the need for the ordained and lay members of the church to be trained together ecumenically for mission; Christian Aid as mission and the place of Voluntary Service Overseas; the preparation at home for people going abroad which enabled them to train trainers rather than simply serve directly; and the importance of realising that mission means always two-way traffic between countries. Areas of collaboration were noted for further reflection and action. These included deputation work, immigrants, regional conferences, candidates, and the extension of the Overseas Fellowship so that it provided an ecumenical service. The concern for mission at home aroused interest in the possibility of having a place such as Scottish Churches' House at the heart of the Aviemore development, but this was not pursued further, since this did not seem to be the right group to follow the idea through.

Contributions from Christians from other countries have greatly enriched these successive gatherings. It was particularly fortunate that in 1968 Bishop Sadiq of Nagpur was able to remain in Europe after the Uppsala World Assembly and act as catalyst for the consultation (that year shifted to September). He spoke on doors which were opening in the missionary situation and other doors which were closing – both of them a test of Christian imagination and enterprise. This consultation on 'The Churches' Missionary Calling' was the first at which was implemented a decision that main issues coming up in the Conference of British Missionary Societies should have a regular and substantial place in the annual deliberations. There was also a sign of the development of joint concerns in the attention given to immigrants, Mrs Claude Barbour illustrating by her own work the kind of concern and type of approach which was appreciated (Christian/Muslim and Hindu/Muslim groups had developed naturally as a result of the trusting relationship which had been established). A further step forward took place that year in the planning of two regional conferences, one in the Borders and one in the North East. When a sounding-out process took place in these respective areas it was agreed that the time did not then seem right for a North East conference; but a one-day conference was run near Melrose in November 1968. Features of this conference were:

1)   the full participation by discussion of all the delegates in the thinking on 'World Mission in World Change';

2)   the use of young people especially on the final panel to which they brought freshness and enthusiasm and;

3)   the experiment of asking groups to shape the conclusions of their dialogue into forms of thanksgiving, intercession and adoration

which two from each group contributed in the closing worship. This experiment allowed the whole thinking of the conference to be summed up in the final act of worship in which about 15 people took part without confusion or a loss of sharpness. The result of this venture was that three or four regional conferences in different parts of Scotland are planned for the autumn of 1969. It was hoped in this way to spread the sense of community-in-mission engendered in Scottish Churches' House through annual consultations.

One 'rogue' consultation does not fit in, in this series, and yet does! At the Faith and Order Conference at Montreal in 1963, Dr John Fleming, who was then Executive Director of the Association of Theological Schools in South East Asia challenged the Church of Scotland delegates about a loss of nerve from which he thought his church was suffering. Before the Montreal conference finished, a plan had been sketched out, to which the missionary societies and committees agreed when it was put to them, as follows. Missionaries who had returned to Scotland after a very short period of service abroad, disgruntled or disenchanted, were to be invited to share their feelings about the mission of the church overseas with other missionaries on furlough who had served for a long period, and intended to return for further service – without the participation of officials from the missionary organisations. It proved to be possible to bring together just the different kinds of missionaries envisaged: and the discussion opened out issues which were picked up in the other consultations on mission overseas. One of the most drastic of these was the idea that there should be a complete break from traditional commitment to small denominational enterprises on the part of home churches: that instead there should be a world survey of need and a world bank of finance and personnel so that resources were directed, not to places to which they had been traditionally sent, but to the points where they were most needed and could be of most use.

Note on some ecumenical contacts

In Scotland, the temptation is great for the National Church, the Church of Scotland, to 'do the ecumenical thing' and shout the others in. Normally it is from joint consultation that joint action should flow. There are exceptions however. The industrial work of the Church of Scotland was so substantial in proportion to that of other churches, that a partnership had been established under the wing of the Home Board of the Church of Scotland which allowed other churches to work together with the Church of Scotland appointees in industrial mission work, without being dominated. There are other instances of theories of ecumenical activity not being able to stand up to the realities of the actual situation! In October, 1961 the Policy and Programme Committee of Scottish Churches' House gave their minds to Church Extension in Scotland. They were convinced that the problems met with in new housing areas were so similar basically that people from different denominations must have very common pressures coming upon them and very similar opportunities in their work in these areas. They therefore started an investigation into the possibility of holding consultations for different regions of Scotland, in the first instance for the ministers in these areas. When, however, the areas were investigated it became clear that church extension work was mainly covered by the Church of Scotland with other churches lightly sketched in, in this part and that. In other words the basis for ecumenical meeting regionally did not exist, and this proposal was brought no further.

A summer conference at Leicester University in 1965 played a significant part in the development of Roman Catholic/Protestant relationships in Scotland. The Warden and his wife attended a gathering which had a large majority of Roman Catholics in it, many from Scotland. One of the main lecturers was the then Roman Catholic theologian Rev Charles Davis. One of the Scottish delegates from The Grail was Miss Florence Henderson. Looking back on that occasion a year or two after Charles had left the Roman Catholic Church and married Florence, several things stand out. One was the warm relationship between these two, who obviously admired and respected one another – though at that point no one expected this to issue in marriage. Particularly striking, on looking back, is the integrity of Charles Davis. He presented the position of his own church with sympathy and understanding; and at the same time showed how thinking must be opened out into new dimensions of study and service. This loyalty and openness had much to do with the formation of an Ecumenical Study Group which met three times per year for some years thereafter, in Glasgow, Edinburgh and Dunblane in turn. The purpose of this group was to allow people who had made contact at Leicester to develop that contact so that it was a contribution to the life of the churches in Scotland. After a year or two the Study Group fell into abeyance, but not before a crucial work was done. And when in October 1967, a party of Roman Catholic delegates and Protestant observers attended the Laity Congress in Rome, their relationship matured to the point where it was possible for Roman Catholic Laity to enter into association with the Laity Committee of the Scottish Churches Council for joint study and action in Scotland. This Ecumenical Study Group illustrates the value of the kind of thing which might be like the first stage of a rocket, which provides initial propulsion and then falls away when the major development has taken off.

Stewardship seemed to be a field which ought to be pioneered ecumenically. Several denominations were undertaking it denominationally. Over four years, starting June 1963, representatives of these denominations and of others interested were drawn together for consultative meeting on the promotion of stewardship work in Scotland and the possibilities of joint action. Certainly, through these residential gatherings, people were helped to deepen their understanding of stewardship, and were brought in to a natural relationship which established a sense of common enterprise. But a failure must be registered. Those who took part were clear that an ecumenical approach needed to be worked out so that whole areas were dealt with in a co-ordinated way, so that the larger dimensions of stewardship, the stewardship of the earth's resources and the claims of the world's poor, were taken seriously into account. But pressure was so severe upon those who were developing stewardship in the different churches, that co-ordinated ecumenical initiatives were really thought of as an extra claim, and there was too much strain to continue planning time for them.

When the question of chaplaincy provision for Stirling University came up, Scottish Churches' House offered to be of service by drawing together all concerned to look at the situation and see if there was a common mind on what should be done. Representatives of Committees and Courts of the Church met with student and staff representatives of Stirling University. It was asked radically whether chaplaincy provision was needed at all – whether, if facilities were provided for students, they should not be left to develop religious activities themselves. Note was taken of the opinion of Dr Horace Walker, the Home Board of the Church of Scotland, that the best person who could be found should be appointed as chaplain to the whole university, and that the denomination of that person need not be that of the national church. In the end it was agreed that chaplaincy provision was needed, and that, at the present ecumenical stage, a team of chaplains from different denominations should be appointed.

Scottish Churches' House had a humble part to play in the field of religious education. There have been two aspects:

1) There was a continuing evaluation of the role and work of the religious specialist in schools, and

2) an encounter of Roman Catholics and Protestants about questions which face them commonly in the field of religious education.

In February 1964 the Association of Teachers of Religious Education in Scottish Secondary Schools, in co-operation with the Policy and Programme Committee of the House, invited people concerned from many angles in the field of education to a consultation entitled 'Instruction in Religion'. The stated intention was to 'take a careful look at new developments in religious education due to the greater use of specialist instructors, and with impending changes in the training of teachers in view'. Substantial working papers were provided for this gathering. The link with ATRESS was strengthened over the following years. At the request of Miss Katerina van Drimmalen, Secretary for Study and Development of the World Council for Christian Education, eight Protestants and the balancing number of Roman Catholics were invited to a two-day consultation in early April 1968 to consider 'the elements which come into adequate preparation for mature church membership'. The word Catechise, for which we have no matching word in English, was used to describe this process whereby people are educated to play an adult Christian role in church and society. Although teachers from different denominations were new to one another's thinking, they soon found themselves on common ground and became a real community. Growing collaboration was marked by a consultation on religious education in schools held in early January 1969. Again, a good number of those who took part were new to one another and to one another's way of thinking. What was clear was the ground they shared and their need of one another; and it was a message such as 'we intend to stay together' which may best describe the feeling of the meeting. So much that was coming up in education put pressure on the concepts, attitudes and educational processes favoured by different churches that they had every incentive to take the measure of them together. The work of collaboration moved forward at its own quiet pace.

On one occasion Roland Walls was leader of a group of Episcopal ordinands who were meeting in the House. Morning prayers were habitually led by all kinds of members of staff. After the bible reading there was a word or two from the leader and time for brief comment from those present. On this occasion Valerie, the cook-caterer, presided. Her comment after the bible reading was brief: "That is supposed to the be Word of God, and I don't believe a word of it!" Roland's eyes grew round with wonder and delight as he listened to 'theologs' stumbling to say anything relevant in response to her decisive comment.

When, after eight years work in a residential centre in the heart of Scotland, Ian and Margaret Fraser moved to Geneva where Ian had been asked to join the World Council of Churches' staff, the last Dunblane event, apart from the farewell service in the cathedral, was also memorable. For a week the House was filled with an equal number of Roman Catholics and Protestants on the young side; and Drs Willie Barclay and Bernard Haring were set among them for the whole time. Programming had to emerge from encounters.

It was a dynamic week!

The last service was to be a mass on the Saturday in the local Roman Catholic church. The question of partaking was debated on the Friday night. It was agreed that the stringent position of that time, should be observed – no partaking for those who were not in the Roman Catholic tradition. Dr Haring, who was to lead the worship, concurred. But when the service came to that point. He threw his arms wide in invitation and several from different traditions responded.

He confessed afterwards 'When it came to the bit, how could I separate those who were clearly one community in Christ at the sacrament of unity?"

Participants in a consultation on Ministry – lay and ordained.

Involvement and Reflection

The Retreat Tradition

The change made in the middle of a gathering of laity who met to reflect on 'The Christian's Life in the World' provides several pointers to the development of the retreat tradition in Scottish Churches' House. When one of the laity came forward, exactly as a shop steward would negotiate with a foreman, a change in the programme was immediately made to try to make it meet the people who took part.

It is early winter, 1964. About fifteen people are gathered in a circle in the common room of the House. They are all laymen including a group who are obviously used to a tough life, mostly miners. This group is clearly ill-at-ease about what is happening.

Step inside now. Find out what is going on.

You can see from the programme that the theme of the weekend is 'The Christian's Life in the World'. It must be some kind of retreat that is taking place though it is not called that explicitly. Nor is it very recognisable as such to those who are accustomed to go on retreat. But it is called 'Time for taking stock, for getting one's life into perspective before God.' That suggests the bracket within which you might expect it to come.

There is a leader who will be available for pastoral consultation throughout but the material for meditation comes from tapes. Dr Han-Ruedi Weber from the World Study Centre in Bossey and Dr Nikki Nissiotis from the same centre, the Rev Albert van den Heuvel of the Youth Department of the World Council of Churches and Dr Tom Simpson, whose scientific work is done at the Torry Research Institute, Aberdeenshire, have all made contributions specifically for this gathering, most of them having been interviewed at World Conferences or Congresses.

For this session Hans-Ruedi has provided some cardinal insights into the Christian's life in the world which provides excellent food for thought. The leader picks out some of these and gives them emphasis so that they might stay in the mind and produce a quiet ferment.

But now people are sitting around and that is why some of those who are new to such an exercise are not at all sure of themselves. Sometimes there is silence. It will be broken by a participant who starts off 'Here is something that has become clear to me for the first time. Maybe if I say how the thought came to me, someone else who had the same difficulty might want to share what I have gained.' In a few sentences the speaker develops his point of new awareness. Then the silence resumes.

The next to break it is someone who has quite a different contribution. 'I have always had difficulty in finding how to make reasonably clear Christian decisions in the following circumstances". She elaborates. "Can anyone help me? I think Dr Weber put his finger right on the spot when he was talking about the decisions we make in the world. I felt there was something important there – yet I could not quite get hold of it!" This one and that one in the group try to make a bridge from Dr Weber's thought to the speaker's circumstances. After some minutes of this, silence again ensues.

The leader then announces the beginning of a period of silent appropriation, inviting those present to remain in the common room or go to their rooms or keep vigil in the Chapel or in the Cathedral, as each think best. After two sessions, a miner approaches the warden as if he were a shop steward mandated by the whole group. His is a mixture of shyness and determination, which makes it clear that he is not at all sure of the ground on which he is walking: but he is sure that things are not working out right and has screwed his courage to the sticking point, resolved to see something done about it.

"It's this silence business", he says, "It's killing us. We get something out of the ideas that the speakers give us. We are not too happy about the time for chewing things over that follows it: but we are beginning to see what it provides and could make quite good use of it. But the silence petrifies us. We just go blank. The idea of spending the rest of the weekend with slabs of silence to cope with is more than we can bear. So the boys sent me to represent them and to ask if you would make a change."

You asked for it, you may say. I am familiar with retreats where, after a period of social meeting and getting acquainted, people move into silence for days at a time with a leader for their thinking and a pastor to consult. Those to whom this amount of silence is quite a new thing have time to get accustomed to it and before long positively appreciate the opportunity to get their minds on God and God's purposes which silence offers. Alternatively there are plenty of conferences where there is talk and discussion and a teasing out of things.

But this is neither retreat-fish, conference-flesh, nor good red herring. Is it?

The warden and 'shop-steward' get their heads together. They develop what the warden calls a 'streaky-bacon' approach throughout each session, 3 minutes input, 3 minutes sharing, 3 minutes silence. It looks queer. It has only one merit – it works.

Before the last session the representative once again takes the chance of getting the warden by himself. Awkwardly as ever he makes a fresh request: 'Would you plan half-an-hour's silence into the last session, please. We think we can use it now.'

One of the most powerful elements in the drive which brought Scottish Churches' House into being was conviction about the importance and contemporary relevance of opportunities for reflection, perspective on life, meditation on God's ways, prayer. The House followed through a specific concern for the retreat tradition (the word 'retreat' was thought to be unsatisfactory, but no alternative word was found). The other dimensions of the House, inter-church counsel and service to the national community, are eminently reportable, and what happened in those areas became known, to some extent at any rate. Work within the retreat category is simply not reportable in the same way. It must be emphasised, accordingly, that this had not only been as important an ingredient in the life of the House as the other two but that it had bulked even larger than the other two. To make a rough estimate, a third of the life of the House was taken up with accommodating groups which came on retreat or responded to opportunities planned from the House.

The work completed at Scottish Churches' House turned out to be both a critique of the classical retreat tradition and a critique of the non-retreat tradition. In the churches which develop common action from Scottish Churches' House there were those which had an emphasis on a regular habit of retreat and those which would not touch such activity with a barge-pole. It became clear that the assumptions of both had to be questioned and new ways explored.

The 'streaky bacon' approach provided an illustration. It was clear by the end of that retreat that a time to take stock of our life was appreciated by lay Christians who had never let themselves in for such an experience before. It was equally clear that if they were not to abandon the terms of the lay world for some pre-packed 'religious' conditions, even an adjusted version of the customary retreat approach would not do. The life of lay people, the modes of reflection which are natural to them, have never been investigated seriously and taken sufficiently into account. They have been asked to step into a different world; and it is arguable that those who have accommodated themselves to a practice which stems from a monastic or some other clerical tradition (such as that which might have been developed in a theological college) have sold their fellow laity down the river. They have been collaborators in the contention that traditions from the past, whose time, content, and form of development suited the ordained, remain valid today, and one has simply to adjust oneself to them. One alternative, that followed by Scottish Churches' House, was to encourage laity to enter into a partnership with clergy in which they discover together the forms of reflection which are native in the daily life of ordinary people. An industrial chaplain recognised one such form and hoped to develop some experiments, using it as a basis. He was present when trade unionists met to discuss trade union affairs. At the end of the gathering the convener of the group would say something like this "Now, boys, let's take three or four minutes in silence before we leave to get straight in our minds the decisions we have made and the actions we will take when we are back on the shop floor." The minutes up, he put on his cap – which was a bit like the Benediction. This was an entirely natural act with no 'religious' intention behind it: but it was a very teaching act. To 'get straight in our minds' how we are to live straight in the world is what retreats should be for. It would appear that the lay mind keeps reflection and action in much closer association: such an attitude challenges the "Let's get away from life to some remote spot behind trees where God is" idea of retreats. If it is believed that human beings must not be continually activist but must take time to reflect on what God is doing and what their own priorities should be in the light of this, then there must be a re-minting of the retreat tradition so that such opportunity is available to all kinds of people in the church 'in the clothes they stand up in'. To get any distance in fulfilling this purpose, occasion must be provided which are flexibly enough prepared for a complete change of approach to be made when it is seen that the original approach is not effective in meeting people where they are – however strange the adjustment might seem. If this meeting of minds takes place the adjustment is thereby shown to be right. The assumption that silence is a means of grace (it is not in fact officially described as such in any church, but the assumption remains) is challenged by lay people, and may be particularly under fire from young people who find that they are able to enter into natural relationship with one another through the release provided by noisy music not silence. Silence has no virtue in itself and does nothing for people by itself. The use of silence must be sensitively appreciated, and the part it plays must be gauged with discrimination and must be subjected to good timing. It is fair to say that every step in this area undertaken by the initiative of the House has been learned before the next step has been taken.

Already by May 1961 the relationship of reflection to action was commented on. Meeting in that month and year, the Policy and Programme Committee showed its appreciation of the value of the definite group on a definite job which comes aside to get perspective and then returns to its task. One of the great disappointments was the breakdown of a retreat planned by churches in Perth in 1967, which was to be related to a survey of local needs, and was to be a way in which Christians of different denominations stood together, with the city's needs in their hands, stretching them out to God to learn God's will for them together. Even though this did not come off the relationship of a retreat to the assessment of a community's needs, and maybe particularly to a sociologist survey was given fresh statement by the attempt to bring it about.

In the early years of the life of the House the approach was fairly traditional and people who already valued the retreat habit met under the leadership of those who were recognised retreat leaders. The intention was to break into new fields, but this proved difficult. The Warden's Memo for the meeting of the June 1962 Committee reports: "Retreats have been held in considerable numbers, but there has been no breakthrough in terms of constituency – most of whom have been old-ish and well-tried in this form of devotion." Two promising points are however also mentioned:

1)   groups which show an interest in going into retreat as groups, and

2)   some people, quite unaccustomed to the retreat habit, who see something in this field as belonging to their need for renewal.

In the Memo sent out for the meeting of the Committee in February 1963 it is reported that more time, office work, and finance have been devoted to soundings taken throughout the life of the churches in Scotland to discover what response their might be to retreat provision than was given to any other aspect of the life of the House. The reaction of those who will have no truck with such a practice is recorded and also the reaction of those who say "We are well supplied within our own denomination." Regarding the latter it is pointed out that there seems to be little realisation that ecumenical retreats will be new ventures, that in fact new experiences may be difficult to fit in if a substantial amount of time is already laid aside within one's own denomination, and that the only invitation we would offer would imply that the well-tried and clearly-articulated should yield, to some extent at any rate, to the 'experimental and confused.' A customary reaction came from people who said that they were too pressured to take advantage of any opportunities which might by provided however relevant and well-timed: and it was clear that these were exactly the people who most needed this type of provision, since their lives were running them. The Committee, when it met, showed its mettle by deciding that sufficient time should be laid aside throughout the year to persist in discovering and supplying what in the end might be recognised as relevant, whatever the economic consequences of small numbers and occasional breakdown might be.

The development from 1961 to 1969 was very fragile. In this development failure and heartbreak were gifts to be treasured. To find doors closed prevented one from banging one's head against them and pointed to possibilities of open doors elsewhere. It was painfully, and literally step by step, that some significant discoveries were made. But they were made. Effective means of meeting people on their own ground and drawing them into a fruitful essay in reflection appear and leave their mark. New constituencies are reached. People are encouraged out of traditional attitudes into new acts of venturing. A different style of retreat leading and type of retreat leader emerge. Many years on, the fact of greatest significance may be that tentative explorations into acts of reflection from groups whose form of meeting seemed quite unrelated to the retreat tradition were taking, with great seriousness, some of the emphases placed, in past centuries, on such things as the value of silence and the benefit of an overall framework of discipline within which there could be flexibilities; on the other hand retreats in the classical mould (and these were encouraged wherever there was conviction about them) opened out to accept quite untraditional elements.

Before describing some of the lines followed it may be worth recording that Scottish Churches' House was used for retreat occasions by presbyteries, dioceses, synods, kirk sessions, office bearers, congregations, youth fellowships, Woman's Guilds, presbyterial councils, Mothers' Unions, theological colleges, ecumenical groups, deaconesses, women's fellowships, ministers' fraternals and the Scottish Church Society.

In 1961 and 1962 attempts were made to provide devotional occasions, mainly for the ordained, drawing upon different regions of Scotland and starting with the Stirling-Dunblane area where presbytery, diocese, Methodist circuit and so on met. These attempts were completely unsuccessful. However in May of 1961 a School of Prayer took place which was effective and significant. Two people were asked to be leaders. The Dean of the Diocese who was not normally turned to for such provision, and an assembly-line foreman from Greenock whose qualifications for leadership were that he had only become a Christian a few years back, he was unsure about the place prayer should have in life and was struggling to find out, and he had never before in his life been asked to give any leadership of this kind! We learned early in our voyage of discovery the value of straight and honest speaking such as came from the Dean in contrast with people who give the impression that they have arrived. Experience had by now pointed to possibilities of building on existing group-interest; and between 1963 and 1966 five retreats for those involved in Stewardship Campaigns, concerned basically with stewardship and prayer, were promoted, the last one failing and indicating that the theme had run out. Between 1964 and 1967 time for reflection upon their responsibilities and the resources to meet them was set aside for those engaged in youth service, at their own request. This provision, entitled 'Resources for Leadership', illustrated the interplay of different aspects of the life of the House. People who came for meetings concerned with the needs of youth, discovering their own need for a more unhurried consideration of the pressures upon themselves and the means to cope with these, realised that the House could provide for both. It was in the end the pressures themselves and the difficulty of finding a common time which was free, which defeated their intention – but only after four fruitful gatherings form 1964 to 1967 inclusive. The basis of most of these gatherings was provided by case-studies of awkward situations participants had to face in a reflective type of discussion, and sorted out in quiet. More general provision for lay people, besides that entitled 'The Christian's Life in the World' already referred to, included a time of meditation on the theme 'Giving People Their Freedom' in the following year (November 1965) A husband-wife team provided the leadership. At much the same point of time, he in his industrial work and she in marriage guidance work, were made aware of the temptation to manipulate people to get them subtly to serve their own ends. This had awakened them to the dangers of manipulation which attended Christian testimony. They explored areas of freedom and influence upon others, making these the substance of meditations.

The programme of the House shows clearly an oscillation between the attempt to provide separate opportunities for the ordained or unordained, men or women, since the character of their responsibilities freed them at different times to take part in retreats, and the conviction that they also needed to be in one company for this purpose. Provision which had the ordained in mind shows this quite clearly. For five years, starting in 1963, the ordained who were in universities, hospitals, and special groups such as the deaf and dumb etc themselves advised on and then took part in a series of retreats mainly concerned with taking secular life seriously. Contributions on tape came from world personalities who had something to say about this, as well as at least one resource person who was present. The 1967 retreat, centred on the 'The Style and Structures of Lay Education Today.' Dealing with lay education, the Christian in politics, and tomorrow's cities, with Mark Gibbs as catalyst, brought together some lay people with the ordained, but not so as to give sufficient confidence to continue. Once again pressures on people's time was the bogey. It struck the committee that people in different denominations who were in the first few years of ordained ministry must be facing similar tensions, problems and opportunities and might be glad to gather to reflect on these. In 1964 a 'First Five Years' group met, and in this and three succeeding gatherings, one of which was led memorably by MM Thomas of India, took time to think of the churches' mission and the missionary structure of the congregation. It turned out that the stage of life did not provide a sufficient focus of interest. The main provision for the ordained in all denominations began in February 1963. Its title 'Strength for this Task' indicated the intention of those who planned the retreat – here was time to take stock, not only of the claims of one's vocation but the resources provided to meet these claims. Two forty-eight-hour occasions, one during or just before Lent and one in the autumn, were offered. From quite early on one had to reckon with a fall-out immediately before or actually on the day on which the retreat started, about two-thirds at times succumbing to emergencies and work-demands. It is curious but true that a reduction of the total price combined with a substantial increase of the (non-returnable) booking fee dealt fairly successfully with this difficulty! The February 1965 retreat is mentioned in sufficient detail to provide the plan of development. A lead for thinking was provided; there followed a period of appropriations then the whole company went to the chapel and gathered up their meditations in thanksgivings and intercessions; and then, in a period of silence, tried to see their way more clearly. It became characteristic of these meetings that the longer sessions between afternoon tea and evening dinner was made a free-ranging one in which people could share pastoral concerns with one another and come clean about their needs and failures in some kind of personal confessional. This clearly met a need for those in ordained situations - talking freely about their inadequacies and failures gaining strength to return to the work. By 1966 it was clear that the thinking was breaking out over the boundaries which mark off the ordained ministry into the whole Church in its ministry and its relationship to the process of secularisation. In 1967 the concentration point was a fresh understanding of the main Christian festivals. In 1968 hospital matrons were also invited, to reflect on 'The Ministry of Healing'. Later that year a retreat centred on the devotional outlook of Teilhard de Chardin was planned.

The Warden's Memo for the February 1967 Committee shows signs of despair at the situation. Probably too general a work was being attempted. The matter was considered and in the June meeting of the same year it was decided that there should be a switch of concentration from before Lent to after Easter, that a timing which allowed for a two-day programme only one night away from home, and a link-up with the Scottish Pastoral Association, might provide a good new development. It did. The timing proved to be more realistic. The association with the Scottish Pastoral Association was a happy one. The ordained, and later, lay people who had similar pastoral responsibilities appreciated themes which were less of general interest and were more specifically related to responsibilities they would handle immediately upon their return to work. (Relationship with the Scottish Pastoral Association had been established when a group of ministers and psychiatrists met in conference on several occasions, starting in May 1962; and later a local branch of the Association was formed which had Scottish Churches' House as its meeting place). The subjects for these gatherings, in November and April each year indicate their depth of concern 'Coping with the Normal Crises – Birth, Marriage, Death.' 'The Ministry, Sin and the Unconscious'; 'Relationships with Individuals and Groups; and Clues from Christ's Practice'; 'Developing Roles in Pastoral Care.' A limited number of people were invited to take part and warned that, if they did not reply or replied only at the last minute, they could well be preventing an invitation from going to someone else. This resulted in a group which really saw this type of gathering as important and developed a continuing conversation. Although at different points the concerns expressed were summed up in acts of meditation and intercession in the chapel, thoughtful discussion was the keynote throughout. Indeed one had to reckon with a kind of dogmatism about talk in this approach which was very similar to the dogmatism about silence in some other approaches. Case material was largely used to get the juices of thought flowing.

Retreats for women began in August 1962 and continued until 1968, two being held each year from 1964. the main factors which caused them to tail off then were the unchanging character of the constituency gathered, whereas the intention was to draw in fresh people, and a growing conviction that the group needed to be of both sexes. The retreats for women centred on Practising Personal Prayer (the subject of the very first gathering), understanding one book of the Bible or one biblical character against the background of our times and as food for contemporary obedience, and a consideration of the centrality of Christ and the character of the fellowship of his followers.

A group of people who were convinced about the value of the silent retreat tradition began meeting in April 1964 and have met for at least one four-day period each year. Their main concern over the years appeared to be to reckon with the reality of God in life and to understand the Church as a community of grace. The organiser (in concert with Scottish Churches' House) of these retreats, reflecting on the highly experimental one which took place in April 1969, made some observations on the whole process. The material he provided he himself described as 'Stories leading to a released imagination rather than sustained thought.' The teaching and practice of the Society of Friends was evident in the acts of silent worship. Contrary to their previous practice, except during planned periods of reflection they were not silent – and in the planned periods only intermittently. No equivalent of the traditional Pastoral Counsellor was present to hear confessions and be pastorally available. A sign of the maturity of this group was that a new member who was incessantly vocal and disruptive, was not isolated and defused – but the very contribution he made was accepted as a gift and in the end contributed to the depth of dialogue and communion. The Methodist Covenant Service sent people out of this retreat back into life, with a real sense of commitment. On reflection, the organiser thought this the most effective retreat that they had held; and thinking on her own Anglican background and the wholly silent retreats to which she had been accustomed, she observed 'That was twenty to twenty-five years ago, and in a different world!"

One idea was not followed up – in the Committee of June 1966 it was suggested that there should be experimental retreats for activists, on a work-camp basis. This would seem well worth pursuing: because those who wanted to get into retreat to get out from under daily pressures had discovered the need to relate their standing in the presence of God to daily responsibilities, and those who had been most aware of the claims upon them of meditation and reflection as realistic ones only when they were related to such responsibilities, had been seeing the need to discover forms of disciplined activity which might provide them with a sustaining framework. The Sharing of the Gospel group, feeling in May 1969 that it had talked itself out, planned a work-and-worship weekend.

A great deal of the probing work on a small scale was done by Leighton House.

In March 1969 there was a consultation on Retreat Traditions to assess the present situation. As a working paper the article on 'Involvement and Reflection' in the World Council of Churches' magazine Laity No 25 was used. A small company of people was gathered from the main traditions which took the retreat as a serious part of the work of the Church. Since the territory in which people moved now had no longer the clear edges that it used to have in the past, it was felt necessary at the beginning to say what was meant by a retreat rather than a conference or consultation. The following was generally agreed.

'A retreat is a deliberate step taken within the whole onward movement of life. It is a withdrawal from business and distraction, but not an opting out of life. It is a time specially dedicated to careful listening to the Word in an effort to search out God's will for us in every aspect of our lives, through an encounter with Christ at every possible level. The aim is a conversion experience and deepened commitment. A retreat is characterised by a mood of expectancy and waiting upon God, rather than by any particular programme or form.

Human beings encounter Christ in many different areas of life – notably, though not exclusively, in Scripture, in worship, within oneself and in others. Retreats should in different ways, according to the particular needs and circumstances of individuals and groups, give opportunity for a variety of means of encounter. The traditional silent retreat on the one hand, and the totally vocal on the other, may have neglected some of those areas, and to that extent may have been inadequate and incomplete.'

Forms of private and corporate retreat were given exposition – and, in the process it became clear that there was already more flexibility in the planning of these than had been appreciated by those who did not experience them.. In Fatima House, Coodham, with which Scottish Churches' House co-operates from time to time, parish retreats, youth retreats, family retreats, and retreats for engaged couples are run. The elements of dialogue, worship and silence were examined. The question of recruitment was gone into. Certain projects were planned as a result and the group agreed to stay in contact through a twenty-four-hour annual meeting. Coodham and Scottish Churches' House retreats for young people who were giving service, and for clergy of different denominations were planned in a preliminary way.

A curious feature of these years is that the need for the Scottish Churches' Ecumenical Committee and later the Scottish Churches' Council, to go into retreat, so that it might consciously stand before God with the responsibilities undertaken has never been followed through; and the retreat element in their residential meeting has diminished rather than increased.

The Week of Prayer for Christian Unity

The most obvious festival occasion in the life of the churches to call for observance in Scottish Churches' House had historically been the Week of Prayer for Christian Unity. Yet what should be done then had proved hard to discern. It had been recognised that the main emphasis must be on local activity, particularly prayer activity. Dunblane must not provide an alternative attraction, drawing people out of the local scene who were needed there to initiate and support forms of co-operation. Yet it seemed that Scottish Churches' House might provide a focus for all that dispersed activity and pilot some work which might be relevant elsewhere than in Dunblane.

In 1963 a Quiet Day was held during the Week of Prayer for Christian Unity with a group of Roman Catholic priests under the Abbot of Nunraw participating with an equal number of Church of Scotland ministers. This proved to be valuable at the point of history when such contact was rare; at the same time there was frustration because, at that point of history, it was not possible to share together in even an agreed closing liturgy.

In the autumn of that year the observance of the Week was discussed. The basic idea was brought forward that the House should co-operate with groups such as the Prayer Union and the Women's World Day of Prayer in all the churches, holding a consultative period which would lead into an all-night vigil and be followed by a further morning of consultation. The theme was to be the serious danger of praying in separated churches without expecting unity; and the unity of the church was to be linked to the need for the unity of humankind in international relationships and industrial relationships in particular. The material for the prayer vigil (which was to be sustained by a chain of prayer with at least one person in the chapel at every hour through the night) was to be provided by the consultative sessions, so that the two were closely interwoven. As early as this the need for a supplementary leaflet to the one produced ecumenically and internationally, a leaflet which would bring to people's attention issues for prayer in Scotland, was being mentioned. Four doctors provided the lead for this first prayer vigil and consultation in January 1964 – Drs AC Craig, RC Mackie, WG Baker and FR Stevenson (the last a doctor in architecture).

In considering the Week in 1965 a Policy and Programme Committee reminded itself that any event prepared in Scottish Churches' House should be of the nature of an act of corporate response and not be some form of demonstration. The subject for the prayer vigil and consultation was the difficulties and opportunities which faced the churches as the result of the Nottingham Conference; and how common obedience can be furthered through prayer.

In the following year theme material was supplied in the words of great personalities of the ecumenical movement, John R Mott, William Temple, Yurgve Brilioth, Yves Conger, LA Zander, Leonard Hodgson, Visser T'Hooft, Lesslie Newbigin, and Joseph A Settler.

In 1967 there was a double event, Dr W Stewart and Miss Mary Kalapesi (an Indian Roman Catholic) grouping people around them with 'Fellowship in the Spirit' as their concern and chapters 3 and 4 of the Epistle to the Ephesians as their basis. The prayer vigil followed under the general heading 'Focus on Prayer'.

By 1968 although there was a further prayer vigil and consultation, it was felt that some new departure was needed. The people who gathered, originally covering a fair spectrum of denominations and ages, were coming more from an older age group. It was decided to try quite a different focus for the Week. A prayer vigil was attempted, with people from the committees of the Scottish Churches' Council invited to take part, but this was not picked up. However the main intention was fulfilled. A Walk/Folk and Prayer experiment took place on the Saturday of the Week. Two charities were chosen, one home (Shelter) and one abroad (The Prague Ecumenical Centre). Young people were invited to walk from the surrounding country, sponsored by friends; when they arrived and had taken some food, they were entertained by folk singers in the cathedral hall, and could rest, listen, or sing; they were then to offer prayers that they had made up themselves, related to the concerns for which they gathered money, in the cathedral. It was thought that some vigil of prayer over a few hours might be possible, but the irregularity with which people turned up pointed to a service which gathered these prayers at the end of the day as the most satisfactory ways of providing the element of prayer. The weather, fortunately, was dry. Local groups also took part and were invited to go out and meet incoming groups, thus making up their own mileage. Some however made a circular tour. This proved to be a thoroughly imaginative way of providing focus for the Week of Prayer for Christian Unity. It may not be appropriate to do this every year.

Groups on Prayer and Worship

At different times small groups have been assembled to assess developments in thinking about prayer in our time. One such group owed its origin to a request that help be given to those who wanted to take part in the Week of Prayer for Christian Unity and found prayer difficult. The group when it met in November 1967 occupied its time with the difficulties of personal prayer in this age, help which might be provided to enable people to put heir own real concerns into they their prayers, weaknesses in the provision of the churches for the prayer of life of their people, and success of renewal of that life.

This impetus to form a Group on Worship came partly out of this discussion, partly from the concern of the Galliard Press to discover and publish relevant liturgies for our time. In March of the following year, 1968, the Group came into being, about half ordained and half lay, and from the start cocked a very keen listening ear to the understanding of worship that lay people had. The very first meeting was started off by a lay man asking drastically "Can modern people worship God?" From that point the whole field of worship was dug around, sometimes this, sometimes that aspect given concentrated attention. At the second meeting a Protestant professor and a Roman Catholic priest led off on the question "What do we do on Sunday morning?" After some general discussion about what was real and unreal in public worship for the members of the group, they were each asked to say what made good sense to them and what not. Before the conclusion of this meeting it was agreed that those who did not go to church needed to contribute to the thinking as well as those who did.

For the third meeting of the Group people were asked to say, in not more than a hundred words, what beliefs they held so passionately that without them life would be radically different. Thus the relationship between belief and worship was investigated.

By the beginning of 1969 the Group of Worship was beginning to be a real fellowship of exploration.

Mr John Calder always took part in acts of worship in Scottish Churches' House, though he was a professed and convinced atheist. In case this was done as a courtesy he was reminded that all those who came to Scottish Churches' House had their convictions respected – it was a matter of his own choice whether he did or did not attend worship. He replied by saying that he was quite aware of this and it was by his own choice that he took part. His questioner could not resist asking how this was since he was a professed atheist. His reply was something like this: 'I cannot believe in the God that you believe in. But the things you pray for in the chapel are real. They are important to me too. I can share with you in your worship by making them into an act of meditation.' Acts of worship which do not have hard lines of set belief drawn through and through them, but open people up with awe to a God who is mysterious and marvellous, can draw atheists and agnostics into participation without their feeling that their integrity is assaulted.

When a group is experimenting in worship, or thinking out belief and trying to express this in worship, the form of service which most effectively provides for this is one which they construct and conduct themselves.

No habitual practice in worship must in any case be used as a lever for people who come to a place of open encounter. They must know that they will be accepted whatever beliefs they hold.

Leighton House

An invaluable addition to the provision made by Scottish Churches' House came with the opening of Leighton House on 8th April 1967. An old relief kirk, across the Braeport from Scottish Churches' House, with a hall attached to it which was still in good condition was made into a residence for Rev Dr JW Stevenson and his family, plus six rooms and a fine common room for guests. After retiring from the editorship of the Church of Scotland magazine 'Life and Work' Dr Stevenson came to Dunblane to be of service to the Scottish Churches' Council in relation to Scottish Churches' House. There had been a lack of provision for individuals and for small retreat groups in the main House. Now individuals who were under the weather and needed some pastoral care or contact, who wanted some time to take stock of their lives, or who simply wanted a place to study and think – had provision made for them. Day retreats could be held. Small groups which were discovering useful elements of reflection and meditation in their daily life which might be built upon, could come to think those things through more deeply. Leighton House could also be used as additional accommodation for larger gatherings in Scottish Churches House.

In its first year, the house was used chiefly by individual ministers, missionaries and deaconesses and with day retreats for Fraternals, a Synod and two Councils of the Woman's Guild. In 1968 there were retreats of Episcopalian clergy, of ministers of the Churches of Christ, of Methodists, of the Baptist and Congregational Colleges; and the religious department of the BBC in Scotland, Scripture Union staff, industrial chaplains, the Cephas Youth Club Committee, and the Prayer Union of the Church of Scotland took time to stand back from their work and evaluate their responsibilities under God. The same year a sign of awareness of the potential of Leighton House was provided by Glasgow Presbytery, which sent 50 ministers from central area parishes for two-day retreat periods, in groups of 6 –8, the Presbytery meeting the expenses.

In 1969 a further 60 ministers for two-day retreats came from Glasgow Presbytery from January to March. In May of that year the Presbytery of Stirling and Dunblane decided to have day retreats for all ministers of the Presbytery, gathering in groups of eight, over the September to October period. The same month and year the Overseas Council of the Church of Scotland approved a programme for groups of men and women missionaries financed by the James Wood Trust, this to consist of directed reading, discussion periods, meditation and worship over five-day periods beginning in the autumn of that year.

In the first full year of operation the number of people using Leighton House for group or individual retreats added up to 330.

Teilhard de Chardin

Work begun on Teilhard de Chardin in 1965 could have come almost under any section heading. Consideration of the contribution of this thought brought together people of very different disciplines and proved to be a means whereby they could begin to relate to one another in terms of these disciplines. His understanding of life provided pointers for religious education, possibly particularly the foundations laid in the primary school. His views on the dynamic development of society could be related to many social issues and to industrial development. Certainly, his whole life and thought could be understood as exploration into God.

The amount of material thrown up in this consultative work is vast in quantity. No attempt will be made to summarise it. But a description of the development of consultations might be in place.

Mrs K Croose Parry was one of the small group with formative minds who brought the Teilhard de Chardin Association into being in Britain. In December 1965 she led a two-day consultation, which was really used to discover the amount of interest in Scotland; and whether it could be used as a base from which work could develop. Mrs Croose Parry was herself principally responsible for the material fed in. The report on this meeting notes "His work allows of discussion between areas and disciplines of thought which are at present disastrously disrelated." There was concentration on the validity of the terms and concepts that Teilhard used, particularly of new ones which he introduced. Warnings were given against making him 'The Master', his ideas into a new religion, his works into holy books. Those who had some knowledge of his own personal characteristics provided these, so that a human picture emerged with Teilhard's failings and limitations given prominence as well as the gift he was and the marvellous gifts he brought.

This first gathering led to a fuller consultation, over several days, with Anthony Dyson as the leader and catalyst. There was consideration of the meaning of Teilhard's thought for public worship and for private devotion. That formed one part. There was also consideration of his scientific work and a physiologist, a biochemist, a zoologist, an economist, and two engineers contributed reflections on his thinking from the angle of their own fields of study and responsibility. In this consultation nearly all the work was done in small groups. There is no adequate report, just different pieces, because Anthony Dyson was to write it up – but suffered a nervous breakdown so that the whole matter had to be laid aside.

In April 1967 theological implications were examined by AD Galloway (Church of Scotland) and James Quinn (Roman Catholic). A lead was provided by Dr Joan Tartaglia who examined implications for political and social ethics of his thought.

1968 was a red letter year. It was possible to show a film, the possession of Dr George Barbour who had worked with Teilhard in China, a film in which Teilhard himself appeared from time to time. Dr Barbour's son, Dr Ian Barbour, trained as a scientist and theologian, made a great contribution including a paper 'Five Ways of Reading Teilhard.' Difficulties of interpreting Teilhard's thought, French/British, Roman Catholic/Protestant, were examined by Hugh Cairns. Behind the whole series the interest and contributions of Hugh Cairns, who was doing a doctorate on the philosophy on Teilhard, were of crucial importance.

In 1969 the attempt was made to hold an extra-mural consultation on Teilhard in the Roman Catholic residential centre at Coodham. This failed through insufficient registrations, although a special job was done through the office to try to assess the breadth and scope of interest in Teilhard de Chardin in Scotland.

What seems to have happened was this. A core group had by that time spent about four years in study and discussion of Teilhard as their main interest, and they had simply come to a stop – they had followed up that interest as far as they could together and they had come to a term. The way forward, it was thought was possibly to contact a different group of those who had no expertise in the field of Teilhard's thinking but who would be interested to have a clear and fairly simple exposition of his basic ideas. To relate this to those who have responsibility for the education of young children, it was thought, might be profitable.

Principals involved in the Scottish Churches House enterprise at a farewell to Margaret and Ian Fraser on their move to Geneva in 1969

Views from the Bridge

a)   by a 'victim', Wilhelm Steffens

b)   by the first warden, looking back on eight years' experience of residential gatherings

c)   by Gillian Carver, brilliant creative first assistant warden, looking back from a longer perspective.

Step inside now.

We are back in April 1963. Wilhelm Steffans can contain himself no longer.

"It is both unkind and unfair" he insists. "You get people here to discuss some issue of Christian faith or practice. You ask them to contribute from different denominational standpoints beforehand, so that you know some of the main intersection points of doubt and difficulty. You set these out in a working paper before they come; and when they come you make sure that they take seriously not only the common points of agreement but also the crucial difficulties and differences. You let them work away at this for two days at a time and they have great difficulties in finding the answers to the questions that have been posed. You are a theologian and you could have put them right in the very first session. It is both unkind and unfair to let them struggle like this to find the answers you could give them".

Willhelm is one of the German students who has taken a graduate course of the World Council of Churches at the Chateau de Bossey, Celigny, Switzerland. He completes the course by doing field work and has been attached to Scottish Churches' House for three months to experience the workings of an ecumenical centre and appraise it critically. Half of the three months has gone. Some of the ideas and methods he encounters have bewildered him. But he has kept patience and has set himself to absorb the environment which is strange to him, had stored up impressions and questions until he felt he had at least a provisional assessment of some of the things, and now speaks in all humility but with a concern which means that he will not be fobbed off.

What can one say to him?

These things have to be said.

If someone produces an answer from the end of the book, however relevant that might be, people have not got there by journeying together in thought.

Any such journey, taken with integrity, would end in fact in a place which could not have been anticipated by people when they set out.

It is the process of journeying together in honest thought which builds people up in an understanding of the faith and equips them theologically. The professional theologian does not have all the answers at the end of his book.

As a theologian he is crippled by his situation, too cut off from the mainstream of life, too dependent on books for insights instead of on people struggling to express their faith in the world. In the equipping of the whole Church to be alive and alert theologically the professional theologian has a decisive role. But it is only one role; and the lay insights of those who struggle with decisions in the world are as necessary for good theological thinking as are the scholarly contributions.

If the leader has answers up his or her sleeve to produce pat-like - a raft onto which people in difficulties might climb – when is he or she to be instructed? A meeting of minds at which the instructor is not instructed has no relevance for the upbuilding of the Church.

Years later a letter is received from Wilhelm, from a mission station in South Africa. In it he says: 'I have learned from hard experience that the approach in Scottish Churches House has merit which I did not appreciate at the time. I have found it essential to adopt a similar approach for my work here."

A Listening Availability
A particular approach and procedure was characteristic of the life of Scottish Churches' House. It may be described as a listening availability. Far from assuming that they knew what is what in different fields of study church-centred and world-centred, the Policy and Programme committee believed that the service they could render was only possible if they did enough listening to discover in what directions to make exploration, and then made available residential accommodation, the resources, and the staffing which could allow things to happen.

Early on, the word 'conference' was dropped for nearly every purpose and the word 'consultation' substituted. Sometimes these words are used with shades of meaning which make them almost identical. The intention in fastening on the word 'consultation' was to suggest mutual contribution, the building up of thought, the drawing together of minds so that they might reach commonly agreed points of discernment and action or get clarity about basic disagreement. Thus, in the minutes of the Programme Committee of 22nd December 1959 – more than a year before the House was opened – the laying on of programmed courses with an expert to act as leader got the thumbs down sign.

Not only in the case of issues and importance in the life of Scotland and of the world, but in the case of inter-church relationships and a re-minting of the retreat tradition, a characteristic procedure was detected. It was recorded: 'A possible line of action will be raised in the committee through the warden, the chairman, or some member. The committee will give it careful consideration and either decide against it, keep it on the agenda to pick up at some more timely point, or give the go ahead.' If the last was such the decision, it would have been quite exceptional for a consultation to be set up immediately. It was further noted in the Policy and Programme minutes of October 1961 that the practice was established of getting the warden to meet with a number of people in the field of concern, listen to what they had to say, and report back. Thus it would suggest that there would have been an accumulation of potential work in the pipeline which was being considered at different stages of committee thinking. As has been said, this may not have necessarily been a reference to a St Andrew's House type group concerned with housing, (though it was on two occasions); it could have been related to conservative evangelicals, that their view and the people they trust might be drawn into a consultation on church unity; or with a group of young people who were aware both of the need for a retreat tradition and for the inadequacy of the existing traditions in all denominations.

Two basic routine questions were presented to those who were thus gathered, say over a meal, once the concern had been shared and some general discussion had taken place. They were: "Is anything in this field needed at all?" and "should Scottish Churches' House have some part to play?" These were applied as rigorous tests, since the aim of the House was not to fill itself with some kind of activity but to select that work to which it might relevantly or even uniquely contribute. Sometimes it became clear through the discussion that any action on the part of the House would be merely going over ground already covered. Sometimes it became clear that what could be done, could most effectively be done locally, not through some central meeting point. But very often the reaction was to explain how thoroughly and adequately everything was being covered by existing provision: then (one could say inevitably) someone would confess failure and the whole group would reorientate itself and begin to look seriously at the service the House could render. From that point, by a process of meeting and correspondence, both ideas and people who had significant contributions to make were snowballed towards the time of consultation. Thus people became participant long before the event itself, and got that cutting edge of interest which only comes when they feel fully involved and feel that what they have to say is taken seriously into account. Near the time of the consultation, four or six weeks beforehand, the material which came in from all quarters would be set out and examined. Almost inevitably four, five, six points of intersection of interest would become apparent. It became clear that main sessions must be devoted to each, and maybe two sessions to some. In nearly every case a working paper or outline was prepared, setting out the material so that community and difference of mind was shown and so that the questions and insights that came from different types of expertise bearing on the same subject were set before participants. This allowed for a defined and economical use of time; and shows how seriously the commitment is taken which is mentioned in the memo of 1961 – of using as a trust the time, which people, particularly professional people, offer. In the building-up process and in the arrangement of the consultation itself the custom is to go bald-headed for the people who matter, however distinguished or busy they might be. This has paid dividends all along the line. It is recorded in the Policy and Programme Committee minutes of 18th June 1962: "people of standing have considered it worthwhile to carve out the time to be in on them (consultations) and to contribute beforehand to the preparation of the ground".

It was, naturally difficult to get the right access to start with. As the reputation of the House for giving people the consideration due to their professionalism spread, there was a greater awareness and willingness to take part: but, initially, one had to insist on and wait for some appropriate form of personal meeting with the strategically-placed person, or work one's way through lower minions, determined to meet face to face the person who mattered most.

The people who mattered were by no means always the 'top' ones. In industry, for instance, they might well be people who, in five years' time, would be in positions of major responsibility – much more important to meet with them than those who were above them, but who were not catalysts in the thinking that was to shape the future.

It was a grave disadvantage that, in Scotland, one did not have on hand MPs who could be lobbied as was the case in the South of England. Money for the development of Enterprise Youth would almost certainly have come more speedily and in greater adequacy had this development taken place in South East England instead of in Scotland, at that time.. But there are great compensations. Scotland is a compassable country. One can be in touch with people who have important contributions in every area of the nation's life. One can develop an informal relationship with government departments to allow work of joint interest to proceed at an informal, yet mutually-committed level, which would have been quite impossible in England.

Care and thought were given to the size of the group. Nearly all the consultative groups which met at Scottish Churches' House were in some sense working parties with work cut out for them. Almost universally, twenty five to thirty was the maximum size for the interplay of thought and the building up of mind which was necessary. People were to meet in conversation face-to-face not stand up individually to address an audience! If the subject needed to be broken down in order that more particular scrutiny be given to parts of it, or if it was clear that, in plenary session, far too few people were making a contribution and that there were some who just did not look as if they felt involved, then the need to divide people in groups became clear. Again and again it was found that people who did not have sufficient confidence to speak in plenary, once they found that what they had to say was taken seriously in small groups, gained confidence to take their full share in further plenary sessions.

Only on the rarest occasion would an individual speaker be allowed to address the consultation at length. A good instance of an appropriate situation for a more detailed speech of greater length was the introduction to the Housing Consultation. JB Cullingworth charted out the housing situation in Scotland as far as it was known, giving appropriate statistics and showing where both statistics and hard tack information were missing – thus a factual, up-to-date context was provided for all the thought and discussion which followed. But in nine cases out of ten people assembled not only having made some contribution to the preparation, but having been issued with a working paper in which the main ground to be covered was already pegged out by such contributions. What was needed, if the time were to be used fruitfully, was to get people to work straight away on the working paper, using the material as the introduction to each section; or if someone was, as was most often the case, invited to lead off a session, all that was wanted was points-making covering crucial aspects of the subject. Those who were most distinguished in their own field were the readiest to see the point of this brevity – and almost always everyone invited played in.

To get the ingredients that were required for the thinking, it was sometimes necessary to make a direct approach to firms or institutions to get a lay person freed in mid-week. A great deal has been achieved by a simple explanation to the person invited why he or she had been asked and what he or she could give, and an encouragement to find out whether he or she could get free. Sometimes a letter to a superior, pointing out the particular service that this person could render, added sufficient weight to do the trick. When ten young people were suggested as those who were knowledgeable and articulate at the age of seventeen to eighteen and as young people who could stand up to adults in discussions on sex, the firms were written to individually and the importance of having young people in from the start such an important subject was stressed. Seven out of the ten were released. On one occasion the Admiral of a dockyard was prepared to adjust the holiday arrangement of a whole section to let one man free for a distinctive contribution he could make. You need to be convinced about the value of the work you are doing, you then need to go straight for the people you want. All things are possible to him that believeth! You then need to use with relevance and economy the experience, skills and time thus put at your disposal.

Chairmanship is an art and a craft. For several reasons initial attempts at providing outside chairmanship had to be given up in favour of a different conception of the work. At first, people were invited to chair who had some distinction in the field in question. It was not sufficiently taken into account that such distinction has no necessary relationship to the art of chairing, far less to that of chairing small groups so that the mind of a company of people can be built up, discerned and registered. Moreover it was not the chairman but the warden who was meeting with people, listening to them, corresponding with them, getting contributions from them – the threads of preparatory thinking were in the warden's hands. Later it became clear that it would be a further deficiency of chairmanship if the chairing of one consultation were unrelated from the thinking of other consultative work which had some affinity – and this would mean the isolation of different strands of thinking within the one House. The remedy was taken quite early and, in the first instance, the warden, and later the warden or assistant warden undertook chairing duties.

The type of chairing which was required needed an unusual blend of commitment and tentativeness. At the beginning of any consultation, often at the beginning of each session, there had to be a free rein so that people might find their way naturally into the discussion at their own time and pace. There came a point when the chair had to sense that enough of this has been done and more focussing had become necessary.

By this time the chairperson, with the help of the working paper or outline, and alert to the reactions of those present, could begin to do a delicate job described in a memo of 1963 as 'sensing, from those technically qualified, issues which were important, and keeping discussion centring on them.' If the whole company is surveyed quietly from a central position, it is possible to note contributions which make the eyes of many brighten with interest, or which even get them sitting forward in their chairs. These indications point to a concern which many share. It is therefore perfectly fair for the chairman to stop the general flow of discussion and ask for more concentrated attention on a particular matter so that the company might yield what they have to say on it before continuing. It is not only fair but necessary to halt discussion and say something like this: "Your reaction to the contribution of so-and-so in the first session, the contribution of group B in the following one, and the trend of discussion in this third one suggest to me that a common conviction is growing among you, and that it is such-and-such. Am I right or have I misinterpreted your thinking?" Where it looks as if the thinking of the group can be woven together the chairperson needs to sense this. On the other hand his or her own judgement might be faulty. The group has to affirm whether the direction indicated is the one that it was beginning to take as a group and the conclusions suggested were the ones towards which it was moving – or not, as the case might be. Chairmanship, accordingly, for this work, must be neither neutral nor disengaged but committed – and yet humble and tentative. In the same way, when it is clear that, beneath all the discussions, specific divisions or disagreements are showing themselves, these need to be brought out into the open, presented to the company for confirmation of their authenticity, and faced. It is often a good thing if the chairperson can take jottings and report, himself or herself, on the gathering. It may be possible then to bring into the report not only the ideas supplied by different people but to preserve something of the idiom and outlook of the persons contributing. It was encouraging that Industrial Training Officers claimed that apprentices were able to find in the reports of apprentices' conferences the things individual apprentices said, made recognisable in the way in which they were reported.

If members of consultations have been doing their work, there should often be as the result of their meeting some lines of further enquiry or study which have clarified themselves and certain forms of action which have commended themselves. If these are gripped and pinned down in the reporting, there is some hope that changes will take place in the climate of opinion and in actual practice. Without this, all that has happened has been a talking-shop. Very often those who have taken part in consultations have channels themselves into which they can direct their fruits so that it is through already existing channels that further thinking is done and action undertaken. Sometimes a group has to be set up since responsibilities have shown themselves which are not being dealt with – as a committee of representatives from St Andrew's House and Edinburgh University was set up to carry questions of rural studies as far as a group of that kind could. At other times (as has been the case with Enterprise Youth and the pre-school child) a considerable amount of energy and thought has to be expended outside the House to get some adequate service established. Once it is established, there can be withdrawal. Sometimes it is clear that, just to have brought a group together and clarified certain issues, has been enough itself. Sometimes (as in the case of National Service) a basis is laid which it seems to be possible to build on – but the time of the circumstances are not quite right, and the work done remains on tap for future development.

In some cases one consultation leads to another and it takes years to do a reasonable job which might then be sent before the public (all in all, seven years were spent on sex and sex education and topics arising therefrom). Sometimes a group appears for which a service might be rendered regularly (eg Housing Associations and Societies appreciate a locus for regular annual meeting, and the consultation on Scotland provides something like a soiree occasion for people of many interests and fields of activity together once per year). It is when a continuing service like this can be rendered that an advisory group from people in the field of concern is beyond rubies in value.

The most important thing is to be quite rigorous about the question of any further meeting. People who have been separated for too long often get quite excited about coming together and would accept some reason for doing so, however inadequate that reason. The case for further meeting must always be proved after thorough examination and a clear indication of what further work requires to be done. It will be only too easy to get slack and plan meeting for meeting's sake. To be thus disciplined does not necessarily mean choking things off. Some area of social work for instance may have been worked over as far as can be done through central consultative work – but, two years later, another aspect may appear commandingly, and then there is the benefit of the background of work already done, and the awareness of people who are invited to do a fresh job that there really is a fresh job to do. At the same time a continuing critique of events enables the staff to learn from failures and to spot new areas of work which cry out to be tackled.

The habit of reporting is a quite essential habit. It allows people to show how the whole consultation has developed, what growth of mind has taken place, what deep differences have to be reckoned with; and sketches outlines for further study and action which allow those who participated to get moving so that change takes place in church and society.

To be available is not only to offer service: it is also to stay out of fields in which those who are consulted and are in a position to advise, believe no useful service can be rendered!

The following is a contribution
to the Audenshaw foundation
by Gillian Carver (May 1970)
and is based on talks and
discussions held during a
visit to Dunblane of the
1970 'CLLT' course, sponsored
by the World Council of Churches
and the laity centres in Europe.

The seed from which Scottish Churches House grew was sown at the first World Council of Churches assembly at Amsterdam in 1948. The Scottish delegates came back convinced that they must begin to work together in their own country, and soon realised that what was needed was a house which the churches might own and use in common.

The House was formally opened in January, 1961. The site at Dunblane, just north of Stirling, has proved very good. It is difficult for people from the far north and the borders to get to us (and the House must seem rather remote from visitors from England and abroad) but it has proved central and accessible for both Edinburgh and Glasgow people.

Dr Ian Fraser, became warden in 1960, and I joined the staff in 1965. Richard Baxter came back from the laity centre at Chilema, Malawi, at the end of 1969 to replace Dr Fraser as warden, who had accepted a post with the Laity department of the World Council of Churches, in Geneva.

In the early stages I doubt if the churches which set up the House quite realised the extent of the work we would be involved in. They imagined it much more as a centre for the renewal of the Church, and for the development of retreats and worship: though they did commit themselves from the beginning to use it as a place which would serve the total life of Scotland. As our programme developed, it very soon became involved with all sorts of aspects of our national life, which were very little related to the institutional churches. The keynotes of our work have been: Where is the action? Where are things happening that are really crucial for the future? Where is there conflict and tension? Where are people out of communication with one another? We are trying all the time to develop a listening sensitivity to these points, whether they be in the secular world or in the Church.

We don't have all the answers

We certainly do not bring people to Dunblane because we think that we have all the answers. We try much more to be catalysts who can bring people together so that they may share their understandings and get to know each other. So often in Scotland – and I imagine in any other country – there are specialists working in the same field who don't ever really communicate. For example, when we had a consultation on 'The Care of Problem Families' we brought together about sixteen different types of people – social workers, teachers, social security officers, officials, housing managers, health visitors, probation officers, and police. Some of them had received medical training, some a social work training; some were concerned with collecting the rents. They spoke completely different languages, and yet they were all concerned with the same families. It was about 24 hours before they could really speak to each other. Then there was suddenly a breakthrough. They said: "We have simply got to keep in touch with each other"; and the result was a working party which contributed to the whole reorganisation of the social services in Scotland.

So we try to work in those areas in which people may meet occasionally on the committee, they may phone each other or write curt memos to each other, but they very seldom meet as people and share their common concerns. I remember after another series of consultation: a social worker emphasised very strongly: "We all meet officially on committees: and I know exactly what everyone is going to say. The great thing about Dunblane is that you never know what anyone is going to say." One of the main ways in which we can serve is that at the House people are released from their official labels. They do not have to represent anybody.

The Dunblane Style
We have few formal conferences, in which you come to listen to experts, speaking knowledgeably about a subject. We don't like people to lecture. We organise consultations in which all the people who come have a contribution to make. Maybe we have an introduction for something like fifteen minutes to open up the discussion; but still it is essentially a sharing rather that an instruction session.

If we think that some particular problem may be a good area for work, we do not then and there set up a consultation. We first spend a good deal of time – perhaps over two or three years – in talking to individuals and small groups, say over lunch in Edinburgh, and asking them "Is this worth trying?" If they consistently say "No", we accept this and drop the topic.

If we feel we have identified some crucial questions, then probably we will persuade somebody to draft a short working paper. Then we circulate this to some people who may be interested and ask them: "Will you come along? How do you feel about the issues raised? Who else ought to be asked to come?" Sometimes it is important to invite 'top people' from Government departments, education, industry or the social services, but we seldom have a consultation consisting only of people of one level of competence. Specialists and members of the general public have different but equally important contributions to make.

Eventually we fix a date and issue invitations. And we send them out a revised working paper and ask for further comments. We often receive in return some useful material which can be slotted into the programme. And so, before a consultation actually starts, a number of the participants have already been involved, and they come committed to work hard.

Consultation design

As an example of the design of a consultation, let me take one on 'The Creative Use of Television.' This was inspired by earlier work on communication and a Government report on television policy. After talking with representatives of both the BBC and Independent Scottish Television, invitations were sent out in May for a meeting in September. The official report was published in July, and in August a summary of important points was sent to participants with a suggested programme. A final programme was drafted a few days before the consultation, which incorporated many suggestions received from the people invited. These included not only staff and broadcasters, from both TV channels, but also educationalists, church representatives, writers, sociologists and members of the viewing public.

The event itself lasted only two days; and we normally find that we have to limit ourselves to this length of meeting, as people find it so difficult to take time off from their jobs. We try to give at least six months' notice of such consultations, unless one has suddenly to be arranged in response to some urgent demand.

We aim to come to some conclusion at each consultation. Perhaps we will agree: "OK it was a good thing to meet. We've learned something. Let's leave it at that." It may be that some aspects of the problem need to be worked at more thoroughly. Possibly the members decide to meet again in a year's time, or two or three people are asked to hold a watching brief and to alert us if further work seems necessary. Very rarely do we continue something simply because we might enjoy another reunion. We strongly discourage meeting together for meetings' sake!

We try to send out rather full reports on consultations. Sometimes these are simply for the benefit of the participants, and people do seem to appreciate them: it seems much more likely that they will take positive action later, if three or four weeks after they have met they receive a report and are refreshed on the topics considered and decisions made. Very often these reports have a wider circulation than just the members. They are however rather rough drafts; and this is one of our worries at the moment. We need to do a better writing job on some of our meetings.

Industrial trainees

I can only list here some of our major topics for consultations; and in particular a proper report on our experiments in new styles of retreats and worship will have to wait for a later paper. We have of course been much concerned with ecumenical questions in Scotland, and the House has been invaluable for inter-church meetings. But a large proportion of the events which we plan are secular. For instance, we have organised two events a year for apprentices and trainees from industry. These young men are sent by their firm for a week's course which is definitely work and industry centred. We have speakers from management and from the trade unions, and some comments about future changes in Scottish industry and possible new jobs and training possibilities. There is no specific Christian teaching in all this; but we give them the chance of coming to our informal House prayers, and we have a period in which they can bring up any questions they want to. Nearly always then – or in late night discussions – they bring up of their own accord all the classic subjects: sex; religion and politics. These men come here more than a bit apprehensive about a meeting in a church house, but afterwards they often comment on the amount of freedom they have had.

Before we set up these meetings, we consulted both the training officers and also some young men themselves. We brought a pilot group to Dunblane, and they spent half their time on a work camp and the other half deciding on a draft programme.

National life

Another important series of consultations have been concerned with Scottish national life, which have brought together people from the arts, from education, from science and technology and from the civil service. And a great many concerns which have been defined in our consultations have now taken on their own life, away from the House. For example we had a meeting on the hazards which face young people today – drugs, early marriage, and so on. From this there grew a working party called Youth at Risk which went on to organise three meetings with older people, to argue out some of the points of tension, and define where young people want to be left on their own, where they need support, and how it can best be given. There are quite a number of such working parties which are now only loosely connected with Dunblane. We have had to learn to let a thing go, so that it can develop a life of its own.

Enterprise Youth

Probably the most significant of these has been Enterprise Youth. In our early days, when we had work camps on the property, we realised that there was almost no cohesion in Scotland among the many different organisations for voluntary service. So we brought them together for a consultation, and now there is an umbrella body, set up with a good deal of Government money, for the whole area of voluntary service by young people in Scotland.

Other groups

In theory we try to space out these consultations over the year, so that our very small staff can take them in their stride. In fact we have been bad at this, so that we often find we have a rush of some work and then a slack period. Of course the number of consultations that we can organise is limited (it is almost incredible how much Ian Fraser managed to pack into his calendar when he was warden). To cover our running costs, it is essential that the House is fully used, and so at the moment more than 50% of all the events at Dunblane are run by groups which come with their own staff and programme – such as a church youth organisation or a university group. The majority of these visitors are church related in some way or another, and provide a very valuable link with the life of the churches in Scotland. This House has been called "an impossibility or a miracle" because in spite of the deep difficulties of inter-church relations in Scotland, it is a genuinely joint enterprise of seven churches, the Salvation Army and the Society of Friends. However in spite of the official commitment of leaders, parishes are still rather indifferent to our work, and such visits have made us many new friends.

Epilogue

TO BE CONTINUED.........................

'I remember a house where all were good
To me, God knows, deserving no such thing:
Comforting smell breathed at every entering,
Fetched fresh, as I suppose, off some sweet wood.

That cordial air made those kind people a hood
All over, as a bevy of eggs the mothering wing
Will, or mild nights the new morsels of Spring:
Why, it seemed of course: seemed of right it should.'

The opening verses of Gerard Manley Hopkins' poem *'In the valley of the Elwy'* might have been written not in Wales but in the valley of the Allan Water, and with Scottish Churches' House in mind. For what Ian Fraser's account of the early days of the House reveals above all for me is the image of *'a house where all were good'*. That is, the stories from that first decade of Scottish Churches House demonstrate that underpinning the energetic creativity which animated its life there lay a deep sense of the human and of the possibilities of human relatedness. Although the House was committed to social transformation it was even more profoundly committed to the transformation of persons, to the conversion of Scotland through the conversion of its people to a more generous and just vision of what that Scotland might be. It is one of the most signal fruits of that time in the life of the House that this now seems, in Hopkins' words, *'of course:seem[s] of right'*. What began as innovation became normal, at least in aspiration. That is testimony both to the courageous imagination of those first years and to the freshness of the summons to the contemporary church.

The fundamental purpose of Scottish Churches House has not changed. Each of the Wardens who followed Ian and Margaret Fraser responded to the same vocation, to form the House as a place for enhancing human relatedness, for imagination and for challenge. Each brought distinctive gifts to the enterprise, and because the House was and is attempting to respond to the character of the contemporary, priorities and programmes have continually reformed. In fact the life of the House as Ian charts it, and as succeeding Wardens might, is in itself a social document, capturing the flavour and nature of the Scotland which it sought to serve. How different and yet how recognizable is the Scotland which emerges in Ian's account. The House, far from attempting to be a place apart has sought to be a place at the heart of things, but with just sufficient detachment to offer a point of view which allows trends and patterns to be glimpsed.

The role of the House in 2002 is inextricably linked to the life of Action of Churches Together as it was earlier to the Scottish Churches Council. There is, perhaps, a growing intentionality in the relationship. This implies that it is harder to disentangle the life of the House as a place of work, reflection and formation from the life of the ecumenical instrument. In fact this is made explicit in the Review of the ecumenical body which the Central Council of ACTS initiated in February 2001, just over a decade after its creation. The location, the placing, of ACTS within Scottish Churches House is not accidental but deliberate. Each is seen as expressing the Scottish churches ecumenical vocation, that will to unity of which the unity of the churches is only one expression. The interrelatedness of the House and of ACTS sets up an expectation that each informs the life of the other, broadening and deepening their common life.

That 'informing' of the wider life of ACTS by the House can be evidenced in a number of ways, but all can be described in one metaphor. One of the dominant contemporary images within the ecumenical movement is that of 'ecumenical space'. It is a metaphor much reflected on within the World Council of Churches and in particular by its General Secretary, Konrad Raiser. It has its root in the image of the tent developed by the prophet Isaiah and carries with it a view of a broad, open, welcoming space in which the unlike and the like come together. The charism of the provider of such a space is to keep the space open, to guard against the temptation to close off and close down encounters which are difficult or painful, and to ensure courtesy and safety for those who come together. It is an idea which in earlier decades found expression in the image of the House as a 'third space', a place belonging to no single institution and therefore belonging to all.

In the 1960's it is clear that the Scottish churches themselves required such a space. Such is the growth in trust and love over the succeeding decades that the coming together of Christians is 'of course' in Hopkins' phrase, unremarked upon. Yet, even in the common life of the Scotland's churches, committed to one another, there remain difficult contested areas, what the ACTS Review calls 'neuralgic' matters, which set the House and the ecumenical instrument it houses a task.

The task of creating 'ecumenical space' has a dynamic which has a new urgency in the Scotland of 2002. On the one hand there is what is sometimes, perhaps misleadingly, called 'wider ecumenism', the interaction of the different faith communities within Scotland. Interfaith dialogue sits alongside interchurch dialogue as an urgent and enriching vocation. Alongside the recognition of the multiple, diverse character of Scotland's religious map the creation, or re-establishment, of the Scottish Parliament is the most obvious new political reality for Scots. The House was one of the places where the vision of a new politics for Scotland was kept alive during the dark days after the 1979 Referendum, and a place where the vital contribution the churches could make took shape.

'Ecumenical space' can be seen then as the offer to the churches of a place where the difficult and still neuralgic questions can be addressed as they continue to extend the common ground which was the theme of the first Scottish Ecumenical Assembly in September 2001: a place where the different faith communities can learn of one another and seek common ground, where women and men of good will all are at ease as they explore what it means to be people with a heart to build the new Scotland. The existence of the Parliament and of the Scottish Civic Forum have changed the way Scots conceive of consultation and civic reflection. Yet, even in the context of a consultation culture, discussions within the House on matters such as sexual abuse, racism and domestic violence have a character which comes from the context itself.

The character of the House, its particular mix of conversation space, chapel and dining room is the key to its distinctiveness. That is, it is a place which is not to be defined by formal programmes so much as by its desire to be a place of community. There have been times, particularly when sisters of the Order of the Holy Paraclete were living in the House, when that sense of community had continuity and visible expression. Yet what is at work day to day is a commitment to form community however transient. The coming of each group, the hospitality given to each conversation, conference, dialogue or retreat is rooted in the vision of community. That forming of community, whether of discourse, challenge, exploration or of celebration is what underpins the life of the House and gives coherence to its life.

It is a fundamentally religious insight which animates the House and those who carry forward its work, a commitment to offer ecumenical space responsive to the world around it expressed in the context of life in community. This is what makes the life of the House an adventure, an enterprise which is never dull or tame.

In his poem *'Settlements'*, in a final section entitled *'What we know of houses'*,
John Burnside writes:

'Our holy ground is barely recognised...
it's bright as the notion of home:
not something held or given
but the painful gravity
that comes of being settled on the earth
redeemable inventive inexact
and capable of holding wat we love
in common
making good
with work and celebration
charged
to go out unprepared into the world

and take our place for granted
every time
we drive back through the slowly dimming fields
to quiet rooms
and prayers that stay unanswered.'

And in that last phrase we read the reason for Scottish Churches House and
the continuing joyful urgency of its task.

Kevin FRANZ
General Secretary of ACTS

Advent 2002

'In the Valley of the Elwy', from The Poems of Gerard Manley Hopkins
Oxford University Press 1970, pages 67/68
SBN 19 281094 4

'Settlements' from The Asylum Dance by John Burnside
Jonathan Cape 2000, pages 28/29
ISBN 0 224 05938 6